AF553873

Caste Politics and Socioeconomic Mobility

Caste Politics and Socioeconomic Mobility

Sadanand Paswan

ADHYAYAN PUBLISHERS & DISTRIBUTORS
NEW DELHI (INDIA)

Published by
ADHYAYAN PUBLISHERS & DISTRIBUTORS
4378/4B, 105, J.M.D. House, Murari Lal Street
Ansari Road Darya Ganj, New Delhi - 110002
Ph.: 011-23263018, 011-23277156, Fax: 011-23280028
Email: adhyayanpublishers@yahoo.com

Caste Politics and Socioeconomic Mobility

Edition 2011
ISBN 978-81-8435-231-3

Printed in India

Published by Harish Chandra Yadav for Adhyayan Publishers & Distributors, Laser Typeseting at A.V. Rao and Printed at Tarun Offset Printers, Delhi

Preface

The political process of any society is influenced by the nature of the society., i.e.social structure India's social structure is best understood in terms of the caste system. Over the years, the caste system developed into an elaborate system to maintain socio-economic inequalities in the society. Individuals belonging to the lower castes and the out-castes suffered from many disabilities and were oppressed and exploited by the upper castes.

The first major challenge to the caste system came with the advent of the British rule. Under the impact of modern ideas and institutions the caste system was undermined. Caste as group identity, however, got strengthened in the new context of modern ideas and institutions. This happened because it became one of the bases of political mobilisation in the course of freedom struggle. The emergence of caste based organisations such as the caste associations and caste federations, by mediating between the caste groups and the political process, further helped the politicisation of castes.

By the time India gained Independence, the Backward classes, because of politicisation, had become a force to reckon with. Their claims and demands could no longer be ignored. The constitution makers enjoined upon the new state to take positive measures for bringing the backward classes at par with the rest of the society. They realised that without the positive intervention by the state it would not be possible to remove their historically accumulated backwardness.

Politics in contemporary India is marked by the resurgence of caste politics. Lot of caste based political parties sprung to life across the length and breadth of independent India. Caste-based political parties have initiated a brutal process of concentrating on the large vote bank of a particular caste. Caste-based politics is surely a negative phenomenon to the Indian political arena. Political parties and leaders should understand that caste based politics might act as a hindrance to the nations development.

The present book describes the histroy and development caste politics over the years. It narrates the advatages and disadvantages of politicisation of caste groups and also discussess the socioeconomic development of schedules community in India after Independece. It will be highly useful refernces tool for students and reserhcers in the fields of sociolology and politics.

Sadanand Paswan

Contents

1

Overview of Indian Caste System

India's caste system is perhaps the world's longest surviving and most rigorously enforced system of social hierarchy. The caste system encompasses a complex ordering of social groups on the basis of ritual purity. Caste is descent-based and hereditary in nature. It is a characteristic determined by one's birth into a particular caste. Caste denotes a traditional system of rigid social stratification into ranked groups defined by descent and occupation. While the particular ranking of castes may vary among regions, the extremes of the spectrum are fixed with Brahmins sitting atop the hierarchy and Dalits, or so called untouchables, at the very bottom.

The caste system is an intrinsic part of Hinduism, the dominant faith practised by Indians. According to Hindu scripture, individuals are born inherently unequal into a graded caste-based structure that defines their status and opportunities in life. Caste-based discrimination is also openly practised by Sikhs, Christians, and Muslims against Dalits who have converted to these faiths in an effort to escape their persecution.

Though the origins of the caste system have long been a subject of dispute, as has the question of whether it tracks racial groupings, the following theories are worthy of note. Caste is said to have its basis in the Hindu religion, as it is referred to in scripture. The *Manu-Smriti* sets out the main castes as each having been created from a different part of God's form, and codifies the respective God-given duties of each of these castes. Alternative sociological theories posit the caste system as a ritual solution to the Vedic cultural preoccupation with distancing oneself from pollution. A popular, but contested, suggestion has been that this Vedic culture arrived in India with the migration of the Indo-Aryans, from whom the Brahminic "upper castes" are allegedly descended. Still others have focused on the role of British colonial rule in cementing caste-based divisions.

Differences in status are traditionally justified by the religious doctrine of *karma*, a belief that one's place in life is determined by one's deeds in previous lifetimes. Traditional scholarship has described this more than two thousand-year-old system within the context of the four principal *varnas*, or large caste categories. In order of precedence these are the Brahmins (priests and teachers), the Ksyatriyas (rulers and soldiers), the Vaisyas (merchants and traders), and the Shudras (labourers and artisans). A fifth category falls outside the varna system and consists of those known as "untouchables" or Dalits; they are often assigned tasks too ritually polluting to merit inclusion within the traditional varna system.

Though most closely associated with Hinduism, the practice of untouchability the social imposition of particular disabilities against individuals deemed to be untouchable permeates all major religions in India and the entire subcontinent. Within the four principal castes, there are thousands of sub-castes, also called *jatis*; endogamous groups that are further divided along occupational, sectarian, regional, and linguistic lines. Collectively, all of these are sometimes referred to as "caste Hindus," those falling within the caste system.

The Dalits are described as varna-sankara, falling outside the system. They are considered so inferior to other castes that they are deemed polluting and therefore "untouchable." Even as outcasts, they themselves are divided into further sub-castes and practice untouchability against those ranked below; the discrimination is wholly internalised giving way to what Dr. Ambedkar termed a system of "graded inequality.

Whereas the first four varnas have over time enjoyed significant occupational mobility, a majority of Dalits in India continue to involuntarily inherit occupations assigned to the caste into which they are born occupations deemed too filthy or polluting for others to carry out.

1.1. Caste-based Discrimination and Inequality

In much of South Asia and India in particular, caste has become co-terminous with race in the definition and exclusion of distinct population groups on the basis of their descent. For over 167 million Dalits or "untouchables" in India, caste remains the determinative factor for the attainment of civil, political, social, economic, and cultural rights.

1.1.1. Untouchability

The practice of "untouchability" the imposition of social disabilities on persons by reason of their birth into "untouchable" castes continues to blight the lives of millions of Indians today who are relegated to life below the "pollution" line. The manifestation of such oppression has taken and continues to take many forms. Age-old customs included prohibiting Dalits from walking public streets lest their "polluting" shadow should fall on an "upper-caste" Hindu, and requiring Dalits to mark themselves with black bracelets; string a broom around their waists so as to sweep the "polluted" dust they walked on; or hang an earthen pot around their necks "lest [their] spit falling on the earth should pollute a Hindu who might unknowingly happen to tread on it."

Modern India has improved little by way of untouchability practices. Dalits are still prohibited from entering temples, are segregated into Dalit ghettoes, and in some areas are still forced to get off their bike or take off their slippers when walking past non-Dalit homes gestures that force Dalits to repeatedly self-affirm their inferior status. Caste divisions between Dalits and non-Dalits dominate in housing, marriage, employment, and general social interaction divisions that are reinforced through the practice and threat of social ostracism, economic boycotts, and physical violence. Dalits are denied access to land, forced to work in degrading conditions, and routinely abused at the hands of the police and "higher-caste" groups that often enjoy the state's protection. In what has been called India's "hidden apartheid," entire villages in many Indian states remain completely segregated by caste. As noted by Ambedkar,

> "India is admittedly a land of villages and so long as the village system provides an easy method of marking out and identifying the untouchable, the untouchable has no escape from untouchability."

"Untouchability" relegates Dalits to a lifetime of discrimination, exploitation, and violence, including severe forms of torture perpetrated by state and private actors. Because of the castes into which they are born, Dalits are forced to work in "polluting" and degrading occupations and are subject to exploitative labour arrangements such as bonded labour, migratory labour, and forced prostitution. Dalit children are vulnerable to trafficking and the worst forms of child labour in these and other areas. Dalits are also discriminated against in hiring and in the payment of wages by private employers.

Migration and the anonymity of the urban environment have in some cases resulted in upward occupational mobility for Dalits, but the majority continues to perform its traditional or "polluting" functions. A lack of training and education, along with the discrimination faced in seeking other forms of employment, has kept alive these traditions and their hereditary nature. A majority of the Dalit rural workforce subsists on the menial wages of landless agricultural labours, earning less than US$1 per day. Those in urban areas work mostly in the unorganised sector. India's much touted system of reservations or constitutionally reserved quotas for scheduled castes assists less than 1 percent of the Dalit population. In all forms of labour, women are consistently paid less than men, compounding the dual discrimination of caste and gender detailed below.

Segregation between Dalits and non-Dalits is routinely practised in housing, schools, and access to public and private sector services. Ninety-nine percent of Dalit students are enrolled in government schools that lack basic infrastructure, classrooms, teachers, and teaching aids. Government schools by and large teach in local languages, as opposed to private schools whose students are predominantly "upper-caste" that teach in English. Their inability to speak English further disadvantages Dalits in the private sector and the global market.

Dalit children also face abuse from teachers and non-Dalit students as well as segregation both in the classroom and in the provision of midday meals. Dalit school children and teachers also face discrimination from "upper-caste" community members who perceive education for and by Dalits as both a waste and a threat. Their hostility toward Dalits' education is linked to the perception that Dalits are not meant to be educated, are incapable of being educated, or if educated, would pose a threat to village hierarchies and power relations.

Indian economist Sukhadeo Throat analyses data generated by primary surveys conducted in four regions of India as well as data generated by the National Commission for Scheduled Castes and Scheduled Tribes' all-India annual reports. He argues that the regional data generated by the primary surveys is important because it underscores severe caste-based abuses that may not have been reported to the local authorities and have been left undocumented. The studies highlight persistent patterns such as: denial of Dalits' access to water; refusal of essential and/or public services to Dalits, or provision of such services in a discriminatory fashion; physical violence against Dalits; and Dalit political disenfranchisement. Throat concludes that "upper-caste" social behaviour in rural India is governed by the norms and codes of the traditional caste system. Consequently, Dalits are separated from other communities, denied freedom of movement, and otherwise ostracised from shared social activities.

The practice of economic exclusion and discrimination is also evident in the differential pricing for Dalits in the sale and purchase of items ranging from raw materials to finished goods, and in Dalits being denied the ability to purchase land for both agricultural and non-agricultural use. A study published in 2006 on the forms and prevalence of "untouchability" in rural India based on an extensive survey of 565 villages in 11 Indian states conducted in 2001-2002 confirmed the extent of "untouchability" practices in rural India today. But contrary to conventional wisdom, "untouchability" is not an exclusively rural phenomenon perpetuated by the uneducated masses. Egregious incidents of caste-based discrimination and abuse at the New Delhi-based All India Institute of Medical Sciences ("AIIMS"), the country's premier medical college, and other institutions of higher education bear testament to the depth and breadth of anti-Dalit sentiment in education and illustrate that such discrimination transcends the urban/rural, educated/non-educated divide.

1.1.2. Endogamy

Strict prohibitions on inter-dining, inter-living, and general social interaction come together with the practice of endogamy as the means for which the caste system is the end. Prohibitions on intermarriage are not only a hallmark feature of the caste system designed to ensure rigid social norms of purity and pollution but are essential to maintaining its very existence. As a result, inter-marriages between Dalits and non-Dalits frequently become flashpoints for conflicts and can result in extrajudicial punishments that include the public lynching or killing of couples or their relatives, rape, public beatings, and economic sanctions. Many such punishments receive "official" sanction from the "upper-caste" dominated *panchayats* (village councils). The prevalence of online matchmaking sites, which explicitly offer to match individuals according to their caste (both within India and abroad) provides a clear example of the practice of endogamy in its twenty-first century avatar.

1.1.3. Gender Discrimination

Caste discrimination has a unique and specific impact on Dalit women who endure multiple forms of discrimination. Dalit women are especially vulnerable to violence by the police and private actors. As the majority of landless labours, Dalit women come into greater contact with landlords and enforcement agencies than "upper-caste" women, rendering them more susceptible to abuse. Landlords use sexual abuse and other forms of violence and humiliation against Dalit women as tools to inflict "lessons" and crush dissent and labour movements within Dalit communities. Vulnerability to sexual violence also results from Dalit women's lower economic and social status, leading many of them to turn to prostitution for survival.

Dalit women have unequal access to services, employment opportunities, and justice mechanisms as compared to Dalit men. In relation to employment opportunities, Dalit women are allotted some of the most menial and arduous tasks and experience greater discrimination in the payment of wages than Dalit men. In relation to services, Dalit women have less access to education and health facilities, ensuring that their literacy, nutrition, and health standards fall far below that of Dalit men and non-Dalit men and women. The number of Dalit women in decision-making positions is also very low, and in some central services Dalit women are not represented at all. Benefits of various development programs for Dalits, such as distribution of land and other productive assets, have essentially gone to Dalit males and have failed to improve the status of Dalit women. Investment in projects targeted to the development of Dalit women is also far lower as compared to those for men.

The practice of *devadasi*, in which a girl, usually before reaching the age of puberty, is ceremoniously dedicated or married to a deity or to a temple, continues in several southern Indian states including Andhra Pradesh and Karnataka. Literally meaning "female servant of god," *devadasis* usually belong to the Dalit community. Once dedicated, the girl is unable to marry, forced to become a prostitute for "upper-caste" community members, and eventually auctioned into an urban brothel. The age-old practice continues to legitimise the sexual violence and discrimination that have come to characterise the intersection between caste and gender.

1.1.4. Status of Manual Scavengers

Dalit women make up the majority of manual scavengers a caste-based occupation wherein Dalits remove excrement from public and private dry pit latrines and carry it to dumping grounds and disposal sites. Indeed, the "occupation" of manual scavenging is the only economic opportunity available to many Dalit women hailing from scavenger sub-castes, with the result that more Dalit women and girls work as manual scavengers than Dalit men. Manual scavengers are situated at the very bottom of the graded inequality structure of the caste system and as a result face discrimination from other non-scavenger caste Dalits who treat them as "untouchables," creating an unquestioned "'untouchability' within the 'untouchables'" The entrenched discrimination against manual scavengers makes it difficult to find alternative employment and even more difficult to convince scavengers that they are able to take on, or are "worthy of performing," different occupations.

"Though long outlawed, the practice of manual scavenging continues in most states, and will continue as long as dry latrines are used." Similarly, dry latrines will continue to be used as long as there are Dalits forcibly designated to clean them.

> In 2002-03 the Union Ministry for Social Justice and Empowerment admitted the existence of 6.76 lakh (676,000) manual scavengers in India and the presence of 92 lakh (9,200,000)

> dry latrines, spread across 21 States and Union Territories.... According to unofficial estimates, the number of manual scavengers in India may be as high as 1.3 million.... Manual scavengers are employed by private and public employers, including the military engineering services, the army, the railways, and other organs of the state.

Manual scavengers work under extremely hazardous conditions. A manual scavenger from Paliyad village, Ahmedabad district, Gujarat, described how in the rainy season,

> Water mixes with the fees that we carry in baskets on our heads, it drips onto our clothes, our faces. When I return home, I find it difficult to eat food.... But in the summer there is often no water to wash your hands before eating. It is difficult to say which [season] is worse.

Manual scavengers are routinely exposed to both human and animal waste without the protection of masks, uniforms, gloves, shoes, appropriate buckets, and mops, resulting in severe health problems. Many scavengers have died of carbon monoxide poisoning while cleaning septic tanks. More than 100 die every year due to inhalation of toxic gases or drowning in excrement. The fear of being fired by municipality officials keeps manual scavengers from demanding higher wages or sanitary instruments.

The persistence of the outlawed and inhuman practice of manual scavenging speaks to the resilience of caste-based discrimination. That human beings should continue to clean human waste and be lowered into sewers in a country that boasts of technological innovation and prowess demonstrates the stranglehold of caste in India today a system set up to *enforce* the poverty of those it considers "outcast."

1.1.5. Unequal by All Measures

Although "untouchability" was officially abolished under Article 17 of the Constitution of India, the practice remains determinative of the social and economic outcomes of those at the bottom of the caste hierarchy. Though "untouchability" is normally considered as a religiously prescribed system of separating the pure from the impure, it is, at its heart, a system to support and sanction an exploitative economic order. As a result, Dalits in India today continue to rank below other social groups in all major social and economic indicators. While Dalits have achieved some gains across a behind non-Dalits. Broadly speaking, the gap between Dalits and non-Dalits in education, health, income, and land ownership has either remained constant or widened.

The practice of "untouchability" in schools has contributed to an alarmingly high dropout rate and illiteracy level among Dalit children, particularly Dalit girls. According to the 2002 India Education Report, school attendance in rural areas in 1993-94 was 64.3 percent for Dalit boys and 46.2 percent for Dalit girls, compared to 74.9 percent among boys and 61 percent for girls from other social groups. According to a 2001-2002 report prepared by the Indian government, "the dropout rate in Scheduled Castes during 1990-91 was as high as 49.35 percent at primary stage and 67.77 percent at middle stage and 77.65 percent at secondary stage." The statistics for higher education are just as alarming—the same government report states that enrolment of Dalit students at graduate, postgraduate, and professional/research/PhD levels is "abysmally low," at 8.73 percent, 8 percent, and 2.77 percent respectively. The 2001 population census reveals that the literacy gap between Dalits and non-Dalits remains significant at 54.7 percent for Dalits as compared to 68.81 percent among other groups.

Discrimination in schools and the resulting dropout rates for Dalit children are intimately linked to child labour. Illiteracy results in a lack of gainful employment options for Dalits. Even educated Dalits face discrimination in the labour market, as seen through the systematic exclusion of Dalits from jobs that they are considered too "impure" or unintelligible to perform. Selective inclusion of Dalits in various employment sectors still results in unequal treatment in the payment of wages, in different terms and conditions applied to their work (including the number of hours worked), in discriminatory treatment in the workplace, and in the prevalence of compulsive or forced work governed by traditional caste-related obligations.

There are an estimated 40 million bonded labours in India, of whom 15 million are children. The vast majority of these labours are Dalits or tribal community members. Bonded labour is sustained by the caste system, in particular through the traditional expectation of free labour and/or inadequate remuneration for work, and by the lack of Dalit ownership of land. Bonded labour also results from indebtedness to employers or moneylenders on whom Dalits must rely because of inadequate wages and because of the reluctance of institutional agencies to lend to the poor in general and to Dalits in particular. Landlessness encompassing a lack of access to land, inability to own land, and forced evictions constitutes a crucial element in the subordination of Dalits. When Dalits do acquire land, their right to own property including the right to access and enjoy it is routinely infringed.

As a result of their poverty and discriminatory treatment, Dalits also fare poorly in health indicators. Over half of India's Dalit children are undernourished, 18.5 percent are classified as "severely underweight," while 8.8 percent die before their fifth birthday. Dalits are often refused admission to hospitals, access to healthcare, and medical treatment. Those who do gain access frequently receive discriminatory treatment. In addition, caste-based occupations that Dalits are made to perform, such as manual scavenging and forced prostitution, frequently expose Dalits to serious and sometimes fatal health hazards.

1.2. Impacts of Liberalisation on Dalits

Beginning in 1991, and under the direction of the International Monetary Fund ("IMF") and World Bank's Structural Adjustment Programme, India's New Economic Policy introduced dramatic shifts in macroeconomic policy and aggressively pursued the privatisation of industries and the liquidation of policies and controls in economic planning and regulation. While these reforms may have ushered in an era of astounding progress in the areas of technology, infrastructure, machinery, space, and even nuclear research, much of this progress has meant little to Dalits; most continue to live in grinding poverty, lacking food security, and without the basic amenities of electricity, sanitation, and safe drinking water. Almost two decades later, economic reforms in India cling faithfully to the flawed "trickle down" theory a theory that holds even less relevance for Dalits for whom few benefits can permeate the caste ceiling or trickle below the "upper-caste" stranglehold on the fruits of economic growth. Unprecedented economic growth has coincided comfortably with a post-reform reversal in poverty reduction trends. Economic liberalisation, for Dalits at least, may be fuelling economic inequality.

As liberalisation leads to a capital-intensive mode of production requiring a greater proportion of highly skilled workers to manage automated production processes, a large migration of unskilled labour to the agricultural sector has led to lower wages for agricultural workers as a whole. In addition to a reduction in agricultural subsidies, Dalits are also affected by the increased acquisition of coastal lands by multinationals (via the central government) for aquaculture projects. Dalits are the main labours and tenants of coastal land areas and are increasingly being forced to leave these areas—to live as displaced people as foreign investment rises.

A reduction in the budget and fiscal deficit, devaluation, privatisation, the elimination or reductions in subsidies, and export promotion have all contributed to inflation. As is true the world over, inflation hits the poorest the hardest. With most of their earnings spent on food, shelter, and clothing, any rise in prices has had a direct negative effect on Dalits' level of consumption. A lack of purchasing power is compounded by the devaluation of currency and has led to a rise in prices for general essential imports.

Empirical studies seem to confirm that poverty rates are uniformly higher in Dalit households (as compared to "higher-caste" households). Eighty-five percent of Dalits live in rural areas while over 75 percent of Dalits perform land-connected work; 25 percent as marginal or small farmers and over 50 percent as landless labours earning less than US$1 per day. Though only 16 percent of the population, Dalits comprise 60 percent of those below the poverty line.

According to government estimates in 2000, the unemployment rate for Dalits and tribal groups was double that of non-Dalits/tribals. Additionally, public sector divestment to private owners is estimated to have left two hundred thousand Dalit employees jobless. Dalits continue to be significantly under represented in most professional strata and their representation in India's high industries, exports, imports, and electronic industries sectors is dismal. Economic liberalisation has not translated into economic liberation for Dalits and other marginalised communities in India. The market, in short, has not served as an equalising mechanism. Economic reforms must be scrutinised for the work that they leave undone and for the inherent assumption that such work can be done by either economic or legal means. Legal reforms to address caste-based inequality and discrimination, though astounding in their vision and reach, have been sabotaged in their implementation due to the conflation of casteism and corruption.

1.3. Caste-based oppression

Caste-based oppression in India lives today in an environment seemingly hostile to its presence: a nation-state that has long been labelled the "world's largest democracy;" a progressive and protective constitution; a system of laws designed to proscribe and punish acts of discrimination on the basis of caste; broad-based programs of affirmative action that include constitutionally mandated reservations or quotas for Dalits, or so-called "untouchables;" a plethora of caste-conscious measures designed to ensure the economic "upliftment" of Dalits; and an aggressive economic liberalisation campaign to fuel India's economic growth.

On December 27, 2006, Indian Prime Minister Manmohan Singh became the first sitting prime minister to openly draw a parallel between the practice of "untouchability" the imposition of social disabilities on persons by reason of their birth in certain castes and apartheid. In a speech delivered at the Dalit-Minority International Conference in New Delhi, Prime Minister Singh explained that,

> "Dalits have faced a unique discrimination in our society that is fundamentally different from the problems of minority groups in general." He pledged support for affirmative action programs specifically targeting Dalits, stating that India's government "is deeply and sincerely committed to the equality of all sections of our society and will take all necessary steps to help in the social, educational and economic empowerment of dalits."

The analogy is an apt one on many levels, and an uncomfortable one on others. Like South Africa, those who sit atop the caste pyramid are a numerical minority. When combined, the population of Dalits, "tribals," "Other Backward Classes," and religious minorities far outnumber those of "upper-caste" Hindus. But the analogy reveals something far deeper, that the system of "untouchability" in India continues to operate as though a form of legal apartheid were effectively still in place.

In many ways the Dalit condition naturally invites such comparisons, and in others it is a singular category, cutting across the Indian subcontinent, but categorically different than discrimination on the basis of race. To begin, the visual cues that accompanied apartheid in South Africa, or racial discrimination in other parts of the world, are lacking in India. Caste is like oxygen it is both invisible and indispensable. While the absence of obvious racial cues does not prevent the system from functioning to the detrimental exclusion of those who fall below the "pollution line," a general lack of Western familiarity with a nonracial paradigm does frustrate international attention and intervention.

The Indian government has taken great pains to insulate itself from international scrutiny by repeatedly pointing out that this is not discrimination based on race, as though such confirmation nullifies the abuse in question. Their protests ignore the fact that the prohibition of "racial discrimination" under international law, and in particular the International Convention on the Elimination of All Forms of Racial Discrimination, Article 1, applies to discrimination on the basis of descent. Regardless of how the abuse is defined, its noxious and pervasive character should be sufficient to invite international attention and condemnation.

Though scholars have pointed to the racial dimensions of caste, this is not a Black and White issue, or a clear Black and Brown issue. The caste system is one of *graded inequality* that invites people to share in the spoils of iniquity even as they suffer from it. By offering individuals a rank in a pecking order, the system strengthens itself and keeps the equality revolution at bay.

India is also an example of injustice in the extreme: the numbers affected are greater, the poverty is deeper, the atrocities are an every day affair, and enforced servitude and segregation is the norm. The population of Dalits equals more than half the population of the United States. A majority of Dalits live on less than US$1 per day. Every week, thirteen Dalits are murdered and five Dalit homes are destroyed. Three Dalit women are raped and eleven Dalits are assaulted every day—a crime is committed against a Dalit every eighteen minutes. Aspects of the contemporary Dalit reality therefore find greater resonance with the 1950s American South, American slavery, and, as noted above,

South Africa under apartheid. But, as discussed below, a number of contemporary communities do exist.

The cross-fertilisation of ideas between India and the United States on approaches to ensuring equality is not new, nor is it surprising. As two of the world's largest democracies and as common law countries with a profound history of *de jure* discrimination, India and the United States have learned much from one another. The very language of the Indian Constitution borrows heavily from the U.S. Constitution. During his time at Columbia University, Dr. B.R. Ambedkar architect of the Indian Constitution was inspired by such legal constructs as the Fourteenth Amendment. As written by one commentator: "Ambedkar's revolution for the emancipation of untouchables was significantly influenced by American ideals of equality."

In 1947, the constitutional drafting committee's advisor B. N. Rau visited the United States and solicited the views of leading American judges and scholars. Almost every fundamental right in the Constitution of India finds its corollary in its American counterpart. Moreover, according to some scholars, the process of drafting the Constitution of India took into account not only the textual wording of the American provisions, but also the eventual interpretation of those provisions offered by American courts.

Both countries also continue to be mired in the politically charged debate around affirmative action as either a suitable remedy to compensate for past injustices or as a means to level a playing field tilted in favour of whites and "upper-caste" Hindus. Indian judges have often cited U.S. Affirmative action decisions and law review articles in their opinions, although U.S. Case law has not been cited as legal precedent. Indian Supreme Court Justice Matthew in the 1975 case *State of Kerala v. Thomas* noted the following in reference to the landmark U.S. Case *Brown v. Board of Education*:

> Beginning most notably with the U.S. Supreme Court's condemnation of school segregation in 1954, the U.S. Has finally begun to correct the discrepancy between its ideals and its treatment of the black man.... These actions, while not producing true equality or even equality of opportunity logically dictated the next step: positive use of government power to create the possibility of real equality.

It comes as no surprise that the richness of the field of comparison has invited critical and thoughtful comparative legal scholarship on the Indian and American experience with affirmative action. Less well-considered are the contemporary struggles faced by both movements to counter the mechanisms and rhetoric through which the objectives of that legal framework now stand to be defeated.

The narrative of oppression, and of racist and casteist denial, is strikingly similar from continent to continent and each country's equality project is decidedly unfinished for similar reasons.

Inviting American scholars and advocates to turn to India and the lessons it offers to illuminate their own racial justice project is not an anomaly, it is the natural continuation of a long tradition of inspiration and solidarity shared between Indian and American civil rights leaders and movements. The following examples are offered as a sampling of that tradition, though they are by no means exhaustive.

In 1936, Howard Thurman, a famous black preacher and educator, visited Mahatma Gandhi in India—who at the time was waging India's civil disobedience campaign against the British—to discuss issues of racial segregation and voting rights in the United States. Better known is the fact that Martin Luther King, Jr. utilised the Gandhian concept of "Satyagraha" or "nonviolent direct action" in his teachings and leadership. Less well known, but equally significant, is the relationship Ambedkar forged with Web. Du Boys during the founding year of the United Nations. The similarity of their situations was not lost on either individual. In efforts to take the struggle for racial justice to the international level, Du Boys used Ambedkar's example in appealing to the Secretary of the National Association for the Advancement of Coloured People ("NAACP") to lodge a petition with the newly formed United Nations General Assembly concerning the plight of American Negroes.

Formed in the Indian state of Maharashtra in the 1970s, the Dalit Panthers aligned themselves ideologically to the Black Panther movement in the United States. During the same period, Dalit literature, painting, and theatre challenged the very premise and nature of established art forms and their depiction of society and religion. Dalit Panthers visited "atrocity" sites, organised marches, election boycotts, and rallies in villages, and raised slogans of direct militant action against their "upper-caste" aggressors. Panther leaders were often harassed and removed from districts for speaking out against the government and Hindu religion. And like the Black Panthers, the Dalit Panthers became frequent targets of police brutality and arbitrary detentions. Intellectual solidarity between Dalits and African-Americans has been found in the school of discourse called "Afro-Asian Traffic," which finds commonality between the two groups in their similar experiences of slavery.

Like the civil rights struggle that began in the 1950s and was led by African-Americans, Dalits in the twenty-first century are forming human rights movements, challenging local governments, and demanding equal access to services and equal protection before the law, often in alliance with international partners. In 2001, African-American and Dalit activists found themselves sharing the same contested space at the World Conference against Racism in Durban, South Africa. Both groups faced the racist and casteist denial of their respective governments who either refused to allow consideration of their concerns in the international forum or diluted their delegation's involvement to the point that their participation was rendered meaningless.

As the battle lines are drawn once again in the debate around affirmative action in both countries, the same ideologies are used to discredit the state's use of race or caste-conscious measures to ensure real equality of opportunity for minorities in the United States and Dalits and other "lower-caste" groups in India. Meritocracy, equality, efficiency, and liberalism are the catchwords that resonate in both countries to either defeat or redefine constitutional pronouncements that were heretofore invoked to ensure substantive equality on the basis of race or caste.

Affirmative action is attacked as either having sufficiently served its purpose, or as not being up to the task of alleviating a broad-based social problem. In the latter category, the alternatives that are offered in its place rarely find traction, let alone implementation in policy terms. Reservations, once the mask that India wore to hide the real face of caste oppression, are now being attacked as an affront to (formal) equality and a barrier to achieving a caste-blind society. Yet formal equality assumes a level playing field which it certainly is not for minorities in the United States or for Dalits and other marginalised communities in India. As critical race theory scholar Crenshaw notes in the context of the rhetoric of colorblindness in the United States, this remarkable strategy is a "breathtakingly bold act of cooption" wherein colorblindness "now delivers its reputation and historical capital to a specious claim that the journey to the promised land is nearly complete."

African-Americans and Dalits are also now made to compete against other marginalised communities in their respective countries for sufficient attention to their demands and their rights. It seems the small slice of the pie reserved for non-whites and non-upper-caste" Indians has not grown much bigger, and attempts to broaden the collective share invites swift protest and condemnation in the conservative media, on the streets, at the polls, and in the courtroom. Regrettably, the attendant claims of women in both struggles, and the compounded discrimination they face, get lost in the debate.

Like the United States, India exhibits a temporal tension between striving for equality as a space where caste categories (or, in other countries, racial categories) do not matter, and the need to continually identify and name the categories that have been used to create hierarchy or exclusion for the purposes of ensuring social inclusion. Such a tension is reflected at the level of policy, of social movements, and of political discourse, both for and against caste-conscious measures to ensure social inclusion.

In both countries, caste- or race-based stigma has not been erased by upward class mobility. Even for the minority of Dalits who have managed to defy their religiously proscribed economic lot, social oppression has not fallen away. As poignantly noted by a Dalit surgeon,

> It is India's most shameful paradox—this country has made almost unimaginable progress in nearly every sphere of human life, but the one thing unchanged is the condition of its dalits and backward communities. I am a microsurge on specialising in hand and spinal reconstruction, and am [a Member of Legislative Assembly] from Bihar, but I still remain very much a dalit a dhobi, to be precise open to routine humiliation from the upper castes.

The inter-category diversity among Dalits that comes about as a result of the creation of a new Dalit middle class is cited not as the success of affirmative action that it represents, but as the reason to now defeat the affirmative action project. Class operates in both countries as a displacement strategy. And in both countries the criminal justice system and its application to particular groups suffers from the twin malaise of over and under-enforcement. Dalits are routinely rounded up for crimes committed in their vicinity, yet summarily ignored when they themselves are the victims of abuse.

Like the United States, India's social transformation project is stunted by its increasing dependency on courts as a source of redress; its recourse to the legislature and courts is seen as the dominant avenue for social reform. The disproportionate focus on proportional representation or policies that aim to increase the representation of marginalised groups in the legislature, institutes of higher education, and now the private sector is where this conversation gets debated and defeated. Left out of consideration is the broad range of possible race or caste conscious measures that exist on paper but are neglected or undermined in practice. Even more neglected is the work that must be done on both continents to dismantle the racist and casteist mindsets that fuel the discrimination and generate inequality.

The social transformation project that began in India with adoption of the constitution in 1950, and in the United States with the civil rights struggle leading up to and following the landmark case of *Brown v. Board* in 1954 has left some with greater opportunity and political mobility but has "transformed" little. The "Dalit ordeal" is an example of a comprehensive legal framework with little to no execution. The "African-American ordeal" is an example of an emasculated legal framework that sees little hope of revival. The gap between constitutional vision and social reality is therefore far greater in India where the progressiveness of the constitution and the broader legal framework is belied by its almost complete under-enforcement. The rule of law lives in the shadow of the rule of caste. Though crafted as a bulwark against caste discrimination, the juxtaposition of egalitarian laws against an inherently unequal system acts as an open invitation to frustrate constitutional intentions.

As a case study, the condition of Dalits in India brings into clear view the limitations of the law and economic growth as antidotes to inequality. India's high levels of poverty concentrated among particular social groups, its epidemic of violence meted out in the name of upholding caste-based norms and traditions, and the prevalence of Dalit segregation, exploitation, and untouchability as the rule, rather than the exception, all expose the ways in which discrimination wears poverty as its mask.

Poverty is deceptive. It makes one conclude that all suffer from it equally. Poverty also masks a lack of political will to change the status quo by shifting the debate to a lack of resources. But a closer look at India's poverty reveals the discrimination inherent in the allocation of jobs, land, basic resources and amenities, and even physical security. A closer look at victims of violence, bonded labour, and other atrocities also reveals that they share in common the lowest ranking in the caste order. Poverty in India is, of course, not limited to Dalits, but as is the case with African-Americans in the United States, if you are a Dalit in India, you are far more likely to be poor. Moreover, the poverty endured is abject, violent, and virtually inescapable.

In both countries, economic progress has not led to equitable growth. In the United States which is the most economically powerful country in the world and India whose economic growth is celebrated as a success of the ethos of economic liberalisation the rising tide has not lifted all boats; rather, it has caused many to drown, in some cases all too literally. Just as African-Americans bore the brunt of Hurricane Katrina in 2005 due to their concentration in the areas where the flooding was worst, as well as the lethargic response of the U.S. Federal government, Dalits too were twice victimised in India's recent natural disasters first by nature, and then by the apathy of the state.

Dalits are particularly susceptible to loss of life and property in times of natural disasters due to the precarious conditions in which they live. A survey conducted by the National Campaign on Dalit Human Rights ("NCDHR") following catastrophic flooding in the eastern state of Bihar in August 2007 which affected 14 million people in the state and killed 2,253 in the region found that Dalits were the worst hit. Relief rarely reached Dalits, testifying to the fact that "[t]he culture of discrimination which runs through Indian society intensifies in times of crisis." In some cases, Dalits were forced to wait for their share of relief supplies until all other groups had received aid.

Even during moments of shared hardship, communities are divided by race or caste. Similarly, caste-based inequality, like racial inequality, survives dramatic economic growth. Even as India celebrated its triumphant testing of nuclear weapons, exploding them underground in the deserts of Rajasthan, Dalit manual scavengers were being manually lowered into open sewers without protective gear to unblock toxic and noxious sewage. In India, the rise of a nuclear state and a technological powerhouse has been accompanied by the rise of the number of manual scavengers in the country today. The militarism and jingoistic nationalism of both governments has also depleted state coffers in the name of ensuring "national security" and fighting the global "War on Terror" a fight in which both states are now staunch allies to the detriment of the poor in both countries who enjoy neither physical nor economic security.

Inequality, Indian-style, is a valuable case study for a variety of reasons: it exposes the pitfalls of relying on the "rule of law" as a self-fulfilling prophecy, or on the "neutrality" of the state as a guarantor of social justice. The case of Dalits in India also serves to counter prevailing global narratives that an insufficiency of resources is solely to blame for the economic woes of the dispossessed, or, its sister argument, that allowing for aggressive market reforms in the name of promoting economic growth will reduce poverty and lead to equitable development.

The treatment of Dalits as "untouchables," regardless of their educational attainment or their economic class, also serves to summarily reject the argument that "success," as measured by one's level of education or income, can work to displace the stigma associated with caste or will do away with discrimination and inequality all together. Such lessons are particularly apt for general inquiries into the need for and/or legitimacy of affirmative action. Inasmuch as affirmative action around the globe is under attack as an affront to liberalism and "meritocracy," the intrinsically antimerit nature of the caste system offers an alternative space in which conversations about "merit" can take place.

India also presents a unique challenge for those human rights lawyers and advocates who operate exclusively in the framework of international human rights law as a mechanism for achieving social change. International human rights laws and mechanisms, with their over-reliance on the role of the state, and their almost unquestioned faith that the right laws will do the trick, are illequipped to take on systems that define equality in the inverse, and in which human beings are born inherently *unequal*. Finally, a closer look at caste, worthy of academic inquiry in its own right, provides a powerful reminder that race and ethnicity are not the sole dominant constructs around which social and economic oppression is organised to the detriment of a sizeable population of the world.

1.4. Caste and Human Rights

On November 25, 1949, in an address to members of the Constituent Assembly, Dr. Ambedkar declared:

> We must make our political democracy a social democracy as well. Political democracy cannot last unless there lies at the base of it social democracy. What does social democracy mean? It means a way of life which recognises liberty, equality, and fraternity as the principles of life.... On the 26th of January 1950, we are going to enter into a life of contradictions. In politics we will have equality and in social and economic life we will have inequality. In politics, we will be recognising the principle of one man one vote and one vote one value. In our social and economic life, we shall by reason of our social and economic structure, continue to deny the principle of one man-one value.

The Constitution of India now in 22 parts, with 395 articles and 12 schedules embraces an aggressive state role in ensuring both formal and substantive equality (equality of result) in India. Even with its more than 117,000 words, and the volumes of laws to which it has given birth, it has yet to yield its promised result for Dalits. As noted above, the mere presence of laws and constitutionally mandated affirmative action programs has served to mask widespread, egregious, and often violent forms of *de facto* discrimination. In 1943, Ambedkar commented that,

> The idea of making a gift of fundamental rights to every individual is no doubt very laudable. The question is how to make them effective? The prevalent view is that once rights are enacted in a law then they are safeguarded. This again is an unwarranted assumption. As experience proves, rights are protected not by laws, but by the social and moral conscience of society.

The drafting of the Indian Constitution in 1947 and 1948 also coincided with the promulgation of the Universal Declaration of Human Rights ("UDHR") in 1948 and as such emulates the UDHR in a number of ways. Ambedkar's words apply with equal force to the corpus of human rights law to which the UDHR has given birth and which prohibits discrimination in its many forms and calls on the state to take positive measures to ensure equality in effect.

Nowhere is this tussle between law and social conscience more pronounced than in the context of caste. The caste system is inimical to human rights and to the vision of human equality as defined under various international instruments. Article 1 of the UDHR, the foundations document of the international human rights legal regime and the calling card of the international human rights movement, proclaims that,

> "all human beings are born free and equal in dignity and rights. They are endowed with reason and conscience and should act towards one another in a spirit of brotherhood."

By contrast, Dalits are born unequal and slotted into a system of graded inequality wherein the inequality is so ingrained that Dalits themselves practice untouchability against other Dalits below them in rank.

As Throat notes, inasmuch as the caste system and the institution of untouchability continue to govern social behaviours in India, "it makes the enforcement of human rights difficult, if not impossible." Throat adds:

> The provisions in the Constitution and law are secular and equal but the customary rules of the caste system and the institution of untouchability are based on the principle of inequality in social, economic, cultural and religious sphere.... People continued to follow the latter because it provides immense privilege and serves their social, political and economic interests.

What then are we to make of the challenge that the caste system presents to human rights law and human rights lawyers? The implications of such a system are vast and counter intuitive to those who reach for the law as a triggering mechanism for social transformation: in sum, legal measures will make little difference unless and until the inequalities embedded in the social structure of the caste system are confronted head on.

The Constitution of India, with all its celebrated virtues, does not take on this challenge. The constitution explicitly prohibits "vertical" distinctions (i.e., the hierarchical distinctions of caste) while tolerating "horizontal" distinctions (i.e., differential treatment for different religions). The limitations on these vertical prohibitions, however, are seldom considered. As noted in Part III, the constitution explicitly outlaws "untouchability," calls for the social, educational, and economic advancement of scheduled castes, and extends constitutionally reserved positions for members of scheduled castes. It does not, however, abolish the caste system *per se*, only the most extreme injustices associated with it.

Such limitations necessarily beg the questions: will an "untouchable" ever cease to be so as long as there is a Brahmin whose claim over priesthood and even the judiciary is near absolute? What rights does a Dalit have if the privilege of "upper-castes" remains unchecked? And what rights would "upper-castes" have left if Dalits were truly treated as equal? Seen in this light, the active and pernicious subordination of the rule of law to the rule of caste is not surprising; rather it is the logical outcome of a general failure to challenge Brahmanism, in the same manner that white supremacy remains institutionally unchallenged in the West. Legally, Dalits may be "former untouchables" but there is no "former Brahmin," legally or otherwise.

Judicial interventions in the context of caste, though commendable in a number of respects, continue to "disaggregation an issue with religious significance to take account of the various ways it may impinge on secular concerns." Though courts have to date allowed the government "to achieve modern secular goal[s] of helping disadvantaged groups," they do so without interrogating the broader caste categories. The "untouchable" does not exist in isolation from the greater caste structure; rather he or she is socially constructed in order to ensure "upper-caste" privilege. Privileges or rights assigned or denied to a particular caste are determined by that caste's relationship to other castes. The question human rights lawyers must therefore start asking is not simply who is disadvantaged by discrimination, but who stands to benefit from it.

Even with its inherent limitations, a faithful application of the Constitution of India—as human rights and constitutional scholar, Upendra Baxi, reminds us would be a recipe for complete social revolution. According to Jacobsohn, Baxi sees India as having both a written and unwritten constitution where the written is the social justice ideology of the document, while the unwritten is the "anti reform ideology of the privileged classes and castes, who, [Baxi] argues, have been quite successful in entrenching their version as constitutional orthodoxy."

Defenders of each system have burned the words of the other in effigy: just as medical students burned the writings of Dr. Ambedkar in anti-reservation protests in 2006, in 1927, Ambedkar set fire to the *Manu Smriti*, the ancient Hindu law book that Ambedkar believed sanctified and authorised the cruel treatment of Dalits. Both acts seek to annihilate that which symbolically stands between those who are aggrieved and that which they seek. For anti-reservations protesters, Ambedkar and his thoughts are the embodiment of undeserved Dalit "privilege," while for Dalits, the *Manu Smriti* stands in as the veritable Brahmin Bill of Rights.

Even acts of simple revolution like the decision to extend reservations to include other "lower-caste" categories have contributed to the resurgence of the Hindu Nationalist movement in India. The movement's emphasis on cultural nationalism is seen as both an attempt to unite Hindus under one cultural, nationalistic banner and as an effective means of "maintaining the status quo in social and economic privilege."

The success of the anti-reform project is so profound that laws are openly and confidently flouted by those who wear their "upper-caste" status as a badge of superiority and preach the virtues of caste to audiences full of reverence. Rules of caste come pouring out of the mouths of school children who learn from a very young age that these norms must be obediently followed, while families openly and exclusively court marriage proposals (in India and abroad) from families of the same caste.

Any project of social transformation, whether rooted in the language of human rights, human dignity, or in the language of equality, must set its sights on the twin goals of eliminating inequality and discrimination wherein discrimination is understood not simply as a legal term but as a hierarchical mindset that allows race- or caste-based abuses and inequalities to comfortably and openly flourish. Instead of reaching for these twin goals, we have arrived at a moment where social transformation and mobilisation is subordinated to imperfect judicial and legislative action and affirmative action policies are narrowly defined and easily defeated under the rubric of liberalism.

Whatever the limitations, reservations have helped create a Dalit middle class. But the creation of a Dalit middle class has not created a revolution, nor does upward class mobility work to eliminate the stigma attached to one's "untouchable" status. Dalit journalist Chandraban Prasad perhaps the only nationally prominent Dalit journalist poignantly reminds us that even as select Dalits migrate into higher class and occupational categories as a result of reservations, Dalit tea shop vendors are nowhere to be found. Though non-Dalits may grudgingly accept marginal economic success among Dalits, they will not dine with them, allow their children to marry them, or even be served a cup of tea by Dalit hands.

1.4.1. Flawed Trickle-Down Theory

Until recently, attention to India from international human rights nongovernmental organisations ("NGOs") focused on the symptoms of the caste system (e.g., bonded labour, forced prostitution, and police corruption) without diagnosing the disease. Simultaneously, international interventions on caste (and racial) discrimination were limited to inquiries regarding the mechanisms of protection offered by the state, without asking for evidence of their effective enforcement. UN. Human rights treaty bodies have now begun to ask for such evidence while domestic agencies have invested greater energy into exposing gaps in protection.

For the human rights movement, what began as a failure of diagnosis has now transmuted into a failure of strategy. The international human rights framework holds as its organising principle the promotion of a system of laws, universal in their application, but delivered by the state. Inherent to this strategy is an over-reliance on the state as a neutral agent of social change and the assumption that like economic growth, international laws and admonitions directed to the higher echelons of the state will trickle down to the rest of the population. The primacy the human rights movement has given to the system of laws and the state's implementation of these laws merits closer scrutiny, most especially in the context of the caste system. The social and religious sanction, when combined with the economic incentives, all but ensures that the practice of "untouchability" is perpetuated. In turn, attempts to alter the status quo are met with violent recrimination. Where then does that leave the law and the state?

1.4.2. Role of the Law and the State

The introductory paragraph to Narendra Jadhav's family biography, *Untouchables: My Family's Triumphant Escape from India's Caste System*, proclaims:

> Every sixth human being in the world today is an Indian, and every sixth Indian is an erstwhile untouchable, a Dalit. Today, there are 165 million Dalits (equal to more than half the population of the United States) and they continue to suffer under India's 3,500 year-old caste system, which remains a stigma on humanity. However, Dalits are awakening. We are struggling against caste discrimination, illiteracy, and poverty; our weapons are education, self-empowerment, and democracy.

The opening of the book exposes the magnitude of abuses perpetrated in the name of upholding the caste system, and the monumental challenge facing a democracy only sixty years young to dismantle and reconstruct society away from practices that are almost sixty times as old as independent India itself. Of note in the above quote is not just the magnitude and age of oppression, but that in the abbreviated list of "weapons" in the arsenal against caste discrimination (education, self-empowerment, and democracy), the laws are nowhere to be found.

By contrast, the notion that the state must take positive action to ensure substantive equality finds increasing traction in international and regional human rights law. So what role do we give the state? At the very least, we expect the state to remedy the effects of discrimination through the implementation of broad-based policies that seek to outlaw, punish, and provide redress for acts of individual discrimination, while simultaneously correcting or alleviating manifestations of structural and ongoing discrimination that are rooted in a historic legacy of legally sanctioned subordination on the basis of caste or race.

The role of positive state action, defined in this case as any race or caste-conscious measure under the broader rubric of affirmative action, will at its best be to remedy the *effects* of racism and casteism. Though affirmative action may be seen as removing the effects of cumulative and structural discrimination that result in race or caste-based inequality, as currently conceived and operationalised it does not deal with the root of the discrimination itself, which stems from a casteist mindset that does not question, legally or otherwise, the Brahminic hierarchy. Nor does it sufficiently consider that the state itself is far from a neutral actor.

The plight of Dalits in India serves to highlight the paradoxical role of the state in a society that is, in its natural state and left to its own devices, inherently unequal. The role of the state in such a context is to institutionalise checks and balances and intervene against the natural inclinations of the dominant groups for the protection of the dominated. But reaching for the state lands us in a double bind: without government intervention, the system could not dismantle itself, but we incorrectly assume that the state is a neutral actor. The state's law enforcement and administrative machinery is itself constructed along the hierarchy of caste.

Even if we were to assume that the state was both neutral and faithful in its implementation of the law, we still must ask whether the law can be a vehicle for social change, or does it simply divert attention away from the social condition it masks and act as a safety-valve to diffuse pressure for real reform. Moreover, can the law take away that which it did not create? If equality is understood as a value as opposed to a law, then can the state as a non-emotional body ever address it? Any program of affirmative action, no matter how broadly defined, implemented, and enforced, will not work to remove the underlying prejudice as long as it conceives of "the oppressed" as its sole target.

1.4.3. The Touchableness

If the human rights framework is to be critiqued for presuming that the state will ensure that the laws will trickle down, then it must also be scrutinised for setting its sites on those at the "bottom." The downward trajectory of human rights sets its sights on the wrong target and invariably assumes that the persona to be reclaimed is that of the "untouchable victim." As noted by Ambedkar,

> It is usual to hear all those who feel moved by the deplorable condition of the Untouchables unburden themselves by uttering the cry, "We must do something for the Untouchables." One seldom hears any of the persons interested in the problem saying, "Let us do something to change the Touchable Hindu."

Affirmative action policies, as currently envisioned and advanced, fail to sufficiently transform the racist or casteist hierarchy itself. Affirmative action may alleviate inequality but it will not break discrimination, and in the process may end up strengthening the discrimination itself by cementing identity formation along racial or caste lines.

Affirmative action (whether under the mantle of the constitution or human rights law), must be conceived in a way that is compatible with the goal of social transformation while recognising that affirmative action, as currently constructed, is a necessary but insufficient tool for social transformation. The gap between affirmative action and social transformation can perhaps be overcome to some extent by reforming affirmative action policies to reflect the salient fact that rights and privileges are negotiated, assigned, and denied not just in the courtroom, the police station, or even the legislature, but in non-formal social spaces where "upper-caste" privilege and "upper-caste" rights are rarely contested on legal or moral grounds. According to Throat:

> Non-formal institutions; social, religious as well as economic, involve a framework of social behaviour of their own, which may not be in consonance with the principles enunciated by the United Nations, or the Constitution of a nation in which case different sets of values may result in conflicts. It implies that unless inequalities embedded in the social, economics and cultural structure of the Hindu society are addressed, the legal measures will make little difference in providing access to human rights to the dalits in India.

The caste system may be understood as an example of what critical theorist Michel Foucault termed disciplinary power. Viewed in this light, caste oppression can be seen as inhering in diffuse power relations that arise out of socially entrenched practices (including discourse) which have become the "norm." These practices "discipline" individuals by imposing categorised identities on them and others, and set those categories within a hierarchy. Foucault argued that the liberal conception of rights was useless as a means of resisting disciplinary power, as it conceived of domination as negative *repression* by the state, thus overlooking the identity-*constructing* effect of disciplinary power relations which do not emanate from a single, central source, but pervade all of society. He argued for a "new form of right" that concerns itself not with setting limits on state intrusions against the private autonomy of an abstract subject, but altering the constructive effects of disciplinary power. Ambedkar was keenly aware of the necessity of a solution that confronted caste as a constructive power of this kind; as he saw it, caste as a discipline was rooted in religious ideology and he made an effort to tackle it at the level of discourse.

Among Ambedkar's most salient contributions was to define the caste system as not simply a division of labour, but a *division of labours* that is neither spontaneous nor based on natural aptitudes, and which prevents mobilisation because of the system of graded inequality in which it inheres. Perhaps the greatest threat comes not from those who oppose affirmative action or Dalit rights, but from the internalisation of the mentality of graded inequality. "Untouchability" among "untouchables" is a well-documented practice, seen especially in the treatment of manual scavengers by other Dalits. As noted in the Mandal Commission Report,

> "[t]he real triumph of the caste system lies not in upholding the supremacy of the Brahmin, but in conditioning the consciousness of the lower castes in accepting their inferior status in the ritual hierarchy as part of the natural order of things."

While the task of mobilising Dalits to claim a uniform Dalit identity in place of the hierarchical structure they inherited and impose is ongoing, the impetus does not and cannot come from the state. The state and any actor asked with thc projcct of translating the human rights vision into reality must set its sights on the (un)consciousness of the privileged castes. Yet what program exists to ameliorate the pathetic mentality of the bigot? Once the "touchable" condition is problematised, then perhaps the quotas would apply to them leaving the remainder and majority of seats and positions open to the majority of the nation.

1.4.4. Economy of Human Rights

An over-reliance on the law and the state has rendered other paths and options for the realisation of human rights virtually obsolete. While the state must continually be held accountable visa-vis its obligation to respect, protect, and fulfil human rights, an almost myopic focus on the state ends up also ceding to it too much power and fosters a perpetual state of dependency. In India, as elsewhere, the state cannot be seen as the sole locus for social change. While the linking of reservations to broader social welfare strategies exists on paper, even those paper promises are being shredded by economic and ideological liberalisation.

Ideologically, caste categories are constructed and imposed to organise exclusion, yet when those very categories are used as a basis to claim remedies to ensure inclusion, the categories magically disappear and we are invited to revel in the fantasy of a caste- or colour-blind nation that through the very proclamation of equality has achieved an imaginary break with the past.

Economically, the persistence of massive poverty in India and its concentration among particular social groups suggests that, without "wide spread purchasing power," the free market perpetuates caste-based exploitation. An alternative prescription offered by Dalit economists involves *greater* investment in agriculture and public services and positive discrimination for disadvantaged classes that must be expanded to sectors currently out of reach and must include due attention to the implementation of the directive principles of the constitution. These policies and programs, they add, must seek to effectuate those principles through caste-conscious interventions in primary education, housing, and healthcare. A similarly aggressive role of the state is promoted by human rights advocates.

Yet as noted in Part II.C.5, the free market ideology stands in fierce opposition to the notion that the state must take positive action to ensure substantive equality for its marginalised citizens. The prevailing legitimacy of the free market ideology within India also serves to legitimise preexisting anti-Dalit sentiment. The outsourcing of public sector functions to the private sector, unaccompanied by the simultaneous outsourcing of human rights obligations to non-state actors, dismantles both the obligation and the infrastructure of programs that support social inclusion, and along with it, any hopes of Dalit advancement. Less frequently noted, but equally pernicious, is the signalling to Dalits that their hopes for social inclusion, centuries overdue, may now be dashed long before they were ever fully realised.

But the iniquities of liberalisation must be delinked from the potential benefits of globalisation. Inasmuch as globalisation represents the influx of outside forces into the Indian scene, and insofar as it has helped build solidarity among anti-discrimination activists across the world, globalisation allows Dalit activists to reach beyond the state to foreign actors and the international community to press their claims.

Social scientist Ramaiah cautions against unequivocally accepting criticisms of globalisation and instead draws attention to its potential to empower Dalits in ways that the state has failed. Legal scholar Chimni supports such a view and finds that Dalit intellectuals tend to see the threat of oppression by globalisation as secondary to oppression by caste adding that much of the Dalit movement has successfully galvanised international pressure to force some change in their status. Indeed the very success of the demands for private sector reservations may hinge on the willingness of foreign investors, who are not steeped in the same caste culture, to both participate and take the lead in creating a space for Dalit employment in sectors from which they have, to date, been excluded.

That foreign investors, aid agencies, and governments are now more attuned to the deleterious role that the caste system plays in undermining both human rights and uniform economic development is a result of the work done by international and Indian advocates using the language and tools of human rights. The next and necessary step is for human rights advocates to step out of the constraints of the trickle-down legal regime and support the advancement of Dalits rights from the bottom up.

1.5. Policies For Addressing Caste Discrimination

1.5.1. Constitutional Provisions

The Constitution of India, often heralded as a landmark document, was inspired by the emancipatory vision of its chief architect Dr. B.R. Ambedkar a Dalit leader who himself suffered severe discrimination and who sought to ensure equal protection and substantive equality for Dalits in independent India. As a document, the constitution combines broad social purpose, stemming from the social content of the Independence Movement, with practical administrative detail, based on the Assembly members' experiences in government and on the events around them.

Ambedkar cautioned against adopting too "Western" a vision of what constitutional democracy in India should look like. According to Ambedkar,

> [Such a system failed] to realise that political democracy cannot succeed where there is not social and economic democracy. Democracy is another name for equality. Parliamentary democracy developed a passion for liberty. It failed to realise the significance of equality and did not even endeavour to strike a balance between liberty and equality, with the result that liberty swallowed equality and has left a progeny of iniquities.

Indian constitutionalism attempts, however imperfectly, to balance liberty and equality interests and in so doing foreshadows the delicate balance between formal and substantive conceptions of equality in international human rights law. Chief among these fundamental rights is the right to equality. Article 14 of the Constitution of India reads:

> "The state shall not deny to any person equality before the law or the equal protection of the laws within the territory of India." An exception clause allows for affirmative action measures under some circumstances. "Nothing in this article... Shall prevent the state from making any special provision for the advancement of the socially and educationally backward classes of citizens or for the Scheduled Castes and Scheduled Tribes."

The clause marks a significant departure from the American model on which India's equality provision is based and constitutionalists the validity of affirmative action in the Indian context. The Indian model is also one of substantive equality. If formal equality aims at equal opportunity, then substantive equality aims at equal results by considering the social structures in which equal results would not necessarily result from formal equality guarantees.

The Court has interpreted Article 14 on a number of occasions as charging the state with ensuring that there is equality among equals. In *State of Kerala v. Thomas*, the Supreme Court noted that,

> The guarantee of equality before the law or the equal opportunity in matters of employment is a guarantee of something more than what is required by formal equality. It implies differential treatment of persons who are unequal.... Formal equality is achieved by treating all persons equally... But men are not equal in all respects. The claim for equality is in fact a protest against unjust, undeserved and unjustified inequalities. It is a symbol of man's revolt against chance, fortuitous disparity, unjust power and crystallised privileges.

Article 17 of the constitution abolishes the practice of "untouchability" and punishes the enforcement of any disability arising out of the practice. Article 21 guarantees the right to life and liberty. The Indian Supreme Court has interpreted this right to include the right to be free from degrading and inhuman treatment, the right to integrity and dignity of the person, and the right to speedy justice. Article 23 prohibits traffic in human beings and other similar forms of forced labour. Since the majority of India's forty million bonded labours belong to scheduled castes, Article 23 is especially significant for them. Similarly, Article 24 provides that no child under the age of fourteen shall work in any factory or mine or engage in any hazardous employment.

Article 43 calls on the state to secure to all workers, agricultural, industrial, or otherwise, a living wage and conditions of work ensuring a decent standard of life. Article 46 comprises both development and regulatory aspects and stipulates that: "The State shall promote with special care the educational and economic interests of the weaker sections of the people, and in particular, of the Scheduled Castes and the Scheduled Tribes, and shall protect them from social injustice and forms of exploitation." As the article falls under the category of directive principles and not fundamental rights, it cannot be enforced by the state's courts. Article 15 prohibits discrimination on the grounds of religion, race, caste, sex, or place of birth while Article 15(4) empowers the state to make any special provisions for the advancement of any socially and educationally backward classes of citizens, or for scheduled castes and scheduled tribes.

Article 330 provides reservations for seats for scheduled castes and scheduled tribes in the Lok Sabha (the House of the People), while Article 332 provides for reservations in the state legislative assemblies. Through Article 16(4) the state is empowered to make "any provision for the reservation of appointments or posts in favour of any backward class of citizens which, in the opinion of the State, is not adequately represented in the services under the State." Accordingly, under constitutional provisions and various laws, India grants Dalits a certain number of rights, including reservations (quotas) in education, government jobs, and government bodies. India's policy of reservations is an attempt by the central government to remedy past injustices related to "low-caste" status.

To allow for proportional representation in certain state and federal institutions, the constitution reserves 22.5 percent of seats in federal government jobs, state legislatures, the lower house of parliament, and educational institutions for scheduled castes and scheduled tribes. An amendment to the constitution also enables reservations for scheduled castes and scheduled tribes in village councils (*panchayats*) and municipalities, with no less than one-third of reserved seats to be allocated to scheduled caste and scheduled tribe women. Notably, no other reservation programs provides for a sub-category of reservations for women. Reservations have also been provided for "Other Backward Classes" ("OBCs")—a group of castes officially recognised as having been traditionally excluded but who, unlike Dalits, are not treated as "untouchables." Under the premise of proportional representation, OBCs are entitled to 27 percent reservations in public sector employment and higher education.

1.5.2. Protective Legislation

In addition to constitutional provisions, the government of India has pursued a two-pronged approach to narrowing the gap between the socioeconomic status of the scheduled caste population and the national average: one prong involves regulatory measures which ensure that the various provisions to protect their rights and interests are adequately implemented, enforced and monitored; the second focuses on increasing the self-sufficiency of the scheduled caste population through financial assistance for self-employment activities through development programs to increase education and skills.

The protective component of this strategy includes the enforcement of those legal provisions that make up the Protection of Civil Rights Act, 1955, and the Scheduled Caste and Scheduled Tribe (Prevention of Atrocities) Act, 1989; of other state and central government laws; and of "positive discrimination" through reservations in the arenas of government employment and higher education. These protective measures are monitored by the National Commissions for Scheduled Castes and Scheduled Tribes. The development measures for the educational, social, and economic "upliftment" of scheduled castes are administered by the Ministry of Social Justice and Empowerment.

1.5.2.1. The Protection of Civil Rights Act

With an eye to eradicating pervasive discrimination practised against scheduled caste members, the central government enacted the Protection of Civil Rights Act, 1955 ("PCR Act") to enforce the abolition of "untouchability" under Article 17 of the constitution. The PCR Act punishes offences that amount to the observance of "untouchability." These include, *inter alia*, prohibiting entry into places of worship, denying access to shops and other public places, denying access to any water supply, prohibiting entry into hospitals, refusing to sell goods or render services, and insulting someone on the basis of his or her caste.

Perhaps the greatest deficiency of the PCR Act was the fact that abuses against Dalits were not limited to name-calling or denial of entry into public spaces: violence was a defining characteristic of the abuse. Thirty-four years after the introduction of the PCR Act, the Scheduled Castes and Scheduled Tribes (Prevention of Atrocities) Act of 1989, was enacted purportedly to bring these other forms of abuse to an end.

1.5.2.2. The Scheduled Castes and Scheduled Tribes (Prevention of Atrocities) Act

In 1989 the Scheduled Castes and Scheduled Tribes (Prevention of Atrocities) Act was enacted to prevent and punish caste-based abuses, to establish special courts for the trial of such offences, and to provide for victim relief and rehabilitation. Its enactment represented an acknowledgement on the part of the government that abuses, in their most degrading and violent forms, were still perpetrated against Dalits decades after independence. A look at the offences made punishable by the Act provides a glimpse into the retaliatory or customarily degrading treatment Dalits may receive. The offences include: forcing members of a scheduled caste or scheduled tribe to drink or eat any inedible or obnoxious substance; dumping excrement, waste matter, carcasses or any other obnoxious substance in their premises or neighbourhood; forcibly removing their clothes and parading them naked or with painted face or body; interfering with their rights to land; compelling a member of a scheduled caste or scheduled tribe into forms of forced or bonded labour; corrupting or fouling the water of any spring, reservoir or any other source ordinarily used by scheduled castes or scheduled tribes; denying right of passage to a place of public resort; and using a position of dominance to exploit a scheduled caste or scheduled tribe woman sexually.

1.5.2.3. Additional Social Welfare Legislation

In addition to the acts described above, a number of other statutes aim to eradicate exploitative labour arrangements in which Dalits are frequent victims. The Employment of Manual Scavengers and Construction of Dry Latrines (Prohibition) Act, 1993, prohibits the employment of manual scavengers or the construction of dry (non-flush) latrines and punishes such offences with imprisonment and/or a fine. The Bonded Labour System (Abolition) Act, 1976, seeks to abolish all agreements and obligations arising out of the bonded labour system, release all labours from bondage, prohibit the creation of new bondage agreements, and order the economic rehabilitation of freed labours by the state. Other relevant acts include the Inter State Migrant Workmen Act, 1979, the Child Labour (Prohibition and Regulation) Act, 1986, the Minimum Wages Act, 1948, and the Equal Remuneration Act, 1976.

1.5.3. Economic Development Measures

The government of India has also attempted to increase the self-sufficiency of the scheduled caste population through financial assistance for self-employment activities and through development programs designed to increase education and skills. Included among these are post-matriculation scholarships for scheduled caste students (which purportedly reach over 20 million students), special education development programs for scheduled caste girls with low literacy levels, hostels for scheduled caste girls and boys from rural or remote areas (designed to facilitate access to education), and a centrally-sponsored assistance scheme for scheduled caste development corporations, which provide eligible scheduled caste families with low-interest loans and financial assistance for a variety of economic development schemes.

Pursuant to Articles 38, 39, and 46 of the constitution a Special Component Plan ("SCP") was introduced in 1979 with a view to "achieving overall development of SCs/STs (Scheduled Castes/ Scheduled Tribes) and to raise them above the poverty line." The SCP is "an umbrella programme under which all schemes implemented by State and Central Governments are dovetailed for addressing different needs of the Scheduled Castes," and is used by the Central Government to direct funds to critical areas of need to ensure the developments needs of the scheduled caste population. The Ministry of Social Justice and Empowerment's Planning, Research, Evaluation, and Monitoring Division ("PREM") is charged with assessing the effectiveness of these welfare programs. Through PREM, the Ministry provides grants to research institutions, professional organisations, and universities to study its scheduled caste welfare programs.

The plethora of laws and programs outlined above, that collectively comprise India's affirmative action package for Dalits, stand in perverse contradiction to the social realities that Dalits face.

1.6. Rule of Law Vs. Rule of Caste

The Rule of Law in India lives in the shadow of the Rule of Caste. If law is understood as a set of rules backed by sanction, then both the legal system and the caste system can lay claim to the mantle of law with one significant difference: the caste system operates more efficiently, more swiftly, and more punitively than any rights-protecting law on the books. Political theorist Hannah Arendt lamented the "poignant irony" of the discrepancy between regarding as "'inalienable' those human rights, which are enjoyed by citizens of the most prosperous and civilised countries, and the situation of the rightless themselves." The rightless, in Arendt's opinion, were those stateless individuals who had been deprived of what she saw as the most fundamental of all human rights: the right to membership in a political community. According to Arendt, without citizenship status, inalienable rights do not come into effect. Devoid of such membership with a people or a state, individuals lose "the very qualities which make it possible for other people to treat [them] as fellow [human beings]."

If citizenship is understood as a bundle of rights that includes, *inter alia*, the rights to personal liberty, personal security, equality before the law, freedom of speech and conscience, the right to own property, and the right to political participation, then Dalits fall far short of that bundle. As a system of law, the caste system relegates Dalits into an almost permanent state of exception. If castes are understood as nations, then as outcasts, Dalits are rendered stateless in their own country. As shown below, the rights enshrined in the constitution and implemented through a plethora of legislation are not meant to serve them. As victims of both over and under enforcement of the law, Dalit existence is defined by the extremes of brutality and neglect.

1.6.1. Police Brutality against Dalits

India's National Human Rights Commission ("NHRC") a body that India characterises as the apex national institution to protect human rights and redress grievances has characterised the law enforcement machinery as the greatest violator of Dalits' human rights. According to the NHRC, custodial torture and killing of Dalits, rape and sexual assault of Dalit women, and looting of Dalit property by the police "are condoned, or at best ignored."

Under a theory of collective punishment, the police will often subject entire Dalit communities to violent search and seizure operations in search of one individual. Dalit communities may also be perceived by the police as inherently criminal. Dalits and other poor minorities are disproportionately represented among those detained and tortured in police custody because most cannot afford to pay police bribes. Police officers' deeply embedded caste bias (most officers belong to the "upper castes") and a general lack of familiarity with legislative protections for Dalits further compound the problem. Dalits, including those arrested for minor offences, are often held in custody for long periods of time, occasionally at distant and isolated locations to avoid publicity, where they are frequently deprived of food and water, subjected to verbal abuse and humiliation, severe beatings, sexual perversities, and demeaning acts. Often the injuries inflicted can prove fatal. Dalit activists are also accused of being "terrorists," "threats to national security," and "habitual offenders," and frequently charged under the National Security Act, 1980, the Terrorist and Disruptive Activities (Prevention) Act, 1985 ("TADA"), and even older counter insurgency laws such as the Indian Explosives Act, 1884. Dalit activists are often subjected to specious prosecutions, falsified charges, and physical abuse and torture following arrest.

1.6.2. Under-Enforcement

Media, nongovernmental, and official reports reveal that the police have systematically failed to protect Dalit homes and Dalit individuals from acts of looting, arson, sexual assault, torture, and other inhumane acts such as stripping and parading Dalit women and forcing Dalits to drink urine and eat faces.

According to legal scholar Alexandra Natapoff, under-enforcement as a phenomenon "deserves a more central role in the evaluation of the evenhandedness and democratic legitimacy of the criminal system." Though articulated in the context of the United States, her conclusion, that under-enforcement "offers important insights into the government's relationship with vulnerable groups in the context of the criminal system," is equally applicable to the Indian context. As Natapoff contends,

> Over- and under-enforcement are twin symptoms of a deeper democratic weakness of the criminal system: its non-responsiveness to the needs of the poor, racial minorities, and the otherwise politically vulnerable. Because of this weakness, justice and lawfulness are distributed unevenly and unequally across racial and class lines, and some people can trust and rely on law enforcement while others cannot.

In what Natapoff defines as "underenforcement zones," "the state routinely and predictably fails to enforce the law to the detriment of vulnerable residents," with the result that "[f]or residents of these zones, lawfulness is spread unevenly throughout daily life and the legal system is at best unpredictable." For Dalits in India, the under-enforcement "zone" may be as wide as India itself.

1.6.2.1. Under-enforcement of Protective Legislation

In 2004, the NHRC released the findings of an in-depth examination of the implementation of protective legislation for scheduled castes. The report is a strong indictment of the government's failure to carry out its promises to protect Dalits from atrocities and violations of their fundamental rights and to grant remedies for rights' violations. NHRC concluded that there is virtually no monitoring of the acts' implementation at any level. Political leaders have also played a significant role in hindering the implementation of the Prevention of Atrocities Act.

The Protection of Civil Rights Act and the Prevention of Atrocities Act together represent the most important pieces of legislation for the protection of Dalits. The potential of these laws to bring about social change, however, has been severely hampered by their under-enforcement due to institutional prejudice and police corruption. State governments have made no serious efforts to identify areas where the practice of "untouchability" is prevalent, have done very little to make public the provisions of the acts, and have failed to periodically survey the acts' effectiveness.

According to the 2001-2002 Annual Report on the Prevention of Atrocities Act, 30,022 cases were registered under the Act in 2001 and 27,894 cases were registered in 2002. As staggering as these statistics are, they represent only a fraction of the violence committed against Dalits. Systematic non-registration or improper registration of atrocities contributes to under-reporting. Additional failures in investigation once a case is registered also help ensure low conviction rates. According to the Annual Report, only 2.31 percent of cases brought under the Act in 2002 resulted in convictions. The low rate of convictions, compared against the high number of atrocities reported against Dalits, is often attributed to the caste bias of prosecutors as well as other organs of justice, including the judiciary, and to the law enforcement machinery's lack of familiarity with provisions of the relevant legislation.

Dalit women are more likely to suffer violence and especially sexual violence, and are least likely to get redress in the courts. Rape cases are not prosecuted in good faith and Dalit women suffer both caste and gender discrimination in the courtrooms. Prosecutor failures in the context of cases involving rape against Dalit women also serve to encourage the use of rape as a tool to punish and silence Dalit communities.

1.6.2.2. Under-enforcement of Social Welfare Legislation

A plethora of social welfare legislation has been enacted with the goal of eradicating exploitative economic arrangements in which Dalits are frequent victims. Land reform legislation has additionally been passed to help free Dalits from their perennial landless condition. Pervasive under-enforcement, however, along with significant loopholes in the acts themselves, has severely undermined the effectiveness of these laws and their accompanying rehabilitation programs.

While the Bonded Labour System (Abolition) Act, 1976, seeks to abolish all agreements and obligations arising out of the bonded labour system, the extent to which bonded labours have been identified, released, and rehabilitated in the country is negligible. Rehabilitation programs for individuals who have been released from bonded labour are similarly undermined by their failure to secure substantial alternative employment, implement rehabilitation immediately after release, and ensure timely provision of benefits.

The prevalence of the practice of manual scavenging has not been alleviated by the Employment of Manual Scavengers and Construction of Dry Latrines (Prohibition) Act, 1993, or its rehabilitation program. To the contrary, the number of dry latrines has increased since 1989. Despite the fact that the Act was intended to be fully implemented by October 2, 2002, only 151,930 out of the total 676,009 manual scavengers identified as of 2004 by the NHRC have been retrained, while only 394,638 have been rehabilitated. The NHRC has concluded that the objectives of these and other relevant labour laws have been soundly defeated due to the inadequacy and unresponsiveness of the law enforcement machinery, as well as the economic and social dominance of the offending employers.

Land reform laws that were intended to provide reparations for the historic landlessness of Dalits have failed due to: a lack of political will and bureaucratic commitment; loopholes in the laws; the tremendous manipulative power of the landed classes; excessive interference of courts; and problems in ensuring that oral tenancies are truthfully recorded in land records so as to enable implementation of the land to the tiller policy.

While India has adopted measures to abolish forced prostitution and "rehabilitate" *devadasis*, these efforts have been largely unsuccessful. Legislative initiatives are poorly implemented. The socialite perception of *devadasis* as women who are sexually available to men makes it more difficult for them to approach the police with complaints of sexual violence. Moreover, the police themselves have been known to exploit *devadasis*.

1.6.2.3. Under-enforcement of Economic Development Measures

According to the National Human Rights Commission, the beneficial impact of programs aimed at ensuring Dalit development have been hindered by inadequate investment of public resources; non-utilisation or diversion of funds earmarked for Dalit development; a lack of programs specifically targeted to Dalit development; poor preparation of such projects; and a lack of monitoring of development programs leading to the failure of many such programs to reach their target groups. The anti-Dalit bias of personnel in charge of implementing these programs has also hindered their effectiveness. Moreover, Dalits rarely participate in the formulation and implementation of development projects. Many Dalits are also unaware of the existence of such programs, further restricting their participation.

The Special Component Plan described above—a potentially powerful mechanism for ensuring Dalit economic empowerment has itself been thwarted in its application and implementation by administrative agencies at the central and state level. According to the National Campaign on Dalit Human Rights, during the past five-year plan period, an average of 2 billion Euros (US$ 2.96 billion) per year was illegally diverted from these funds. According to some estimates, over the course of the past quarter-century a total of US$93.75 billion has been siphoned from Dalit development programs.

1.7. Casteism and Corruption

While the near epidemic of over- and under-enforcement speaks to a lack of political will on the part of the state to ensure Dalits' rights, it also serves to counter common assumptions about why such abuses persist. The notion that a dearth of resources are to blame for the lack of socioeconomic development of Dalits is belied by the siphoning of close to $3 billion a year away from funds that were meant to advance Dalit economic empowerment. Secondly, the brutality of the police toward Dalits makes clear that they are not merely uninterested in securing redress for anti-Dalit crimes; they view Dalits as criminals and derelicts at best, and subhuman at worst. Local police chiefs have been known to indoctrinate recruits to hate Dalits, and Dalits may be denied entry into police stations. What security do Dalits have when they cannot even step foot into the very office that represents their first line of defence, or worse, when they are tortured or raped by those meant to defend them?

What has alternatively been called a "lack of political will" or "police corruption" benignly represents something far more pernicious. The words "police" and "corruption" seemingly go hand in hand in India; one can hardly avoid using one word without uttering the other. But what is meant by corruption in the context of caste is woefully misunderstood. While petty bribes do certainly play a role, especially when most Dalits can ill-afford to pay them, the lack of "will" to enforce the law is not due to passive apathy but to active complicity in the caste system. The nexus between political leaders and "upper-caste" community members accounts, to some extent, for these failures and for the disincentive to address violations by private actors. That which is under-enforced is done so at the behest of the privileged castes to whom the police and the judiciary owe their caste loyalty and who have a vested (karmic and economic) interest in keeping the system in place. Those who are brutalised represent individuals who are simply meant to be treated that way.

Just as police officers refuse to register complaints brought by Dalits, as complainants "are often treated with indifference by local judges." The caste composition of the police and the judiciary is a significant part of the impunity equation. Dalits are severely under-represented in the higher ranks of the police, the prosecutors, and the judiciary. The reservations regime, discussed below, does not extend to the judiciary with the result that, in 2002, the Supreme Court had only one Dalit out of twenty-six judges, while the High Courts had 25 Dalits out of 625 positions. In January 2007, that Dalit judge, Justice K.G. Balakrishnan, became the first Dalit to rise to the position of Supreme Court Chief Justice.

According to recent studies based on available data, 47 percent of India's Chief Justices and 40 percent of all other judges have been "high-caste" Brahmins, who constitute only 6.4 percent of the population.

Caste discrimination also does not cease once a Dalit is appointed to a judicial position, as discriminatory attitudes prevail among judges themselves. The depth of anti-Dalit sentiment in the judiciary is particularly well illustrated by an incident that took place in July 1998 in the state of Uttar Pradesh, where, as the *Times of India* reports, an Allahabad High Court Judge had his chamber "purified with Ganga *jal*" (water from the River Ganges) because it had earlier been occupied by a Dalit judge.

When the law enforcers become the criminals and the judiciary treats its own colleagues with untouchable contempt, then something far more insidious is at play. The police, and in some cases the judiciary, do not owe their allegiance to the rule of law, but to caste. Casteism must then be viewed as a form of corruption, and a force that invites corruption, rather than something separate from it. Those who occupy a variety of positions in the public administration from the police, to prosecutors, to district collectors, to judges, and to government bureaucrats responsible for implementing social welfare programs are so deeply entrenched in the casteist mindset that the system cannot be anything but corrupt and the state is anything but neutral. The brutality and apathy of state agents is matched by the brutality of the dominant castes. This could only be so if they were one and the same.

1.8. Violence and Caste Entrenchment

In India's perennial struggle between the rule of law and the rule of caste, violence is the trump card that ensures the rule of caste always wins out. Violence against Dalits in India has reached epidemic proportions. Between 1992 and 2005 a total of 398,644 cases involving crimes against Dalits were registered throughout the country. These include the crimes of murder, rape, kidnapping, robbery, and arson, among others. Police statistics averaged over the past five years indicate that every week 13 Dalits are murdered, 5 Dalit homes (or possessions) are burned, 6 Dalits are kidnapped or abducted, and that every day 3 Dalit women are raped, 11 Dalits are assaulted and a crime is committed against a Dalit every eighteen minutes.

These statistics represent only a fraction of the violence committed against Dalits. A lack of police cooperation (including denying Dalits entry into police stations), fear of reprisals, systematic non-registration or improper registration of atrocities cases, and additional failures of investigation have all contributed to underreporting and to the staggering acquittal rates associated with these crimes. Despite these obstacles, fifty-seven atrocities cases are officially registered in police stations across the country every day.

Violence is a principal weapon in sustaining economic and caste-based discrimination against Dalits. Dalits' attempts to enforce their rights, alter village customs, defy the social order, or to demand land, increased wages, or political rights often lead to violence and economic retaliation on the part of those most threatened by changes in the status quo. Dalit communities as a whole are summarily punished for individual transgressions; Dalits are cut off from community land and employment during social boycotts, women bear the brunt of physical attacks, and the letter of the law is rarely enforced.

Over the course of just one week in September 2007, a number of atrocities made the headlines. On September 20, it was reported that a Dalit man, a sixty-year-old landless labourer, was beaten to death by landowners in the eastern state of Bihar over a "land-related dispute." Two days later in the northern state of Uttar Pradesh, a Dalit woman, whose son was accused of eloping with an "upper-caste" girl, was set on fire and killed. The following day it was reported that police had failed to register a First Information Report ("FIR") against suspects in the case of a Dalit boy who was forced to set himself ablase in the northern state of Punjab. On September 26, newspapers reported that in the central state of Madhya Pradesh, a Dalit labourer was reportedly tied to a tractor and dragged, sustaining severe injuries, for refusing to plow the fields because he was sick. That same day, it was reported that the suicide of a Dalit PhD. Student from the Indian Institute of Science in the southern state of Karnataka was alleged to have resulted from caste-based abuse and harassment.

The atrocities outlined above are revealing on many fronts and speak to the degrading, retaliatory, and violent nature of abuse against Dalits; to the impunity enjoyed by perpetrators of such acts; to the geographic spread of such cases; and perhaps most disturbingly, to the fact that these abuses are all too commonplace. A review of cases reported in any other week would likely yield the same results and even then would grossly underestimate the prevalence of such abuses, the majority of which never get reported to the police or make national headlines.

Tellingly, in that same week and in the week that followed, a number of headlines spoke to both the initiatives taken by the government to purportedly protect Dalit rights and to examples of Dalit protest and Dalit activists' engagement with the state machinery in an effort to demand their rights. The headlines, among others, read:

> "National Human Rights Commission issues notice to police for failure of action;" "Dalit Commission constituted in state;" "Collector for speedy disposal of atrocity cases;" "Cells to deal [with] Dalit issues;" "SC/ST orgns to campaign for reservation in Kerala;" "SC/ST hostel students go on an indefinite fast;" "Protectors block Delhi-Dehradun National highway;" "PIL [Public Interest Litigation] moved in HC [High Court] by Dalit outfit."

Hidden beneath the headlines are the parallel stories of resilience and retaliation. It has been suggested that the rise in violence against Dalits since the early 1990s is a direct reaction to increasing resistance on the part of Dalits to defy the social order and demand their basic rights, on the streets and in the courtrooms. The retaliation, which in many instances is directed at entire Dalit communities, seeks to send a clear message that Dalits should not dare to step outside their karmically prescribed duties and occupations. The very nature of the violence signals the dehumanisation of Dalits as lesser humans and speaks to the use of violence as caste entrenchment. The use of sexual violence against Dalit women signals the perception of Dalit women as "sexually available," while the use of economic boycotts ensures that a relationship of economic dependency between Dalits and their "upper-caste" employers remains intact.

In the overwhelming majority of cases, the sheer brute force with which caste rules are enforced, and against entire Dalit communities, acts as a form of collective punishment. As noted above, punishment from the law enforcement machinery against perpetrators of such acts is comparatively nonexistent. The contradiction is not ironic; it is the logical outcome of that which justifies the violence itself. The observance of "untouchability" and the punishment of those who dare step out of their ranking as "untouchables" are acts "of religious merit, the non-observance of which is a sin." If the act of discriminating and punishing is seen as just, and laden with economic incentive, then how can just punishment be punished? Seen in this light, the impunity perpetrated by the police who are products of the same hierarchical system is not impunity from the vantage point of caste, but a form of justice in observance of a wholly different set of laws.

1.9. Collective Unconsciousness

Atrocities of the nature outlined above do not find a home in the collective conscience of the nation. Though the state may respond with the pro forma setting up of commissions to investigate particular atrocities, or with administrative agencies mandated to address the lack of justice to Dalit victims, the outcry from the general public is deafeningly silent. This of course begs the question, "Why?" Some may posit that such cases, by the sheer force of their volume turn outrage into apathy, compassion into fatigue, and normalise that which should be anything but. Others may live in wilful blindness and fail to connect the dots between acts of violence to draw the clear line that such violence helps preserve: the line between the "pure" and the "polluted." Some may offer counter-narratives that pigeonhole such incidents into rural pockets, blame them on a few bad apples, or worse, blame the victims for the violence they surely invited upon themselves. These and other narratives help reconcile such tragedies more comfortably with one's idea of what India represents: a secular liberal democracy (and the world's largest at that), a multicultural tapestry of cultures and religions, and a booming economic powerhouse.

The Idea of India is, of course, in the eye of the beholder. As has been said about the caste system itself, India is "Superman's heaven and the common man's damnation." Some have begun to tell the Tale of Two Indias, wherein inequalities are further polarised by globalisation's steady march, and where Indians are anointed into the Billionaire's Club, while farmers commit suicide to escape their vexing poverty. But the equation is not so simply divided between the "Haves" and "Have-Nots." For caste has turned India into many nations and has kept India from realising true nationhood. If nationhood is defined as the success of securing citizens' allegiance to the nation above all else, then surely India has failed in its nation-building project. For Indians, the nation comes a distant second to caste, religion, and region.

Then there are those who, even while acknowledging the Two India paradigm, argue that reservations will only serve to "enshrine caste differences" and "prevent India from reaching its full potential." For such critics, the vision of the future India can only be realised through the creation of educational opportunities for all, regardless of caste, and through equality of opportunity in a "merit-based system." Reservations, in turn, are emblematic of a "divide-and-rule" approach that has the "potential to break up India."

Ironically, those at the bottom of the caste system would likely make the very same argument with one important difference: it is not reservations that divide and rule or get in the way of equality of opportunity; it is the caste system itself. Set against the backdrop of the "untouchability" mindset described above, and the abuses and inequalities that it foments, reservations *create* the possibility of a meritocracy and of equality of opportunity, albeit imperfectly, rather than undermine it. The space into which reservations enter, the space of caste, is antithetical to "merit" because under the caste system respect and ability (or lack thereof) is determined not by natural talent, but by the karmic *non*-accident of one's birth into a particular caste.

As the reservations debate careens into the corporate board room, many now argue that India will lose its competitive edge and sacrifice efficiency if the private sector comes under the purview of reservations and opens the door to "non-meritorious" candidates. Caste-based affirmative action in India, a constitutional right, is now portrayed as antithetical to the meritocracy that India purportedly represents. An overhaul of the terms of the reservations debate is long overdue.

REFERENCES

Bloch, Francis, and Vijayendra Rao, "Statistical Discrimination and Social Assimilation," *Economics Bulletin*, 10(2), 2001, Pp: 1-5

Conlon, Frank F., "Caste by Association: The Gauda Sarasvata Brahmana Unification Movement," *The Journal of Asian Studies*, Vol. 33, No. 3, Pp: 351-365, May 1974.

Das, Veena, *Structure and Cognition: Aspects of Hindu Caste and Ritual*, Second Edition, Oxford University Press, Delhi, 1982.

Kumar, Dharma, *Land and Caste in South India*, Manohar Publishers, New Delhi, 1992.

2

Caste-based Reservation

The reservations policy has not proved in and of itself to be a sufficient remedy for caste discrimination against Dalits in India. Though reservations have helped support a Dalit political awakening, they are limited in their reach. The reservations policy benefits only a minute percentage of Dalits in the country high illiteracy and drop out rates among Dalits mean that very few are able to avail themselves of constitutional rights in public sector employment and education. A number of key sectors also continue to remain outside the purview of the reservation policy; and caste-based discrimination continues to be practised in the sectors where reservations are secured, leading to under-enforcement.

Problems of enforcement and reach are, however, effectively sidelines in the anti-reservations debate. Reservations are now at the centre of a storm of critique that projects reservations as undermining "meritocracy ideals" and reinforcing caste-based divisions. There has also been widespread public opposition to reservations for Dalits in local government bodies (often leading to violence) and in highly coveted government jobs and seats in higher education because of the economic security these jobs are perceived to offer. While reservations to state legislatures and the lower house of parliament have ensured greater Dalit representation in political bodies, these reservations have not necessarily translated to greater protection of Dalit rights. Finally, the already limited reach of reservations is increasingly undermined by economic liberalisation and its attendant outsourcing of public sector jobs to the private sector where reservations, for the time being at least, cannot reach.

2.1. Reach of Reservations

It is not incorrect to say that for some things are getting better. Dalits have achieved positions of economic and political prominence unimaginable prior to independence. Thanks in large part to greater opportunities created by reservations, Dalits are now engineers and surgeons and feature prominently on the political landscape. The expanding power base of Dalit and "low-caste" political parties, the election of Dalit and "low-caste" chief ministers to state governments, and even the appointment of a Dalit as president of India in July 1997 all signal the increasing political prominence of Dalits, but cumulatively have yet to yield any significant benefit for the majority of Dalits. Indeed, one could argue, as sociologist Jogdand does, that the reservations have really only provided "individual social mobility at the expense of group stagnation," in that gains at the singular level are only loosely tending towards the uplifting of Dalits as a whole.

The examples of a Dalit chief minister, a former Dalit president, and the current Dalit Chief Justice of the Supreme Court of India are called upon to symbolise far more than they represent evidence of real equality for Dalits in India today. Such figures are on the fingertips of those who critique accounts of widespread untouchability, exploitation, and violence against Dalits as "unbalanced." How the identification of a handful of examples balances the treatment of over 167 million people as subhuman is left unquestioned as the curious mathematical feat that it represents. As is often the case in other countries, the existence of the exception is enough to swallow the rule. Rather than strengthening the argument that such *few* examples confirm the sluggish pace of change, they are offered as proof positive of the success of legal reform.

According to a 1996 estimate, only 1.1 million out of the then population of 138 million Dalits were employed in sectors that fell under the domain of reservations, a paltry 0.8 percent. With the privatisation of public sector industries since the advent of economic reforms in India in the early 1990s, that percentage has likely declined. For the minute percentage that has been able to escape the confines of poverty, reservations represent the only viable path to economic liberation and the embodiment of hope for many Dalits that a slice of the economic pie is "reserved" for them. Reservations are an entry point, an opening of the door to institutions that were historically sealed shut by the caste system.

Though limited in their reach and their effect, research suggests that reservations for Dalits in political representation, public employment, and education have benefited those whom the policies were able to reach. Supporters of reservations argue that without affirmative action Dalits would not be able to penetrate the caste ceiling in education and employment that results from entrenched anti-Dalit biases. They add that there are no objective standards of merit applicable to all groups within society, given that dominant groups shape traditions within which they make judgments of merit. Further, they support reservations on the basis of national diversity, arguing that different views should be represented in national institutions to promote diversity, which ultimately benefits the social and the political life of the country.

Supporters also point to evidence that reservation policies have been successful in some areas. Reservations in local government bodies, such as village councils or *panchayats*, for example, have enhanced the delivery of local public goods to disadvantaged groups. Similarly, reservations in higher education have afforded greater opportunities to Dalit students. While the reservation policies tend to benefit the so-called "creamy layer" of the Dalit population, the average socioeconomic status of Dalit students is still significantly lower than that of other students. As a result of reservations, these students are able to secure better career opportunities than they would have in the absence of reservation policies.

2.2. Under-enforcement of Reservation Policies

The few who have been able to avail themselves of the benefit of reservations must still wage a hard-fought battle to overcome the stigma of their "untouchable" status. Caste-based occupational distribution is reinforced in reserved government employment. The National Human Rights Commission reports that Dalits occupy 65.57 percent of the total government posts for *safai karmacharis* (sweepers) and only 16.7 percent of non-sweeper posts. Dalits are also discriminated against when being considered for promotions. Reservations in higher education continue to be met with a great deal of resistance leading to under-enforcement. In the country's 256 universities and approximately 11,000 colleges funded by the University Grants Commission (an apex body of the Government of India), Dalits and tribal community members comprise only 2 percent of the teaching positions about 75 thousand teaching positions reserved for these communities remain vacant.

Dalit students also continue to face discrimination in higher education and are limited in their employment opportunities upon graduation. In September 2006, amidst anti-reservation protests, allegations of caste-based discrimination and intimidation surfaced at the All-India Institute of Medical Sciences ("AIIMS"), India's premier medical institute. In written complaints submitted to the director of the Institute, two first-year Dalit students complained of casteist remarks and various forms of harassment and intimidation from senior "upper-caste" students. The complaints were accompanied by a memorandum signed by forty students recounting similar incidents of harassment and intimidation.

Graduating from an eminent institution also does not guarantee suitable employment for Dalits. Despite earning a Masters degree in economics from Gujarat University, the best job twenty-four-year-old Arvind Vaghela could get was as a road sweeper. Vaghela's story underscored the experience of many other university-educated Dalits. In his city of Ahmedabad;

> "[n]early 100 of its council sanitation workers have degrees in subjects ranging from computing to law, but cannot get better jobs because they are Dalits."

Such outcomes are the result of intentional discrimination in hiring decisions, and the lack of "social and cultural capital" enjoyed by Dalits. As noted in a recent study by economist Deshpande and sociologist Newman, "social and cultural capital (the complex and overlapping categories of caste, family background, network and contacts) play a huge role in urban, formal sector labour markets." As a result, Dalits' historic exclusion and disadvantage continues to undermine their advancement even where they are just as qualified and competent as their "upper-caste" peers.

Where political reservations are concerned, strict party politics has, according to one commentator, resulted in "accommodating rather than forceful, articulate and independent" Dalit elected representatives. More fundamentally, violence and intimidation are used to prevent Dalits from standing for election in local government bodies.

In October 2005, a Dalit woman, Prabhati Devi, was burned alive for contesting a *panchayat* (village council) election against an "upper-caste" candidate in Mirsapur district in Uttar Pradesh in defiance of a local politician's warning not to contest. Those Dalits who are in positions of public office are also often unable to properly discharge their public functions due to intimidation, threats, and physical violence at the hands of "upper-caste" community members.

Additionally, Dalits who convert to Christianity or Islam lose their "scheduled caste" status and the few benefits it affords. While the Constitution of India grants certain constitutional rights to Hindu, Buddhist, and Sikh Dalits, the same benefits do not extend to Dalits who convert to Christianity or Islam, even though they are ultimately unable to escape their discriminatory treatment as "untouchables." At this writing, a petition challenging the constitutional validity of the 1950 Presidential Order limiting reservations to Hindu, Buddhist, and Sikh scheduled castes was pending before the Supreme Court.

Despite the obvious problems associated with the effective implementation of reservations, equality on paper has helped usher in a new conservative discourse. Fuelled by proposals to introduce reservations in the private sector and expand the scope of reservations in higher education, such a discourse skips the step of situating reservations in the context of the social and unequal reality that Dalits face, and moves straight to critiquing the continued "privillaging" of particular groups on the basis of their caste as a mechanism that reinforces difference.

2.3. Reservations in Private Sector

Economic liberalisation in India with its underlying philosophy of increased reliance on market forces, a dismantling of controls, and a drastically reduced role of the state has resulted in a shrinking of the public sector. The reservations model is therefore affecting and able to assist fewer people, inasmuch as government related jobs are being drastically reduced. Though poorly monitored and enforced, there is, as noted above, evidence to support the notion that Dalits have benefited from the quota system. Substantial divestment in the public sector, including the proliferation of joint ventures formed between public sector undertakings and private companies, both domestic and foreign, serves to severely undercut the reach of the reservations policy. According to Dalit theorist Dr. Anand Teltumbde,

> Even if such entities technically remains a PSU [Public Sector Undertaking] and follows the reservation policy sincerely, it would still have little or no scope to absorb the dalits in its staff. Whatever may be the strategic considerations, the fall out of this process practically amounted to shutting the doors of these new age companies to the dalits and to potential neutralisation of the reservation policy.

Reservations in educational institutions and scholarships for Dalit students represent a critical component in Dalit socioeconomic development. Economic reforms have, however, led to a freezing in grants to many institutions. The privatisation of social services is turning education and health services into commodities only affordable to the rich. A blind faith adherence to privatisation as the lone path that India must take, combined with the pretext that reservations undermine India's ability to compete in the global market, is seemliest "superimposed on... Traditional caste prejudice" to all but seal reservations' ominous fate. In response, sectors within civil society and some government actors and agencies have supported a proposed extension of reservations to the private sector.

The National Commission for Scheduled Castes and Scheduled Tribes has stated that the private sector, which continues to enjoy government patronage through concession land, financing, and excise and sales tax relief should also be brought under the purview of the reservation policy. Indian economist, Sukhadeo Throat, has argued in favour of extending reservations to the private sector to redress market discrimination against Dalits. According to Throat, caste-based market discrimination not only exacerbates inequality but is also "retrogressive for economic growth." Throat and Newman argue that discrimination here should be understood as the result of social exclusion of Dalits. The restrictions placed by caste on Dalits' ability to participate in the market, and the fact that the benefits of an exploitative market outweigh the intangible costs to Dalits, mean that we cannot simply rely on a competitive market to self-correct discrimination. Strong opposition to the private sector proposal remains, however, from both private employers and certain political parties. Private employers have criticised the government for failing to provide Dalits adequate opportunities in education and for imposing upon the private sector the obligation to employ individuals they deem unqualified.

2.4. Caste and Anti-power Sharing

Opposition to reservations often centres around the "meritocracy ideal" that "positions in society should be based on the abilities and achievements of the individual rather than on characteristics such as family background, race, religion or wealth." Critics add that reservation policies are inherently divisive and serve only to solidify caste divisions. Instead of lowering the caste barriers, they argue, reservation policies accentuate caste identity and lead to greater social stratification. Opponents have also called for greater reliance on economic indicators of "backwardness," rather than on caste, and have criticised the reservation policies as strengthening "anti-Scheduled Caste attitudes."

The idea that reservations are a *threat* to meritocracy is a farce. The road that begins with Dalit students being made to clean toilets at schools and sit at the back of classrooms, and ends with Dalit students facing ongoing harassment from their peers in institutes of higher education, while examiners stroke students' backs to check whether they are wearing the sacred Brahmin thread, is hardly one that is paved with meritocracy ideals.

The caste system is by its very nature antithetical to merit inasmuch as it assigns value on the basis of birth and not individual aptitude. Similarly, hearings and promotions are dictated not just by the academic credentials of particular candidates, but by the ability of those individuals to effectively deploy caste-based networks that, as in the public administration, corrupt the ability of the private sector system to operate neutrally.

Moreover, if market efficiency is furthered by the freedom of individuals to develop their capacities to the point of choosing their occupations, then that very principle "is violated in the caste system in so far as it involves an attempt to appoint tasks to individuals in advance, selected not on the basis of trained original capacities, but on that of the social status of [his or her] parents." And what could be more inefficient than the denial of opportunity to individuals, in the millions, who are told from birth to death that they will never amount to more than that which has been previously ordained for them? As an economic organisation, "caste is therefore a harmful institution, in as much as it involves the subordination of man's natural powers and inclinations to the exigencies of social rules." By denying so many the freedom to choose their profession, caste also becomes "a direct cause of much of the unemployment we see in the country."

Reservations or quotas are critiqued for their inflexibility, but the rigidity of the caste system, against which more fluid options find no traction, does not get scrutinised. Timeframes for bringing reservations to an end are proposed as though giving legal remedies a deadline will automatically lead to discrimination's time-bound demise.

Reservations as a form of power sharing in India take on new significance given that the caste system is organised around the idea of power consolidation and is, in its division of labour according to caste, antithetical to the very notion of a meritocracy. The absence of choice in employment is also quite stark in the Indian context wherein one's caste, or more specifically one's membership in an "untouchable" caste, remains determinative of one's occupation. Dalits throughout India are forced into an involuntary monopoly over occupations considered too filthy or polluting for others, occupations over which they ironically exert 100 percent reservations. *Inequality* of opportunity is the social norm and one that the state has stepped in to legislate against in order to secure equality of respect and concern for its most marginalised inhabitants. Left to its own devices, Indian society would no doubt swallow Dalits whole. Until now at least, the Indian Supreme Court has agreed.

2.5. Supreme Court Jurisprudence on Reservations

According to comparative constitutional law scholar Jacobsohn, each nation's constitution contains a vision of the kind of polity it seeks to preserve and to become, which combines distinctive aspects of the country's political culture with features of a universal culture of constitutionalism. Jacobsohn refers to the gap between the ideal espoused in a constitution and the societal status quo as the "disharmonic jurisprudential context," within which courts have incentives and opportunities to learn from the constitutional approaches of other countries, although they may also incur costs in doing so.

Indeed the Indian judiciary has on numerous occasions triumphantly stepped into such a disharmonic context to attempt to harmonise India's constitutional vision with the abysmal condition of Dalit social reality (borrowing in some cases from the American experience). The jurisprudence of the Indian Supreme Court has to date lent much credence to this ethos. In *ABSK Sangh v. Union of India*, Justice Chinnappa Reddy noted that,

> [W]hen posts... Are reserved... To members of Scheduled Castes, Scheduled Tribes and other socially and economically Backward Classes it is not a concession or privilege extended to them, it is in the recognition of their undoubted fundamental right to equality of opportunity... And to secure to all its citizens, justice, social, economic and political and equality of status and opportunity... To ensure their participation on an equal basis in the administration of the country.... Every lawful method is permissible to secure the due representation of SCs and STs in the public services.

In that same case, Justice Krishna Iyer noted:

> Trite arguments about efficiency are a trifle phoney.... The fundamental question arises, as to what's "merit" and "suitability?" Elitists, whose sympathies with the masses have dried up, are from standards of Indian people, least suitable to run the government and least meritorious to handle the state business.... Unfortunately, the very orientation of our selection process is distorted and those like the candidates from Scheduled Castes whom from their birth, have a traumatic understanding of the conditions of agrestic India, have in one sense more capability than those who lived under affluent circumstances and are callous to the human lot of the sorrowing masses.

As the following discussion shows, implementing this understanding of Dalit's social reality is far from straightforward. As challenges to the constitutional validity of reservations grow, the limits of the Supreme Court's ability to reconcile the state's duty to take positive action with its duty to ensure the right to equality are increasingly tested.

2.6. Caste and the Other Backward Classes

The period starting in the early 1990s is significant not only because it launched the era of economic reforms, but also because it saw the entry of "Other Backward Classes" ("OBCs") into the reservations conversation—an entry that has resulted in much confusion and backlash, including against Dalits, and has paved the way for Class to enter the Caste debate. OBCs or so-called backward castes are identified as those whose ritual rank and occupational status are above "untouchables," but who themselves remain socially and economically "depressed." Few groups in independent India have made progress on a scale comparable to the OBCs, including in the arenas of politics and land reforms. Yet the inclusion of so many heterogeneous groups within the OBC category has both made for its enormous size and has complicated its demands for reservations.

In *Indira Sawhney v. Union of India*, which challenged the constitutionality of then-Prime Minister V.P. Singh's decision to implement 27 percent reservations in government employment for OBCs, the Supreme Court affirmed that caste may still be used as a criterion for determining backwardness, as long as the caste is primarily socially and educationally backward, as determined by empirical evidence. Furthermore, in order to ensure that the most disadvantaged would benefit from reservations, the Court spelled out a means test, or the "creamy layer" test, which imposed an income limit to exclude those eligible for OBC classification. The Indian government subsequently implemented a more complex means test to be applied to individuals and their families who attempted to claim backward status. This test takes into account a variety of indices of social, educational, and economic disadvantage, such as parents' professional status, and the claimant's occupation and wealth as calculated by agricultural landholding. Notably, the Supreme Court's determination of "scheduled caste" status embodies the critical recognition that one's membership in a Dalit caste *per se* subjects individuals to a particularly egregious form of discrimination ("untouchability") *regardless* of one's socioeconomic status, and merits positive action and special attention by the state. By contrast, the determination of "Other Backward Classes" recognises the socioeconomic gains achieved by many members of backward castes in India—who are not subject to "untouchability" practices—and circumscribes constitutional protections more strictly to those in greatest need by using empirical evidence of economic status.

In December 2005, the Ninety-third Amendment, which inserted Article 15(5) into the Indian constitution, expanded reservations for OBCs to include private colleges, while the Central Education Institution (Reservation in Admission) Act of 2006 provided for 27 percent reservations for Other Backward Classes ("OBCs") in higher educational institutions in the country. When combined with the percentage of seats already reserved for scheduled castes and scheduled tribes, a total of 49.5 percent of seats would be reserved in national public universities. In April 2008, a five-judge constitutional bench in the Supreme Court upheld the 27 percent OBC quota in government-maintained and funded institutions, stating that the Ninety-third Amendment—which empowers the Central Government to make reservations for "socially and educationally backward classes," scheduled castes, and schedules tribes in educational institutions— does not violate the Constitution's "basic structure." Meanwhile, the implementation of the Central Education Institution Act has been stayed by a two-judge bench hearing, which in light of the importance of the questions of law raised in this case referred it for hearing to a higher bench.

At issue in the latter case is whether the Ninety-third Amendment confers on the government the "unbridled power" to make provisions for certain groups without indicating the circumstances under which such reservations can be made, or limiting the duration of such provisions thereby violating the right to equality and the basic structure of the Constitution of India. Petitioners have argued that there is currently no accepted definition of who constitutes the "socially and economically backward classes," adding that the use of data that is either obsolete or based entirely on caste statistics further perpetuates the caste system. A related contention involves the scope of Article 15(5) and whether allowing for reservations in institutions of higher education abandons the significance of merit altogether, adding that such reservations in speciality institutions had been struck down by the

Supreme Court in earlier decisions. Finally, the petitioners have argued that the current Act does not take into account the concept of excluding the "creamy layer" from the reservations policy.

While the category at issue is that of OBCs, the issue of whether Dalit candidates should also be subjected to the "creamy layer" test has now entered the fray. Moreover, the public discourse and ensuing protests have conflicted the Dalit and OBC categories in the symbols used to decry the Amendment and the Act. In the spring of 2006, for instance, thousands of students across the country went on strike to protest the expansion of reservations in higher education. Under the banner of "Youth for Equality," "medical students in Delhi, dressed in their white coats, took up brooms and swept the streets to suggest that they will become untouchable 'sweepers' if the policies are implemented." Students at the All India Institute of Medical Sciences also burned copies of Dr. Ambedkar's books in protest, video-taped the incident, and circulated the video on campus as a means of intimidating Dalit students who were no strangers to name-calling, abuse, and harassment. Oblivious to the irony of degrading Dalits as sweepers while simultaneously marching under an equality banner, or burning the books of the author of the constitution whose equality language now buttresses their fight—an act no less horrific for Dalits than the burning of crosses in front of African-American homes by the Clue Culex Clan—the anti-reservations protests in India are a microcosm of the global trend to co-opt the language of equality for wholly unequal ends.

References

Paul R Brass, *The Politics of India since Independence,* Cambridge, University Press, 1990, pp 210-11.

Professor Parmaji, *Caste Reservations and Performance : Research Findings,* Warangal, Mamata, 1985, pp 174 -75.

Ramaiah, A (6 June 1992). "Identifying Other Backward Classes" (PDF). Economic and Political Weekly. pp. 1203–1207.

3

Politics of Positive Discrimination

The need to discriminate positively in favour of the socially underprivileged was felt for the first time during the nationalist movement. It was Mahatma Gandhi, himself a devout Hindu and a staunch believer in the caste system, who was the first leader to realise the importance of the subject and to invoke the conscience of the upper castes to this age-old social malady of relegating whole communities to the degrading position of "untouchables". He also understood the political logic of inducting this large body of people into the political mainstream in order to make the freedom movement more broadly-based.

By renaming these untouchables as "Harijans" (people of God) he tried to give this policy a religious sanction so as not to disturb the traditional sensitivities of the caste Hindus more than was really necessary. Gandhi's logic was not greeted with enthusiasm by all sections of the untouchables, most notably by their leader B R Ambedkar, who felt that it represented an extension of the patronising attitude of the upper castes, and no more than that. Against the background of the political conflict between the Congress and the Muslim League Ambedkar found the situation conducive to ask for separate electorates for the untouchables on the lines of the Muslim League.

The British government had obvious reasons to support the demand and on 17 August 1932 it announced the Communal Award granting separate electorates for the depressed classes by treating them as a minority. Gandhi protested against the Award and went on a fast unto death if it was not withdrawn. His contention was that the caste Hindus would react violently to the scheme and in rural areas which were dominated by upper castes the lives of the depressed classes would become even more miserable.

Behind this argument of course was Gandhi's political understanding that it would weaken the freedom movement. Whether Gandhi was actually interested in bringing the depressed classes into the social mainstream of Hinduism or was just indulging in a political ploy to gain the support of these classes for the freedom movement without tampering too much with the Hindu caste structure has been a long debate which has become extremely acrimonious of late.

The political crisis that Gandhi's hunger strike had triggered was resolved by the Poona Pact of 24 September 1932 signed between the non-Harijan Hindu leaders and Ambedkar. The pact was a compromise which provided for 148 reserved seats instead of the 78 separately elected members provided for by the Communal Award. It also granted certain privileges to the Harijans such as, educational opportunities, representation in services, and the franchise. It had become necessary to list the depressed castes for purposes of representation at the national and state levels.

This schedule was prepared in 1936 after considerable difficulty following the passage of the Government of India Act, 1935. It covered 43.6 million people in all, which meant 28.5% of the Hindu population and 19% of the total population of British India. By the time of the census of 1941 the number had risen to 48.8 million. It was this list which the Constituent Assembly later adopted. At the 1991 census there were about 135 million SC people in India consisting of 15.75% of the population.

So far as the enumeration of tribes was concerned it was relatively easy because of their cultural and spatial specification. Moreover, the British had already treated them separately for administrative purposes. Since the 1935 Government of India Act provided for the separate representation for the Scheduled Castes, separate representation for the "Backward Tribes" was a logical extension of the principle. Accordingly, a schedule of these tribes was also prepared. At the 1991 census they were about 66 million making up 7.75% of India's population.

3.1. Constitutional Provisions of Positive Discrimination

The Constitution of independent India which largely followed the pattern of the Government of India Act, 1935, made provisions for positive discrimination in favour of the Scheduled Castes and Scheduled Tribes (SCs & STs) which constituted about 23% of the divided India's population.

Besides reserving parliamentary seats for them they were given advantages in terms of admission to schools and colleges, jobs in the public sector, various pecuniary benefits for their overall development, and so on. The constitution indeed guaranteed the fundamental right of equality of all citizens before the law but it also categorically laid down that nothing in the constitution "shall prevent the State from making any special provision for the advancement of any socially and educationally backward classes of citizens or for the Schedules Castes and the Scheduled Tribes".

Some of the constitutional provisions which aimed at positive discrimination are:

— *Article 17:* Abolition of "untouchability" and making its practice in any form a punishable offence.

— *Article 46*: Promotion of educational and economic interests.

— *Article 16 and 335:* Preferential treatment in matters of employment in public services.

— *Article 330 and 332*: Reservation of seats in the Lok Sabha and State Assemblies.

Later, the job-related positive discrimination was extended to government-supported autonomous bodies. A 1974 Government order laid down that all such bodies which employed more than 20 people, and where 50% of the recurring expenditure was met out of grants-in-aid from the Central Government, and which received annual grants-in-aid of at least Rs.200,000 should invariably provide for reservation of SCs and STs in posts and services. The general rule which exempted the scientific and technical posts from the purview of positive discrimination was applicable to the autonomous bodies too.

As a result of this policy of positive discrimination, there has been some improvement in the position of these people. In 1957, the percentage of SCs in the Class I Central Government services was a mere 0.7. By 1971 it had improved to 2.58%. So far as the Class II and III services were concerned the improvements were from 2.01% to 4.6% and 7.3% to 9.59% respectively. In 1947-48, only 650 scholarships were awarded to the SC students for post-school studies costing the state Rs. 540,000. But by 1973- 74, the number of such scholarships had gone up to 270,420 costing the exchequer over Rs. 120 million. Corresponding improvements were recorded amongst the STs as well. In 1993, of the 365 districts of India about 65 were headed by SC or ST Indian Administrative Service (IAS) officers. Several vice chancellors, doctors, engineers, lawyers and other professionals now belong to these categories. But the overall picture has not improved much.

The disparity between the Dalits (a term which literally means the "downtrodden" and which is being used lately to connote the SCs) and others in literacy in terms of percentage points has remained more or less the same during the last four decades. This is much the same in respect of higher education, particularly scientific and technical education. The percentages of SCs and STs in these areas is still abysmally low. Where there are a large number of SCs and STs in the workforce they are mostly employed as workers in the lowest grades and in jobs which can only be described as menial.

The employment ratio of the SCs and STs is even lower in the public sector undertakings. While our data here is relatively old, they still reveal that even after almost three decades of independence the picture remains dismal.

What is particularly relevant to note is that most of the sweepers employed in the central government are still from the SC category. Thus while the SCs and STs are not represented in proportion to their population at higher levels they are over-represented at the lowest level which was the exact situation traditionally and which was meant to be altered.

There has been only marginal improvement in the lot of the SCs and STs. Social discrimination still persists even fifty years after independence and so does the stigma attached to persons belonging to such castes. The quotas earmarked for the SCs and STs are often not filled on account of the indifference of the heads of departments.

According to the Chairman of the National Commission for Scheduled Castes and Scheduled Tribes, this is done systematically through a variety of subterfuge—from destroying application forms from such persons, to filling up posts through *ad hoc* recruitment on the ground that there is a ban on new recruitment on a permanent basis. He is particularly critical of institutions of excellence in this regard : "These institutions are particularly resistant to SC reservation. Not one of them has filled the quota, including the Indian Institutes of Technology. They are also not filled owing to the non availability of qualified people even at the standards specifically lowered for these groups. For example, in 1980, the upper caste Hindus who made up 25% of the population held 89.63% of the Central Government jobs while the SCs & STs who made up for almost the same percentage of population (23%) accounted for only 5.6% of the jobs.

The primary reason for this depressing situation is that caste feelings still persist in Indian society which does not permit an egalitarian approach to develop roots whatever the state might direct. Surprisingly, while the intermediate castes fight for their rights *visa-vis* the upper castes yet when it comes to castes lower than theirs they show the same disregard to these lower castes which they themselves are subjected to by the upper castes. The noted social anthropologist M N. Srinivas sums up this attitude as "I am equal to those who think of themselves as my betters, I am better than those who regard themselves as my equals, and how dare my inferiors claim equality with me? As a natural corollary to this, politics is also caste-oriented and does not allow public policies to be oriented to the upliftment of the SCs and STs. The landlessness of these groups keeps them perpetually poor which also prohibits them from learning new skills which the present liberalisation process demands. The cumulative effect of all this is a lack of effort on their own part to improve their lot. It has been seen that the Dalits in predominantly Dalit villages are the worst off. There is of course the obvious political reason for this as well—no political voice is articulated on their behalf.

There are, in addition, certain inherent flaws in the policies of the government. The unprecedented growth of private Englishmedium schools which are far better than the state funded schools and where it is not necessary to reserve seats for the SCs and STs has totally undermined the policy meant to educate the latter and make them employable in a highly competitive job market. Insofar as the job quota is concerned the fact that they are not category-specific permits most of the offices to fulfill the statutory requirement by filling the posts at lower levels thus leaving the leadership levels largely upper-caste dominated. It is, however, a double-edged weapon. If the situation is altered in favour of the SCs and STs for each category of jobs the allegation against the policy of positive discrimination that it has benefited mostly the elates amongst the SCs and STs would become even sharper and would become more easily verifiable.

3.2. Dalit Ascendancy

Whatever may be said in criticism against the policy of positive discrimination it has served at least one purpose. It has made the Dalits conscious of their rights and they have learnt that in a democratic milieu these rights have to be extracted through agitation and electoral politics and not to be expected as charity doled out by the privileged classes. The old theoretical controversy between Gandhi and Ambedkar seems to be coming to the fore once again. That this conflict would generate increasingly high levels of violence is a foregone conclusion and there is considerable evidence of this. Reflecting on the situation Rajni Kothari writes:

> It poses the question of what to emphasise more: Western hegemony or caste domination within India, reflecting the issue posed much earlier during the independence movement as to what was more important- social emancipation or political autonomy. What is more important: autonomy (and agitation politics) of the community or autonomy of the nation in the international order? If it is both, how to reconcile the two? We seem to be back to the Ambedkar-Gandhi controversy. There is visible evidence of organised violence directed against the Dalits the result of which is an equally visible evidence of Dalit anger.

One saw this in Maharashtra, particularly in Mumbai, in July 1997 when the statue of Ambedkar was defiled by some miscreants. That act of vandalism was obviously not accidental. Behind the outburst of violence on the part of the Dalits were pent up frustrations and anger rooted in deep social maladies. There is no evidence to support the contention that wherever the Dalits are present in large numbers conflicts between them and others inevitably follow. An analysis of the violence, and indeed the atrocities, committed against the Dalits during the period 1977-85 would show that these incidents are largely concentrated in the Hindi-speaking states of Bihar, Madhya Pradesh (MP), Rajasthan and Uttar Pradesh (UP) where agriculture and the land tenure system are still highly feudalistic. Recent reports show the same pattern.

According to data available with the National Crime Record Bureau (NCRB), UP accounted for 47.7% of the total recorded violence countrywide against the SCs in 1994. The corresponding figures for Rajasthan and MP were 14.2 and 11 per cent respectively. Atrocities against the STs were most rampant in MP with 35.3% of the total national figure, followed by Rajasthan, Mahatashtra and Gujarat with 28.8, 8.9 and 8.6 per cent respectively. The data also showed that violence against both SCs and STs, considered together, rose from 24,992 cases in 1992 to 33,908 in 1994, registering a rise of 89.03%. It may be noted that the violence against the SC/STs, which had been witnessed ever since independence and before, increased measurably after 1970 when the political and economic influence of the OBCs increased and the OBCs began asserting their dominance over the SCs and STs, particularly in the rural areas. Against this background the political rise of the Dalits, through their most vociferous voice, the Bahujan Samaj Party, can be easily explained. In UP the party has emerged as a force to reckon with and has twice ruled the state through political alignments with other parties. It would not be surprising if in the near future it develops a stake in national politics as well, with Dalit politics increasingly enlarging its area of operation.

3.3. Other Backward Classes

Unlike the SC/ST there was no clear thinking about the backward classes in the pre-independence period. Yet in provinces such as Bombay, Madras and Mysore there was some reservation of jobs and seats for them in the field of education. Appendix 1 for a complete list of Backward Classes in India.) After independence, Articles 15(4) and 16(4) of the Constitution did make some reference to them but no special provision was made for their upliftment. In 1953, the First Backward Classes Commission was set up by the Government of India under the chairmanship of Kaka Kalelkar. In its report submitted in 1955 the Commission expressed doubts about using caste as the sole criterion to identify the backward classes. Nevertheless it identified 2399 caste groups as socially and educationally backward. The recommendations of the Commission, however, were not accepted by the government on the ground that objective tests had not been applied in making the selections. In some of the states, however, reservation for the OBCs was introduced.

For example, in 1970, on the basis of recommendations of the Manohar Pershad Commission, Andhra Pradesh reserved 25% of seats in colleges for them. This protective discrimination was extended to the level of Lecturers (Assistant Professors) in 1976 and to that of Readers (Associate Professors) in 1983. These policies, however, largely remained on paper; as for example, in the Osmania University during the period 1977-83 the number of teachers belonging to the BC, SC and ST categories all put together did not constitute even 10% of the selected candidates although 43% of the jobs had been reserved for them. The periodic reports submitted by the Andhra Pradesh Backward Classes (BC) Legislative Committee constantly drew attention to this nonimplementation of the rules. In the 1970s and 1980s, however, the backward caste movements picked up momentum in several parts of India and a number of castes such as the Yadavs, Kurmis, Koiris, Vokkaligas, emerged as important political forces. Arguing that their lot was even worse than that of the SC/ST for they constituted 52% of the population while they accounted for only 4.69% of the Central Government jobs, they launched political agitation in the name of the OBCs (Other Backward Castes). The Janata Party which came to power in 1977 represented many of these forces. It was against this background that the Second Backward Classes Commission was set up in 1978 under the chairmanship of B P Mandal. Popularly known as the Mandal Commission its report was submitted on 31 December 1980.

By using eleven indicators for determining social and educational backwardness and by basing its caste data on the 1931 census (the last census in which caste affiliations of Hindus were recorded) the Mandal Report came out with a list of 3,248 castes or communities as OBCs accounting for 52.4% of India's population, which meant roughly 350 million people then. The report pinpointed social disabilities they confronted and their economic, social and educational backwardness.

For the upliftment of the OBCs the Mandal Report recommended a number of reforms including structural changes in oppressive production relations. But its most important and controversial recommendation was that 27% of jobs in government and public enterprises should be reserved for the OBCs. The report also specified the exact scheme and procedures to be followed to implement this recommendation:

1. Candidates belonging to OBCs recruited on the basis of merit in an open competition should not be adjusted against their reservation quota of 27%.
2. The above reservation should also be made applicable to promotion quota at all levels.
3. Reserved quota remaining unfulfilled should be carried forward for a period of three years and de-reserved thereafter.
4. Relaxation in the upper age limit for direct recruitment should be extended to the candidates of OBCs in the same manner as for SC and ST members.
5. A roster system should be maintained for the OBCs in the same manner as for SC and ST candidates.

The rationale behind the 27% formula was that since 22.5% reservation had already been made in favour of the SC/ST (in direct proportion to their number) and since Supreme Court rulings had prescribed that the reservations should remain below 50% it was not possible to reserve 52% of seats for the OBCs in direct proportion to their number. "In view of this," the report said, "the proposed reservation for OBCs would have to be pegged at a figure which, when added to 22.5% for SCs and STs remains below 50%. In view of this legal constraint, the Commission is obliged to recommend a reservation of 27% only, even though their population is almost twice this figure. By the time the Mandal Report was submitted the Janata Party had split and the Congress was all set to return to power. The recommendations of the Mandal Commission remained in cold storage for about a decade. It was in 1990 that Prime Minister V P Singh, partly for the purposes of refurbishing the social base of his ruling coalition and partly to blunt the *Hindutva* edge of the Bharatiya Janata Party (BJP), decided to implement them. With this a new chapter opened in Indian politics and along with it an acrimonious debate over the issue of social justice started.

The government promulgation provided for a 27% quota in government jobs for people belonging to the OBC category. Implementation of the report led to violent protests from the upper castes and eventually resulted in the fall of the V P Singh government. But the movement has continued and at present no political party finds it possible to dissociate itself from the recommendations of the Mandal Report. The arithmetic of numbers at the hustings has made the OBC phenomenon almost a permanent fixture in India's politics. Some of the South Indian states breached the ceiling of 50% laid down by the Supreme Court for reservations. In Tamil Nadu there is a reservation of 69%; in Karnataka it is as much as 73%. Even such a strong critic of the OBC quota system such as Orissa's late strongman Biju Patnaik also gave in to pressure. Announcing the introduction of the OBC quota (within the legal norms) in his state in September 1994 he said "I must admit we should have tried to follow the path enunciated for the backward classes in states like Tamil Nadu, Kerala and Karnataka". In Bihar reservations have reached 76%. The pressure for similar policies has reached north India as well.

3.4. Reservations for Minorities

Lately, a new controversy has been added to the reservations debate with demands from sections of the minorities for their inclusion in the category of affirmative action beneficiaries. The issue is politically sensitive and particularly so because the Hindu chauvinistic BJP, the principal opposition party in parliament, regards it as another ploy to pamper the minorities. Its position on the issue may be viewed against the background of several conflicting realities, namely, that the party claims that the Muslims are pampered while the social indicators tell a different story, that the Muslims are growing in numbers disproportionately compared to the national and Hindu averages which is a fact, and lastly, that while the BJP stands for reservations of SCs, STs and OBCs and also economically depressed classes it is strongly opposed to affirmative action for the Muslims (including Dalit Muslims) and Dalit Christians.

While the policy of reservation for SCs and STs is enshrined in the constitution and reservations for the OBCs have gained political support over the years, the question of reservations on the basis of religious identity remains very controversial and generally leads to acrimony. As a self-proclaimed secular state India shows equal respect to all religions, or, maintains an equal distance from all religions. But there is some ambiguity in the case of India's policy of affirmative action meant for the upliftment of SCs and STs. Hinduism as understood in India's constitutional parlance includes Sikhs, Buddhists and Jains. Therefore, the SCs belonging to these communities should have been granted the quota benefits as was done in respect of Hindu SCs. But it was not the case to start with. In 1950 a Presidential Order made under Article 341 of the Constitution had declared that "no person who professes a religion different from Hinduism shall be deemed to be a member of a Scheduled Caste." In 1956 the Sikh religion was included with Hinduism as part of this order. Thus came the Sikh SCs (Mashabi and Ramdasias Sikhs). So far as the Buddhist SCs were concerned they were granted limited benefits, that too in U P and Maharashtra only, till 1990 when this anomaly was rectified and they were brought on par with the Hindu SCs.

So far as the Jain SCs are concerned they are either non-existent or are too minuscule to make any political demand in their favour. It may be noted that all the three religions—Sikhism, Buddhism and Jainism—emerged as protest movements against the evils of Hinduism, most importantly, the institution of caste. If so, the existence of SCs among them is a contradiction in terms. That many early adherents to these religions would be from the depressed classes is also understandable. Did not the same situation prevail in regard to converts to Christianity and Islam at a later date? The argument advanced by adherents of the *status quo* is that since Christianity and Islam were opposed to the recognition of caste, then depressed caste converts to these faiths should not be allowed to think in terms of affirmative action. The same argument could be used against affirmative action benefits for Sikh, Buddhist and Jain SCs.

The confusion is further confounded if one raises the issue of conversion and compares the SCs with the STs. If an SC converts to Christianity or Islam such a person is automatically deprived of his SC benefits. But if the convert is an ST he continues to take the advantage of the ST benefits because those benefits, as the argument goes, are ethnicity-based and not religion-centric. In short, when the Dalit Muslims or the Dalit Christians are demanding quotas for themselves, their claims are advanced on the basis that in reality, India's Islamic and Christian societies are as much socially stratified as the Hindu society, the difference being only one of scale. The current official position is that: "No scheme for minorities below the poverty line is being implemented in the country. Still, there is a standing instruction of the Government of India "to all the Ministries/Departments of Government of India that whenever a Selection Committee/Board exists or has to be constituted for making recruitment to 10 or more vacancies in Group C or Group D posts/services, it shall be mandatory to have one member belonging to SC/ST and one member belonging to minority community in such Committees/Boards. Where, however, the number of vacancies against which selection is to be made is less than 10, no effort should be spared in finding a Scheduled Caste/ Scheduled Tribes officer and *a minority community officer* for inclusion in such Committees/Boards."

3.5. Issue of Muslim Quota

In several states either the Muslims in general or the Muslim OBCs as part of the general OBCs are on the positive discrimination list. For example, in Kerala 12% of the jobs are reserved for the Muslims. In August 1994, the Andhra Pradesh government included the Qureshi (butcher) Muslims in the OBC list. In September 1994 the Manipur government announced the inclusion of Meitei Pangal (Muslims) in the state OBC list. In early 1995, the Government of Karnataka announced a 75% enhancement in the OBC quota of which 6% was assured for the Muslims. In July 1995, the U P Government decided to issue caste certificates to Muslim sub castes so as to enable them to benefit from the 8.44% reservations under the OBC category.

In national politics too political parties compete with each other in demonstrating their concern for the Muslims. The issue of reservations figures largely in this. In July 1995, when preparations for the 1996 Lok Sabha elections had already started the Welfare Minister in the Narasimha Rao government, Stroma Kesari, advised his party not to ignore the Muslims. He said "In the Assembly elections of Uttar Pradesh, Bihar, Andhra Pradesh, Maharashtra, state party leaders hailing from the upper castes did not highlight the fact that we gave 27% reservation to the backwards which included 110 Muslim sub castes. This led to the poor showing. Kesari's successor in the H D Deve Gowda-led United Front government, B S Ramoowalia, repeated the same promise and announced several schemes for the benefit of Muslim OBCs.

However the current controversies do not relate to the Muslim OBCs, but are over reservations for the entire Muslim community as one social unit and also over the question of quota benefits for the so-called Muslim Dalits. The first demand for reservations for the Muslim community was mooted in West Bengal during the regime of the Congress chief minister Siddhartha Shankar Ray, during the days of the Emergency (1975-77). A delegation led by Sainul Abedin, a minister in Ray's cabinet, met Prime Minister Indira Gandhi and demanded reservation for Muslims. In 1980, the Muslims of the state made the same demand before the Gopal Singh Committee. The committee recommended inclusion of Muslims under the reservation scheme. As the issue of quota matters electorial many of the state governments where the Muslim community figures politically would like to make commitments in their favour however cosmetic they may eventually prove to be. For example, in Bihar the Janata Dal leader Laloo Prasad Yadav had promised 10% reservations for Muslims before the assembly elections of 1995. In Assam, Hiteshwar Saikia of the Congress tried to ward off attacks on his government's inability to stop the killing of Muslims in Bodoland by promising the community 24% reservations.

In West Bengal, the Congress and the Muslim League leaders launched agitation to remind Jyoti Basu of his 1977 poll pledge to provide quotas for Muslims in jobs and educational institutions. In U P the Samajwadi leader Mulayam Singh Yadav wants to make a dent in the growing popular bases of the BJP and the Bahujan Samaj Party (BSP) by advocating reservation for the Muslims in the state. Following the increasing communalisation of politics in the late 1980s and particularly after the demolition of the Babri mosque on 6 December 1992 the demand has been picked up by the Muslims in several parts of the country. In Bihar two organisations—the Bihar Backward Muslim Morcha (BBMM) and the Muslim Reservation Front (MRF)— surfaced, demanding 20% reservations for the community. In April 1995, about 100 representatives of the Muslim community met in Delhi under the leadership of Syed Ahmed Bukhari, the Naib Imam of the Jama Masjid, and demanded reservation for Muslims on a proportionate basis in all fields as the minority community was backward educationally, economically and socially. In September, the 95 member strong Jama Masjid Action Committee adopted a 10-point charter of demands which included reservation for Muslims. Of late, even the National Commission for Minorities, a statutory body, has appealed to the Government of India to do away with the proviso in the 1950 Presidential Order for SCs and STs which uses religion as the criterion for deciding the SC status.

According to Tahir Mahmood, the Chairman of the Commission, there must be the recognition of absolute equality of all religions and, religious communities under the constitution and laws. He believes that the 15- year-old Gopal Singh Committee report on problems of minorities has outlived its utility and there should be a fresh and comprehensive study of the problems faced by the religious minorities. One of the arguments levelled against the demand for quota for the entire Muslim community runs along the predictable line that if the quota is granted to the community as a whole the beneficiaries would be upper caste Muslims such as the Saiyads, Shekhs and other Ashrafs at the cost of the really needy classes. Dalit Muslims tend to subscribe to this logic and ask for a quota not for the community *per se* but only for themselves. To this the Muslim leaders like Syed Shahabuddin have strong objections. They argue that the Muslim community as such is depressed and therefore deserves affirmative action and, so far as the criticism that benefits under reservations would be cornered by the socially and economically privileged group among them is concerned, they argue, that it is equally applicable to the entire question of quota for the SCs, STs and the OBCs.

3.6. Question of Dalit Christians

The question of Dalit Christians is different from the issue of reservation for the Muslim community or the Muslim OBCs. Dalit Christians are those who were originally untouchables and who converted to Christianity. But conversion did not improve their social status and upper caste converts continued to look down upon them. As a result casteism continued to exist in the Church in India. In 1929 a delegation of depressed class Christians stated in a deposition before the Simon Commission: "We remain today what we were before we became Christians-untouchables degraded by the laws of social position in the land, rejected by caste Christians, despised by caste Hindus, and excluded by our own Hindu depressed class brethren. According to socialactivist-cum lawyer Flavia Agnes "For all its homogenous appearance the Christian community is very caste-ridden. Especially, the recent converts.

The converts, largely from the backward communities, now find that they are losing out on both fronts. They continue to be sub-castes without the benefit that would have accrued to them if they hadn't converted. There are about 16 million Dalit Christians in India and they form over 60% of the total Christian population of 25 million. Economically it is a depressed lot. A study undertaken by the Jesuits in Tamil Nadu reveals that 79.6% of the Dalit Christians are landless, with their average annual income put at Rs. 903; 54% live under single layer thatched roofs. The illiteracy rate is 65%. Nearly 35% of households manage with one set of clothes. T

hough Dalit Christians constitute 70% of the Roman Catholics in Tamil Nadu, there is only one Dalit bishop and a mere 3.8% Dalit priests. Several reports submitted by various committees—Kumara Pillai (1965), Santhnam (1970) and Chidambaram (1975), apart from the two Backward Class Commissions reports of Kalelkar (1955) and Mandal (1980) of the Central Government, as well as the several BCC reports of the states including Andhra Pradesh (1970), Tamil Nadu (1970 and 1975) as also the Third and the Fourth Annual Reports of the Minorities Commission of the Central Government (1980 and 1981/82) and the SC-ST Commissioners' Reports—have recognised this fact and recommended remedial measures. The Mandal Commission affirmed that "there is no doubt that social and educational backwardness among non-Hindu communities is more or less of the same order as among Hindu communities. Thus both from within and without, caste amongst non-Hindu communities receive continuous sustenance and stimulus."

The Dalit Christians made their demand for inclusion into the list of the Scheduled Castes as early as in 1950. It was not heeded. But a contemporary letter dated 7 November 1950 from Pandit Jawaharlal Nehru written from the Prime Minister's Office in reply to C X Francis

(President of the Catholic Regional Committee of Nagpur) who had pointed out the injustice done to the Dalit Christians by the Presidential Order, said that "all state aid and facilities are to be given not only to the Hindu scheduled castes but also to all other educationally and socially backward classes whether they profess Hinduism, Christianity or any other religion. Only in the matter of reservation of legislative bodies and Parliament, no person who professes a religion other than Hinduism shall be deemed to be a member of scheduled castes. Lately, the demand has been renewed.

In 1994, the All India Christian Federation in its Memorandum to the Prime Minister, demanded that "there should be an end to discrimination by the state against Christian Dalits only on the ground of religion ignoring other evidences of their social and educational backwardness and, to grant them SC status... On par with the Scheduled Castes belonging to the Hindu, Sikh and Buddhist religions. On 21 November 1995, the Christian educational institutions in most parts of the country went on a day's strike in support of the demand for reservations for the Dalit Christians. In March 1996, the All India United Christians Movement for Equal Rights and the National Coordination Committee for SC Christians advised the community to vote for those political parties which would include Dalit Christian issues in their election manifestos in the forthcoming eleventh general election.

Such efforts did not go waste and in the 1996 parliamentary elections, all the major political parties barring the BJP, included in their election manifestos the demand that the Christian Dalits be treated as Scheduled Castes. The Common Minimum Programme of the United Front also included it. When a 14-member delegation of the All India Christian People's Forum met the then Prime Minister Deve Gowda on 14 June 1996 the latter promised the delegation that a bill would soon be introduced to extend the SC status to the Dalit Christians. But nothing happened, for the reason that the ruling United Front coalition did not have enough confidence to secure its passage in the teeth of a determined BJP opposition.

The BJP is opposed to reservations for the Muslim community as a whole and the Dalit Muslims, as well as to granting SC status to the Dalit Christians. So far as the Muslims are concerned it is not opposed to the idea of the backward caste Muslims asking for reservation under the OBC quota scheme but it is vehemently against introducing any quota for the entire community for it would have "a serious repercussion" for the nation. It is also against individual states deciding on quotas in general. It endorses in principle the Supreme Court verdict that total reservation should not exceed 50% with the exception of Tamil Nadu and Karnataka.

The BJP's opposition is probably based on its *Hindutva* considerations. Its premise is two-fold. If the Dalits of other communities, namely, the Muslim and Christian are granted SC status then it would, on the one hand, make the Hindu SCs feel insecure for there would be more claimants on the quota and on the other, it would discourage "de-Christianisation" of the Dalits, a phenomenon which is otherwise expected in the given situation. The party hopes that the more the Dalit Christians would be denied the SC status the greater would be their compulsion to reconvert to Hinduism. In March 1994 many Dalit Christians of Tamil Nadu did indeed reconverts to Hinduism for getting the SC status. Gopal Sardesai of the Vishwa Hindu Parishad (VHP) argues that: "Scheduled Caste Christians should return to the Hindu fold and then claim the benefits of reservation."

3.7. Perspectives of Positive Discrimination

3.7.1. Merit versus Social Justice

The most common criticism raised against the policy of reservations is that it is at the cost of meritocracy and that it promotes mediocrity which a developing society like India can ill afford. While apparently and theoretically the argument seems well-founded there is neither evidence to support the fear nor is it true to say that meritocracy would be the norm once reservation is lifted. All kinds of undocumented reservations operate in India through kinship connections, caste connections and professional connections. For instance the Delhi University Teachers Association (DUTA) is generally opposed to the OBC reservation but does not mind asking for reservations for the wards of the teachers or for weighted in their favour for university enrolment. Commenting on the impact of reservations on the educational standard, sociologist Andre Beteille writes:

3.7.2. Inherent Contradictions

The more fundamental question, however, is how far have the quotas and other privileges helped the target groups. As we have seen above the progress in this regard has at best been marginal. Whatever progress has been registered by the depressed classes it is more or less proportionate to the overall progress achieved by the nation. As target groups they should have shown a visibly better record, but this has not happened. In a country like India where poverty, illiteracy and deprivation are so widespread, it is a questionable proposition to think in terms of upliftment for particular social groups, that too by emphasising reservations alone. A report on the state of primary education in India brought out by the *India Today* portrays a depressing picture of the Indian state's failure in this regard. The problem as such is much larger and mere targeting particular sections of society would not do. It is surmised that since reservations are the least expensive and politically most rewarding the political parties find them the easiest policy options available to them.

A related question is whether the privileges are being cornered by the elates amongst the target groups. One common criticism against the reservation policy is that it has benefited only a small section of them. According to estimates only 6% of the SC families have benefited from the policy. It must, however, be admitted that even this small number has thrown up leadership for the community to bargain for the larger interests of the community at large. Moreover, it is a fact of life that in any community within a competitive polity the initial beneficiaries are invariably the elates.

This criticism, however, is largely valid in respect of the OBCs where some of the backward castes are way above others amongst them. As such, any reservation policy meant for the OBC community as a whole, is bound to end in ineffectiveness in the long run by this internal contradiction alone. As most of the underprivileged amongst the OBCs would ask for their rights there would be cleavages in the OBC identity as is now being seen in Bihar. There the Kurmis and the Koiris are opposing the Yadavs, both belonging to the OBC category. Moreover, with other demands being raised for quota allocations by women, professional groups, the poor from the upper caste Hindus, and so on, there is a possibility that the entire system of OBC reservation would collapse as a result of these divisions.

3.7.3. Persistence of Caste Prejudice

One other issue which needs to be discussed here is whether there can ever be any real improvement in the lot of the underprivileged sections of the society, whether they belong to the SC/STs or the OBCs, without attacking the caste system itself, this being the essence of the debate between Gandhi and Ambedkar. Can the elimination of the stigma experienced by the underprivileged be achieved through the philanthropy and grace of the upper caste Hindus or has it to be earned or wrested by the underprivileged themselves through their struggles, even violent struggles. If violence is inherent in the circumstances would it not perpetuate the caste cleavages at the cost of social harmony? In any event it has been noticed that the quota system has eliminated whatever goodwill the upper castes had for the lower castes. As one non-Indian scholar wrote in 1979 "In the course of my visits to India over two decades I have noticed an erosion and virtual disappearance of a liberal-minded public opinion supporting private efforts to improve opportunities for the S.C." This lack of concern is manifest in the record of private sector employment. "The pervasive over-estimation of the amount and effectiveness of preferential treatment reinforces the notion that enough (or too much) is already being done and nothing more is called for." A recent study based on interviews of 500 Punjab government employees stationed in Chandigarh reveals the deep-seated prejudice among the non-SCs against the quota privileges meant for the SCs. Particularly prejudiced are the Class II and III categories of the employees. Caste conflicts are rampant as a reading of the Annual Reports of the Home Ministry reveals. During 1996 there were 672 caste-related incidents involving all the three broad caste categories, namely, the Forward Castes, the OBCs and the SCs.

In the current context the most critical question is whether two Indias are being created by two diametrically opposite sociopolitical forces—the demand for modernisation on the one hand bolstered by the opening up of the economy and its integration into the techno-intensive global economy—and on the other, the demand for social justice undermining the core of that theory. One calls for the withdrawal of the state and the other assigns to the state the role of the greatest dispenser of equity.

Against this background it would be increasingly difficult for the state to implement its policy of reservations especially where the OBCs are concerned. On the one hand the number of government jobs is shrinking while on the other pressure for more jobs is mounting. There is yet another related issue. Greater liberalisation of the economy means more modernisation of trade and industry. The traditional vocations of the backward classes such as cleaning, hair-cutting, fishing and tanning are under threat of being controlled by the upper castes particularly in the urban areas. With the growing use of technology in these trades they are no longer looked down upon as occupations. Therefore, the backwards cannot depend any more upon the state; they would have to respond to the market as well. This brings into question the broader recommendation of the Mandal Commission (structural changes in the oppressive production relations). But no OBC leader seems to be much concerned about that. Of course, the market has its own logic and the OBCs are getting drawn into them.

3.8. Transformation of Caste

The caste system has been traditionally analysed as based on the notion of ritual purity. In this view, its holistic character - to use the terminology of Louis Dumont - implies that the dominant values that of the Brahmins, are regarded by the whole society as providing universal references, role models. Low castes may for instance adopt the most prestigious features of the Brahmins' diet and therefore emulate vegetarianism. Such a process reflects a special coherence in society, all the groups admitting the values of the upper castes as *the* legitimate value system. Such coherence is not synonymous with cohesion. In fact, sanskritisation itself bears witness of an aspiration to social mobility and therefore tensions : low castes constantly try to improve their social status by imitating the high castes and contest the position, which has been assigned to them in the system. Moreover, the myths of origin of the low castes are always centered around the idea of an initial decline: even Untouchable castes claim to descend from Brahmin castes and that they have fallen from this rank often because of the malicious intent of upper caste people. The myth of origin of the Chamars is very telling in this aspect : their original ancestor was the youngest of four Brahmans brethren who went to bathe in a river and found a cow struggling in a quicksand. They sent the youngest brother in to rescue the animal, but before he could get to the spot it had been drowned. He was compelled therefore by his brothers to remove the carcass and after he had done this they turned him out of their caste and gave him the name of Chamar. The four brothers epitomise in this narrative the Brahmins, the Kshatriyas, the Vaishyas and the Shudras.

Robert Deliège points out that such a myth is very similar to that of another Untouchable caste, the Paraiyar of Tamil Nadu. In Fact, according to him, 'the untouchable myths are quite distinct from those of higher and even middle range castes', so much so that one can speak of an 'intouchable myth of origin'. However these myths do not reflect the existence of a separate, untouchable identity : 'they take caste for granted, and by stressing their brotherhood with Brahmans, they acknowledge the superiority of the latter. This is pure sanskritisation. A caste moves up above its neighbours and another comes down, but all this takes place in an essentially stable hierarchical order. The system itself does not change. Indeed, the values sustaining the social system remain the same.

While the Brahmins are the main objects of imitation, Srinivas points out that the sanskritisation process does not refer to them only. The Kshatriyas are often chosen as role models too. D.F. Pocock even suggests that there is a 'Kingly model of Hindu society'. However this style of self promotion did not simply rely on the imitation of the superior. In fact the second *varna* has been one of the main avenues for social mobility because the Shudras could conquer power and replace Kshatriyas as rulers on the basis of their mere strength and because Brahmins then legitimised their rise by evolving the needed genealogies. Srinivas indeed points out that 'the Kshatriya category was the most open one in the caste system'.

Historically, low caste groups have also explored avenues for upward mobility through the bhakti movements and the sectarian model. Since the Buddha, gurus have recurrently questioned the caste system on behalf of f the fundamental equality of men before god. Their disciples who were initiated into monastic orders forgot about their caste to form new fraternities. Srinivas emphasised that the 'protest sects' in a way 'offered opportunities for mobility to members of the so-called low castes'. Ambedkar rightly pointed out that 'from the point of view of the annihilation of caste, the struggle of the saints did not have any effect on society'. The traditional caste system was more directly challenged during the British Raj.

3.9. Caste Associations

The development of the means of communications in the XIXth century led to the opening up of the *jati* which, till then, was confined to a reduced territory, delimited by matrimonial relations. Hence the emergence of horizontal solidarities and the territorial extension of the frontiers of caste. The members of a same *jati* were enabled to migrate to find jobs or even obliged to do so, if they were transferred within the British administration for instance. The State building process played an important role since it led to the establishment of an all India bureaucracy. Transfers of bureaucrats out of their native place often generated feelings of anomia and made the finding of the suitable match for endogamous marriages more complicated.

These institutions were also stirred up by the census, which was a key element in the formation of the colonial state. From 1871 onwards the British enumerated the castes and therefore these 'human groups we're treated to a considerable extent as abstractable from the regional and territorial contexts in which they function[ed]'. This effect reinforced those of the state construction process but the census also raised among several castes the sentiment of having common interests since the British did not content themselves with enumerating them ; they also classified them. In 1901, the Census Commissioner, Risley, decided to give the ranking of the *jatis* in their local context and their *varna*, which was a much more delicate enterprise. Castes immediately organised themselves and, as Ghurye points out, even formed councils to take steps to see that their status was recorded in the way they thought was honourable to them. This process was especially prominent among the low castes and therefore gives 'An indication of the widespread desire for mobility among the backward castes...'. Each census provided castes with an opportunity to petition the government for getting a higher place in the order of precedence and for being recorded under new, sanskritised, names. Indeed, this move was in keeping with the logic of sanskritisation since the objective was not to opt out from the system but to rise within it according to its own rules and values.

However, castes associations secularist and became gradually mutual aid structures, in charge of founding schools for the caste's children, creating co-operative movements and claiming new advantages from the state. The caste associations, from then on, tended to become interest groups. The Rudolph therefore underline their modern character – in a western sense. They behaved like a collective enterprise with economic and political objectives, in a way, which brings to mind the image of "lobbies". Generally, their leaders did not come from the most prestigious clans or families but from those of the castemen who were the most educated, able to negotiate with the state and often as ambitious as the political entrepreneurs of Joseph Schumpeter. In many cases, they came from the younger generation. However, the transformational potentialities of caste associations must not be exaggerated since they were not conducive to social change *per se*.

The associations representing upper castes were often very conservative, as evident from the case of the Kanya-Kubja Brahmins, a *jati* widely dispersed across Uttar Pradesh, Madhya Pradesh and Rajasthan. In 1884, a Kanya-Kubja caste association was created in Lucknow. An all India association grew out from it in 1901 and established local branches all over the Hindi belt. It was founded for helping the Kanya-Kubja Brahmins to compete with Kayasths, Banyas and other Brahmins of North India in terms of education and administrative jobs. The number of local branches increased until the mid-1930s when then it declined, partly because of the Congress' opposition to caste movements. However, it started to rise again in the 1950s in order to protect the Kanya Kubja Brahmins against the "threat" that represented affirmative action measures in favour of the lower castes.

Among the non-davits, caste associations often merely served as vehicles for sanskritisation in North India. The Kayasths of North India were probably the first to show the way in that direction. In late XIXth century, Munshi Kali Prasad, a Lucknow-based rich lawyer from this caste, wrote *Kayasthas Ethnology*, a book where he showed 'to which of the four great divisions of the Aryans in India the Kayasthas belonged'. Subsequently, the Kayasths claimed that they were the descendants of the Emperor Chandragupta. In 1873 Kali Prasad set up in Lucknow a fortnightly magazine *Kayastha Samachar* and a Kayasth

Dharma Sabha whose main task was to educate the caste's children. A primary school was opened in Allahabad for poor and orphan children of the caste. In 1877, it became an Anglo-Vernacular middle school, then a high school and in 1895, an intermediate college. The Kayastha Conference was founded in 1886 on the basis of the Kayasth Dharma Sabha. The first resolution it passed at its first annual meeting in 1887 stressed the need 'to improve the educational and moral status of the Community' by opening new schools for which money was raised by the association. It also tried 'to encourage the community to undertake commercial and other respectable pursuits and not to rely solely on clerical or literary avocations'. It established mutual aid programmes for the neediest Kayasth families to enable them to finance the study of their sons or the marriage of their daughters, etc. Parallel to this strong emphasis on socioeconomic developments, the conference did not neglect the initial sanskritisation objectives of Kali Prasad. It had a Temperance section and repeatedly - and allegedly successfully - requested the Kayasths to give up drinking.

The Kayastha Conference is revealing for the ambivalence of caste associations: on the one hand, it endeavoured to promote the status of the Kayasths in the sanskritisation logic; on the other, it was created to fight against the restrictions of job opportunities in the administration of British India. Certainly, this attitude stemmed from modern motives since the main reason for sanskritisation was to standardise the Kayasth culture and to create a homogenous social group, however, sanskritisation remained the key idiom, with its emphasis on positional mobility instead of structural changes, to use Srinivas' words..

The most important social change that caste associations have achieved probably concerns the unity of the caste groups. They have successfully incited the sub-castes to adopt the same name in the Census and to break the barriers of endogamy, even if, within a caste, the members of the upper class still tend to intermarry - but then it is more economic endogamy than purely caste-based endogamy. Once again, the Kayasths are a case in point, not only because their association established a network covering several provinces, including the hindi belt and Hyderabad, but also because, in Hyderabad at least, 'the ease with which marriages across former boundaries are accommodated is striking'. For Leonard, this change 'might confirm an ideological shift from caste to ethnicity and class'. This process has been observed by Robert Hardgrave in the case of the Nadars of Tamil Nadu whose caste association, the Nadar Mahajana Sangam was founded in 1910 and promoted what he calls 'caste fusion', as 'the unit of endogamy expanded'. S. Barnett maintains that this kind of fusion tended to transform castes into ethnic groups. His demonstration is based on another Tamil case study, the Kontaikkatti Vellalars who do not represent a large number of people but are influential since many of them are landlords. From 1920 onwards, the caste association has encouraged them to expand endogamy in new territories and to other Vellallars in order to make up for their numerical weakness. It may then be one of the first examples of caste federations. For Barnett these innovations confront the entire ideological field of caste hierarchy, since 'blood purity', on which according to him relies ritual purity has lost its importance. The relevant unit is not the original *jati* any more, but groups of castes, which represents the transition from caste to ethnical regional caste blocs. "Ethnically" because each such unit is potentially independent of other such units, defined and characterised by a heritable substance internal to the unit itself and not affected, in terms of membership in the unit, by transactions with others outside the unit. Rather than the conceptual holism of caste, we begin to see the antecedent autonomy of its component parts. In an ethnically situation transactional ranking no longer orders the parts of the whole, and caste interdependence is replaced by regional-caste bloc independence. The subjective representation of the collective self is most important for the issue we are dealing with. Caste is partly a mindset. It is based on beliefs in hierarchies relying on purity and impurity – what Ambedkar called 'graded inequality'. Alternative social *imaginaries* might be conducive to the emancipation of the lower castes. As M.S.A. Rao argues: 'The problem of identity is crucial in the formation of protest groups and for collective mobilisation':

> Deprived sections of society in different parts of the world have organises themselves into protest movements to fight against discriminations of various kinds based on colour, religion, caste and tribe. Their problem, however, has been one of establishing a new identity – the kind of image that they want to protect in order to gain self-respect, honour and status.

Such a change in collective identity is precisely at stake in the process of ethnic identity building by lower castes. This kind of ethnicisation of castes or caste federations are much more conducive to social change than caste associations or caste fusion pure and simple.

3.10. Ethnicisation of Caste

The ethnicisation process which took place in western and southern India was partly due to the impact of the European ideas, as propagated by the missionaries and the schools. The ethnicisation process is well illustrated by the Satyashodak Movement developed by Phule in the Bombay Presidency in the late XIXth century, which was not a caste movement since it intended to represent the 'bahujan samaj', the majority of the people, the masses. Jotirao Phule was a Mali, a cultivating caste in close contact with towns where its members sold their products. In one of these towns, Poona, Phule could attend a school of the Scottish Mission. What he learnt about the Blacks in the United States suggested to him a comparison with the lower castes - hence his book, *Slavery* that he dedicated 'to the good people of the United States as a taken of admiration for their sublime disinterested and self sacrificing devotion in the cause of Negro Slavery.

The writings of Thomas Paine exerted a special influence on Phule who discovered the individualist values of liberty and equality in *The Age of Reason* and *Human Rights*. This source of inspiration developed in conjunction with that of Christianity. For Phule, Jesus-Christ epitomises equality and fraternity. He also regards him as the spokesman for the poor people. However, Phule did not convert to Christianity and even translated the Christian idiom into a new discourse focused on King Bali, the subterranean god who reigns in the underground world according to Hindu mythology.

Through the vernacularisation of Christian values and symbols, Phule endowed them with a new, positive identity to his people. He even gave them a new history on the basis of some of the findings of Orientalist. In 1792, William Johne's had deduced from the discovery of the Indo-European linguistic family the notion of a common, original race whose branches had migrated towards Europe and India. This theory was developed during the nineteenth century by many German philologists such as Abreact Weber, R. Both, A. Kuhn and J.

Möhl. In their writings appear the notions of 'Sanskrit race' or 'Vedic people'.

The first Hindu nationalist ideologies of the late 19th century and early 20th century borrowed heavily from the European orientalists. Among other themes, the one they used assiduously related to the common racial origin of the European and Indian people and its corollary, the southward migration which they interpreted to prove that the Hindus were the first race and that they once dominated the whole world. This myth helped the first Hindu revivalists to regain certain self-esteem by claiming that their ancestors were the first inhabitants of the world.

Phule used the Aryan theory to his own advantage: the fact that upper castes leaders traced their origin from Aryan conquerors could be used to argue that they descended from foreigners and that their culture, including the caste system was alien to India's original people. Phule, therefore, portrayed the Aryans as invaders who had settled in India at a rather late period to subjugate the first inhabitants of India and destroyed their civilisation. For him, the low castes were the descendents of these people. In this reinterpretation of the past, the invaders are identified as Brahmins whereas the indigenous groups are described as descending from the original ruling class, the Kshatriyas. In Phule's ideology, this category does not refer to the second *varna* but includes all original Indians, from peasant castes to Untouchables. According to him:

"The Kshatriyas in India that is the original masters of the land here where known as Steaks, Pishachas, Rakshasas, Ahirs, Kakatas, Bhut, Kolis, Mangs, Mahars etc. They were extremely adept in fighting without the aid of arms and were famed as brave and valiant warriors. They were of an epicurean temperament and were given to the enjoyment of the goods things of life. The kingdoms of most of these rulers were in a prosperous condition, and it would be no exaggeration to say that the land of King Bali was literally flowing with milk and honey".

This description does not only present the original rulers of India as brave warriors but also emphasises their sense of manliness and honour while fighting and their good nature. Such a narrative prepared the ground for the stereotype of the 'good salvage' that will be applied to the Indian aborigines. The king of these original Kshatriyas, Bali, is described by Phule as reigning over a rich country and this prosperity was the very reason for the Aryan invasions:

> The extreme fertility of the soil of India, its rich productions, the proverbial wealth of the people, and the other innumerable gifts which this favourable land enjoys, and which have more recently tempted the cupidity of the Western nations, attracted the Aryans. The original inhabitants with whom these earth-born gods, the Brahmans, fought, were not inappropriately termed Rakshasas, that is the protectors of the land The cruelties which the European settlers practised on the American Indians on their first settlement in the new world had certainly their parallel in India in the advent of the Aryans and their subjugation of the aborigines. They originally settled on the banks of the Ganges whence they spread gradually over the whole of India.

Phule's endeavour had a pioneering dimension since he was probably the first low caste leader who avoided the traps of sanskritisation by endowing the low caste with an alternative value system. For the first time, the low castes were presented as *ethnic groups* which had inherited the legacy of an antiquarian golden age and whose culture was therefore distinct from that of the wider Hindu society ; secondly, his efforts in favour of the low castes were not confined to his castemen only: he wanted to unite the *Shudras* and the *Atishudras*. As early as 1853 he opened schools for Untouchables. He projected himself as the spokesman of the non-Brahmins at large and, indeed, kept targeting the Brahmins in vehement pamphlets where he presented them as rapacious moneylenders corrupts priests eager to extort as much as they could from poor and ignorant villagers.

Phule was also the first low caste organiser. In 1875 he was attracted by the Arya Samaj, but he kept his distance from this movement because he did not trust the upper caste reformers who pretended to fight against the social system even though they observed its rules. Phule also remained aloof from the Congress, which he regarded as a Brahmin movement. Nationalism, according to him, was an illusion created by upper caste manipulation to conceal the inner divisions of Indian society. He narrated pseudo-historical episodes bearing testimony of the traditional solidarity between the Mahars and Shudras and protested against the Brahmins' stratagems for dividing the low castes. A major spokesman of the non-Brahmin movement in Maharashtra in the 1910-1930, Mukundrao Patil, the son of Phule's colleague, Krishnarao Bhalekar, was for instance a radical defender of the Untouchables even though he was a rich peasant. He advocated 'the general Satyashodak ideology, of opposition to Sanskritisation and assertion of the " non-Aryan " unity of Maharashtrian natives'. By that time, Phule's view of the non-Brahmins as non-Aryas had made an impact on the small dalit intelligentsia.

The Satyashodak Samaj eventually attracted even Marathis such as the Jedhe family who from Poona realised 'the futility of a purely Maratha politics'.Keshavrao Jedhe adopted 'the long-held Satyashodak view of history: Brahmans were outsiders to the country and to the ethnic community of true " Hindus "; they desired only their own caste superiority and consolidated their power through treachery, through falsification of historical records, and by weaving a web of religious slavery which set up a social hierarchy of superiority and inferiority and divided the masses.'

Maratha princes such as the Maharajah of Baroda strongly approved of Phule's ideological commitments and donated large amounts of money to his movement. A direct descendant of Shivaji, the Maharajah of Kolhapur, Shahu, who reigned between 1894 and 1922 and who was 'intensely proud of his Maratha lineage', was even more supportive. He recruited Maratha Satyas Satyashodaks in his administration. In 1902 he even reserved 50% of the vacancies in the state administration for 'the members of the backward communities'.

Shahu patronised the establishment of the Satyashodak Samaj in Kolhapur in 1911. He promoted inter-caste dining and introduced the Inter-caste Marriage Act in 1918at Kolhapur. In 1920 he appointed Maratha priests to circumvent the Brahmins and soon after established the Kshatriya Vedic School to train Maratha priests. The very name of this school suggests that Shahu was still acting in the framework of sanskritisation. Indeed, he tried to secure for the Marathas the status of Kshatriyas and in fact he broke with the local Brahmins in 1900 when they refused to recognise his family's claim to this status and accordingly refused to perform certain rituals. He called them 'Suryavaunshi', pretending that they could trace their lineage to the sun God, Surya. Shahu cannot be described as a Maratha leader also because of its efforts to federate the low castes. In the communal representation scheme that he introduced in 1920 in the Kolhapur municipality 85 castes were grouped into 20 'unions of castes'.

Yet, the main reason why the Sathyashodak Samaj could not become a common platform for all the non-Brahmins on the basis of a non-Aryan identity had much to do with the attitude Marathas. Most of them refused to mix with lower castes and stuck to the sanskritisation process of other with which Shahu has still affinities. For instance, Bhaskarrao Jadhav, in *Martial ani Tyanci Bhasha*, displayed much ambivalence: on the one hand he admits 'the prevalence of Dravidian customs and racial intermixture among Marathas, and on the other asserts, without any qualification, the Marathas are definitely " Aryan Kshatriyas ". Therefore, even those who had followed Phule's message for some time, eventually joined hands with the Brahmins-dominated Congress, or were co-opted by it. Congress leaders such as N.V. Gadgil, who was very much aware that the nationalist movement could only acquire a mass-basis if it attracted low caste people, contacted K. Jedhe and made an alliance with him in the early 1930s

In spite of this ultimate failure, from Phule to Shahu, the low castes movement of Maharashtra was characterised by very distinctive features with long terms implications. Even though the Satyashodak idiom was imbued with the symbols of kshatriyahood, this movement escaped the sanskritisation process since the upper castes were not seen as role models but as invaders whose culture could be despised. A similar pattern developed in the South with the Dravidian movement.

3.11. From Non-Brahminism to Dravidianism

In Madras Presidency, the Non Brahmin movement was instrumental in engineering forms of caste fusion and succeeded in endowing the lower castes with an ethnic identity relied on two grounds: they were not only presented as the original inhabitants of India, as Phule had already argued, but also as former Buddhists. This twofold argument was first articulated in the first decade of the XXth century by Iyothee Thass, a Pariah converted to Buddhism. He pointed out that ancient India had been prosperous and most humanly governed under Buddhist kings but that they were dislodged from power by Brahmin invaders who imposed the caste system. The Buddhists were then marginalised and considered as unclean and low. Their religion had endowed them with a specific culture that eschewed violence, forbade the taking of alcohol etc. That even maintained that in the past India was called Indirar Desam, the land of Indirar, Indirar being the Buddha after he succeeded in controlling his five senses. This original civilisation was none other than the Dravidian civilisation and Thass therefore chose to call its caste-mates, the Pariahs, 'Dravidas'. Therefore early as the late nineteenth century, the Non-Brahmin movement claimed that the lower castes were the original inhabitants of India. Again, British Orientalism had prepared the ground for this development. The Reverend Caldwell had already suggested that Sanskrit had been brought to South India by Aryan, Brahmin, colonists and that the original inhabitants were Dravidians speaking Tamil, Telugu etc. The Pariah Mahajan Sabha, which had been founded in 1890, became the Adi-Dravida Mahajan Sabha, which, in 1918 appealed to the government to replace the pejorative word Pariah by Adi-Dravida, denoting the original inhabitants of Dravida land. In 1917 an Adi-Andhra Mahajan Sabha had come into existence the same way. In fact, this association was initially called Andhra Panchama Conference but the chairman of its 1917 session, M.V. Bhagya Reddy in his presidential address, declared that the so-called Panchamas were the original sons of the soil and they were the rulers of the country'. Hence the change of name of the Sabha. Varma was a Mala and in the 1931 census about one Ahird of the Malas and Madhigas gave their identity as Adi-Andhras.

One of the most influential proponents of the Dravidian ideology was M.C. Rajah, a Pariah who became secretary of the Adi-Dravida Mahajan Sabha in 1916 and who presided over the All India Depressed Classes Association since in 1928.

This identity-building process was led one step further by Ramaswami Naicker, alias Periyar, a religious mendicant who had been completely disillusioned by the Congress and Gandhi while he was taking part in the Vaikom satyagraha. If Phule had drawn some of his egalitarian inspiration from Thomas Paine, Periyar was much impressed by Robert Ingersoll. Like Phule and Ambedkar, he was egalitarian in a western, individualist vein. The notion of human dignity was so central to his thinking that after quitting Congress in the mid-1920s, he launched the Self-Respect Movement, which immediately endeavoured to pressurise the Justice Party in order to make it the true advocate of the lower castes. Another of his key words was Samadharma that referred to the general principle of equality. But Periyar regarded it as a Buddhist notion. Like Thass, he presented the lower castes as descending from the first Buddhists and endowed them with a Dravidian identity, especially after his mobilisation of the late 1930s against the attempt of the Congress government of Madras at promoting Hindi in the schools of the Presidency. The Dravidar Kashagam that he founded in 1944, though its mouthpiece, *Viduthalai*, considered that the Congress was behind 'the exploitation of the northern bania and his Aryan [Brahmin] mentor'. Thus, 'Samadharma came to stand in for a civilisations and cultural alternative: a social order based on radically different principles from the present, which needed to rest on premises derived from a non-Aryan, non-Sanskrit ethos'. Periyar had an explicitly ethnic conception of the low castes' identity. The Non-Brahmins who all shared a Dravidian identity had therefore to get united. As a result, Periyar advocated the coming together of the Christians, Muslims and low castes Hindus, and, within the latter, of the Untouchables and the Shudras. Such a rapprochement took place indeed since Nadars and Adi Dravidas were the mainstays of the Self-Respect movement and then of the DK. But there were also Vellalas, Mukkulathavar and even Chettis among the lieutenants of PeriyarAs in Maharashtra, the 'non-Aryans' did not form a solid block at all. M.C. Rajah criticised the 'natural animosity' of the Justice Party towards the Untouchables and in 1922-23 his South India Adi-Dravida Congress broke ranks with the party. However, the ethnic ground of the Non-Brahmin discourse which, from That to Periyar combined Buddhist and Dravidian references had enabled its leaders to unify low caste people and mobilise them against the 'twice borns'. As early as 1920, 'a non-Brahmin constituency with its own distinctive political claims had emerged in Madras' and enabled the Justice Party to win the elections.

This ethnicisation process was fostered by the political reforms since the British were much willing to recognise ethnic and/or caste groups as legitimate units for representation in the political arena.

3.12. Impact of Compensatory Discrimination

The formation of caste federations and the ethnicisation of caste, two inter related processes, were fostered by the British policy of compensatory discrimination based on the reservation of seats in the bureaucracy and in the assemblies. The very decision to grant such or such statutory representation to such and such group in these assemblies contributed to the crystallisation of new groups which resented their non representation. Caste groups, often with low status, were prominent among those, which mobilised against the state's decisions.

The Non-Brahmin movement of Madras Presidency was especially active. In April 1920, Lord Chelmsford received a Memorandum protesting against the reservation of only 28 seats out of 65 for the Non-Brahmins in the Legislative Council of Madras. Interestingly, the signatories emphasised their caste and ethnic differences for justifying their claim:

The Brahmins differ from the non-Brahmins in caste, manners, customs and interests and even in personal law in some respects. The former is Aryans and the latter are Dravidians and thus they differ in race. In the past the Brahmins have practically monopolised all or almost all the seats in the Local and Imperial Legislative Councils. The disabilities under which the Non-Brahmins have been suffering were fully set out in the Memorandum which Rai Bahadur K.V. Reddi prepared and submitted to the joint Select Committee on Government of India Bill

The Non-Brahmins asked for more seats in Madras assembly because they were 'different'. During the 1920 election campaign, their leaders requested 'all non-Brahmins in this presidency to immediately organise, combine and carry on an active propaganda so as to ensure the return to the reformed Council of as many non-Brahmin as possible'. This tactic yielded dividends since the Justice Party came first in the elections. In their plea to the British, the Non-Brahmins also emphasised their marginality in the state services and the 'disabilities' from which they were suffering.

This policy made a similar impact on the low caste movement in Western India. In Bombay Legislative Council the Marathas showed the way in the 1920s. Their principal patron, the Maharajah of Kolhapur, Shahu Maharaj, had circulated a memorandum 'on the necessity of separate Communal electorates for the Marathas, etc., for electing members to the new Councils under the Reforms scheme', where he wrote:

The Marathas have distinguished themselves in the war certainly not less, if not more, than the Sikhs or the Mohammedans who have been given separate electorates. They are almost given to agriculture, military service or employment as mill-hands. Being thus not a commercial or educated community, they are poor, and without resources, influence and organisation. In this respect they are even worse of than Telis, Tilaris, Goldsmiths, Sutas, Lohars and even Mahars, Mangs and other Untouchables, to whom many a business line and handicraft are open Five great monsters do a lot of mischief to the village agricultural community which mostly consists of the Marathas. The Kulkarni is the biggest of them all. Next to the Kulkarni is the Brahmin Sawkar moneylender who has appropriated to himself a very large portion of the village lands. The Ahird in this order is the schoolmaster and his brother the college-professor in big cities is the Brahmin bureaucracy watered and nourished by Government themselves. The village priest, securely and permanently installed by Hindu religious puranas invented and developed to maintain the Brahmanic supremacy is the fifth monster.

Shahu demanded separate electorates instead of reserved seats on which, he said, he was 'sure that weak, unprincipled undesirable Marathas will be elected who would be used by Brahmins as cat's paw f or them to draw the apples out of the fire', the same kind of argument used by Ambedkar before the Poona pact. However, the British were not prepared to grant a separate electorate to the Marathas. Some of them preferred to focus their demand on larger quotas and they had understood that to pressurise the British more efficiently they had to appear as representing more than one caste. They held, under the auspices of the People's Union, whose patron was the Maharajah of Kolhapur, a Conference of the Hindu Backward Classes in June 1920. The British, so far, designated the Marathas by their caste name but the conference considered that 'the term "Maratha and allied classes" should include all the Backward communities'. Therefore, the conference made 'an emphatic protest against the misleading statement made in public to the effect that the Marathas, Mails etc. do not belong to the Backward Classes when their percentage of education is very low'. The main demand of the conference was that the 8 seats reserved to the Marathas and allied castes in the Montage-Chelmsford report should be extended to 15. Simultaneously, the

Secretary of the Poona-based All India Maratha Mali Union made a similar representation to the British:

The word 'Maratta' [sic] means all the backward classes. As a matter of fact not only the Marattas but all other allied communities have fought in the last world war for the Empire and all such communities are anxious to get the privilege of reserved seats in the council to be hereafter elected.

Among the allied communities of Marathas, Yadav Gavlis then opportunely discovered that they had strong affinities with the Marathas. The President of the Yadav Gavli Association, Raghunath Vithal Khedekar, was an exceptional personality. Born in Bombay in 1873, his father had been Private secretary of the Maharajah of Bhavnagar, one of the most progressive states so far as the upliftment of the lower castes were concerned. The first Yadav association had been founded in 1903 by a relative of his father. In the early 1920s, Khedekar protested that the Southborough Committee should consider the Yadav Gavlis as Marathas :

The Yadav Gavli community claims descent from the Great Yadav families to one which Shri Krishna the 8th incarnation of Vishnu belonged. The whole of the North India, Gujarat and Deccan were only ruled by the Kings of the Yadav families. They have kept up their Kshatriya caste traditions, customs and occupations. They have given considerable recruits to the government and have been regarded as Marathas and included in the Maratha regiments.

In the end, the Yadav-Gavli association demanded the 'inclusion in the list of the Marathas and allied communities of the Deccan for franchise purpose'. Access to political power was of course the main reason for this social rapprochement. Eventually, Khedekar was deputed by the People's Union, the Deccan Riots Association and the Yadav Gavli Association for making a representation to the Joint Select Committee. He explained:

If the term 'Maratha' be defined as meaning 'anti-Brahmin' in the regulation to be framed under the Indian Act, it will remove all misunderstandings and ill feelings in the Maratha castes and it will allow Jains and Lingayat castes to share the benefit of the reserved seats.

Marathas, who had already forged a 'backward' front with the Mails and the Yadavs were striving for shaping an even larger coalition including the Lingayats and the Jains under the all-encompassing label of 'anti-Brahmins'. Certainly, the loose structure of the Marathas lent itself to this kind of aggregative strategy. They have no clear-cut sub-castes, they are so 'amorphous' that 'it is hard to tell in some cases, whether a group is Maratha or of another affiliation called Kunbi'. This arrangement naturally 'facilitates incorporation into Maratha caste' of other peasant castes. The British approach of compensatory discrimination through quotas in the assemblies have accelerated the transformation of castes into interest groups and have fostered a process of amalgamation among the low castes. Leading castes such as the Marathas initiated federations whose aim was purely political. They had understood that the rules were those of the game of numbers which, alone could enhance institutional representation in the State. In Maharashtra this strategy was rather successful. Its architects could rely on the legacy of Jyotirao Phule's Satyashodak Samaj, which had established an idiom - the Bahujan idiom - encompassing all the Non-Brahmins. Another important factor laid in the pivotal situation of the Marathas who represented 20% of the population. They were certainly not able to federate all the Non-Brahmins but the mere fact that the British designed a category called 'Marathas and allied' showed that they had been successful to a certain extent. Among these allies were the Kunbis, who have always been regarded as more backward than the Marathas but who appeared in the same category.

In Maharashtra and Tamil Nadu, the ethnicisation of caste and the formation of caste federations, helped the non-Brahmins to get organised and to gradually assert themselves in the political arena. However, the most significant caste federations took shape in the South and in Gujarat.

3.13. Rise to Power of the Low Castes

Kothari and Maru have defined caste federations in terms which would have suited well the Maharashtrian situation since they emphasise the role of individual caste associations in the shaping of such coalitions and put a stress on the political motivations:

The concept of caste federation refers to a grouping together of a number of distinct endogamous groups into a single organisation for common objectives, the realisation of which calls for a pooling together of resources or numbers or both. The traditional distinctions between the federating groups are on the whole retained, but the search for a new organisational identity and the pursuit of political objectives gradually lead to a shift in group orientations.

This definition was evolved in the course of a study of the caste federation phenomenon in Gujarat where the 'Kshatriyas' indeed exemplified this phenomenon. Right from the 1910s the state Rajput leaders had constituted caste associations for promoting education. In the late 1930s, the descendent of one of its leaders, Natvarsingh Solanki, wanted to extend these associations to other castes which he considered as Kshatriyas. He tried to refashion the social identity of those groups in order to allow others to join hands with the Rajputs and in this way, to acquire more weight.

Gujarat's largest caste was the Kolis. They had been classified by the British as a 'criminal caste' but claimed that they were Kshatriyas and resorted to genealogists for being recognised aristocratic ancestors. In this, they purely imitated the Rajputs. Some Koli clans had been able to establish matrimonial alliances with Rajputs, as those castes practised hypergamy and/or had established small principalities before the British took over. Many of them met the necessary conditions for being enfranchised when the British established provincial legislative councils. The right to vote therefore enabled the Kolis to use their main asset, their number" : in 1931 they represented about 20% of the population, almost the double of the Patidars the dominant caste, the main rival of the Rajputs, who represented only 4.85% of the population. Solanki opened his caste association to the Kolis for this very reason: for transforming it into a mass organisation.

In 1947, the Kutch, Kathiawar, Gujarat Kshatriya Sabha was created after years of preparatory work. The word 'Kshatriya' was a useful umbrella label to bracket the Rajputs and the Kolis together. The Kshatriya Sabha is a good example of the way castes, with very different ritual status for defending common interests. The Rajput leaders of the Kshatriya Sabha emphasised that a *Kshatriya* is not to be defined by descent but by military values. Political calculations had therefore social implications. Several taboos were abolished. Rajputs and Kolis of the Kshatriya Sabha shared meals and the Kolis elite married their daughters to lower Rajputs –who practised hypergamy anyway – and this process fostered the rajputisation of the upper Kolis. Kshatriyas tended to form a new caste. The use of terms like Koli Kshatriyas and Rajput Kshatriyas certainly show that the merger was far from complete. But important dimensions of the caste system were eroded by the after-effects of basically socio-economic and political strategies. In fact, the main demands of the Kshatriya Sabha after independence reflected a relative indifference to ritual issues in comparison to material objectives. This claim was the exact opposite of sanskritisation. The Kolis benefited more than the Rajputs from the Sabha, which created boarding schools, grants, loan systems etc. in favour of the poorest of their community. This development contributed to the emergence of a Koli intelligentsia of Kolis which, even though it remained small gave the Koli masses a new confidence and self-esteem as a caste. The members of this elite 'interact[ed] frequently and chart[ed] out common political strategies'. Right from the 1950s, the Kshatriya Sabha tended to capitalise its electoral support to the Congress in exchange of tickets for a number of its members as party candidates. The party was not fully responsive, especially because of the Patidars who were very influential in the Congress. The Patidars disapproved of the Kshatriyas demand regarding land reform. The Kshatriya Sabha therefore kept its distance with the Congress before the 1962 elections and the party underwent a setback. Instead, the association gave its support, against large concessions, to the Swatantra Party, which became the leading opposition party in the state. The Kshatriya Sabha then supported the Congress, which regained a more comfortable majority than in 1962.

Caste federations turned out to be political interest groups with more leverage than caste associations, simply because they represented more people. In Gujarat, after the Congress split of 1969, a majority of the party conservative notables remained with the Congress (Of) while a larger number of Kshatriyas joined the Congress. They gradually gained control over the state Congress. Madhavsingh Solanki, a Kshatriya of low birth, became Chief minister in 1976 and appointed a majority of ministers with the same background. During the electoral campaign of 1977 he initiated a new caste alliance regrouping the Kshatriyas, the Harijans, the Adivasis and the Muslims. This KHAM alliance was largely responsible for the Congress success during the 1980 elections. Between 1957 and 1990 the number of upper caste Congress MLAs decreased from 33 to 6%. those with a Patidar background remained stable at about one fourth of the total, whereas the Kshatriyas increased from 12 to 25% and the KHAM MLAs at large from 39 to 55%.

While the 'Kshatriyas' of Gujarat represent the best example of caste federation, other instances occurred in South India. In the early 1960s, the Kallan, the Maravar and the Agamudiar, three lower castes who had already close ties with each other decided to adopt the same name, Mukkulator in order to merge and to influence local politics.

The search for new forms of caste activity did not contribute to social change and to the rise of the low castes in the same way in Maharashtra, Tamil Nadu and Gujarat but the above case studies suggest a western and southern pattern. In these areas, the development of communications, the impact of western ideas-ranging from missionaries' propaganda and school teaching, the establishment of a pan-Indian administration and census operations, fostered the formation of caste associations. However, they prepared the ground for two major developments, namely the ethnicisation of castes, of which the ideology of the 'bahujan samaj' evolved by Phule and the Dravidian movement were the best examples, and the federation of castes which was epitomised by the 'Kshatriyas' of Gujarat. Both phenomena were influenced by the orientalist discourse and responses to the British policy of compensatory discrimination. They were intended to help the low castes to reach power and they were successful to a large extent

In North India, none of these processes reached their logical conclusion even through the British Raj had generated the same context as in the South and in the West. Caste associations often followed the sanskritisation path and neither prepared the group for an ethnic discourse nor developed into caste federations.

3.14. Low Caste Movement in Hindi Belt

In North India also British policies had changed the social and political context in such a way as castes could have felt the same strong incentive to get organised. Efforts were made in this direction but they did not bear the same fruits as in the South and in the West. While caste associations took shape at an early date, they did not join hands into federations and they operated within the logic sanskritisation. The Government was petitioned by the All India Kushwaha Kshatriya Mahasabha, 'on behalf of the kori, kachchi and murao castes'. The fact that the Kushwaha label stood for three sub castes of castes of market gardeners shows that this caste association promoted the fusion process, but not to a very large extent : this process cannot be compared with caste federations in Gujarat. Secondly, the Kushwahas claimed the rank of Kshatriya, and another association of middle caste of peasants, which sent also a petition, the Kurmi Kshatriya Parishad Sabha, did the same. Sanskritisation continued to play a major role among the low caste associations.

3.14.1. Sanskritisation and Lack of Unity

The 'Yadav' label covers a great number of castes, which had different names, initially: Ahir in the Hindi belt, Punjab and Gujarat, Gavli in Maharashtra, Gola in Andhra Pradesh and Karnataka etc. However, traditionally their common function, all over India, was to take care of boffins cattle as herdsmen, cowherds and milksellers. In their 'Tribes and Castes of the Central Provinces of India', Resell and Hira Lal note that 'In former times the Ahirs had the exclusive right of milking the cow, so that on all occasions on their must be hired for this purpose even by the lowest castes'

While the Yadavs are speared several regions, they are more specially concentrated in the Ganges plain where they represent about 10% of the population. They form one of the largest castes in Bihar and Uttar Pradesh with respectively 11 and 8.7% of the population. The 'casteregious' mapped by J. Schwartsberg show that the Yadavs were the largest caste in almost all the districts of northern Bihar and in much of eastern UP in 1931 But the Yadavs are not a dominant caste, as pastoral activity did not go usually hand in hand with land possession and from the ritual point of view, the Yadavs are traditionally regarded as low caste peasants: The very mention of the community invokes, in Bihar, the image o f dull, miserly and loud-mouthed people lacking in grace and culture. Besides, the Yadavs are considered as to be unusually prone to casteism and violence.

In the central Provinces, a proverb says ' A Goalie's quarrel: drunk at night and friends in the morning'. Resell and Hira Lal note that in this region too, 'The Ahirs are also hot-tempered, and their propensity for drinking often results in affairs, when they break each other's head with their cattle-staffs'. However, their association with another image, that of placidity and peace. One of the proverbs cited by Schwartsberg says: 'The cow is in league with the milkman and lets him milk water into the pail'. The Yadavs reportedly descend from immigrants from Central Asia, the Abhiras, who established kingdoms in North India, the most recent of which was built in Rewari, in Haryana in the XVIIth century. The scion of the dynasty, Rao Bahadur Balbir Singh, established the Ahir Yadav Kshatriya Mahasabha in 1910. This association claimed that the Ahirs descended from the Yadu dynasty to which Krishna the cowherd god belonged, and that, therefore, they were Kshatriyas. To promote a warrior ethos and the caste unity, the association leaders could easily rely on the caste history since Ahirs were easily presented as coming from the same ethnic stock and were known for their martial valour. This is probably why M.S.A. Rao considers that the 'term Yadava refers to both an ethnic category and an ideology'. Certainly, the Yadav leaders succeeded in their fusion project since they persuaded their caste fellows to downplay the endogamous units into which they were divided. There have even been some inter-regional marriages. Fusion was made easier from the 1930s onwards when North Indian Yadavs started to migrate from their villages to towns and especially to Delhi. But this project did not incorporate a more ambitious ethnicisation process through which other Kshatriya castes would have been merged. So far as ideology is concerned, it was dominated by sanskritisation.

The Yadavs lent themselves for such sanskritisation because they had 'a special relation to the Hindu religion, owing to their association with the sacred cow'. And the Arya Samaj also exerted a strong influence over the Yadav movement. As early as 1895, the ruler of Rewari, Rao Yudhishter Singh invited Swami Dayananda in his State. Branches o f the Arya Samaj flourished soon after and Rewari provided a base from which Arya Samaj updeshaks operated in neighbouring areas. The Arya Samaj was a reform movement, which has been too often regarded as purely Punjabi and confined to the urban middle class. In fact, it made inroads in the adjacent states at a quite early date and attracted then large numbers of low caste people. Dayananda even started his 'campaign against heresy and orthodoxy' to use the words of an Arya Samajist in the Kumbha Mela held in Haridwar. He stayed eight times in Meerut, for instance, between 1866 and 1880 the Meerut City Arya Samaj was established as early as 1877 and others followed in Farrukabad Kanpur Benares Lucknow. Eventually, the Srimati Arya Pratinidhi Sabha for the United Provinces of Agra and Awadh was founded in 1886. These local branches gradually extended their influence in the countryside. The anti-Brahmin stance of the Arya Samaj was especially appreciated by the low castes of the United Provinces. In *Sathyarth Prakash*, Dayananda has very strong words against 'the sectarian and selfish Brahmins', 'these ignorant, sensual, hypocritical, irresponsible and vicious people' who 'often dissuade persons from learning and ensnare them into their evil ways with the result that they lose health, peace of mind and wealth. Dayananda reproached the Brahmans with exploiting the superstition of the Hindus by projecting themselves as the only intermediary between man and god, a monopoly he compares to that of the Catholic Pope and which according to him was evident from the brahminical invention of idol worship: 'These Popes fill their pockets by playing fraud upon you. In the Vedas there is not even a word to sanction idol-worship or invoking invitation and dismissals'.

Dayananda eulogised the Jats for forcefully resisting the Brahmins' 'popish' attitudes. He narrates the story of a Jat whose father was dying and who was asked to give his only cow to the priest as a 'dying gift'. The Jat had to agree since the priest had already talked to his relatives who put pressure on him. But he went to the priest's house soon after and boldly accused him of being 'a great liar' since he had not taken the cow to the river bank but was milking it. He then contested the authority of the Garuda Purana, the book the priest mentioned as dictating his conduct: 'This book has been written by your forefathers to secure livelihood for you...'. The Jat took the cow back to his home and Dayananda concludes, 'If other persons also behave like the Jat, then alone can the popish fraud be stopped'. Jats were very pleased by the way Dayananda praised one o f them and they naturally shared his indictment of the Brahmins.

However, Dayananda's indictment of the Brahmins did not amount to a complete rejection of the caste system. What he condemned was the hereditary caste. He contended that in the initial *varna vyavastha* children were placed in each *varna* according to their individual 'merits, actions and temperaments'. He specifically recommended that the 'fixture of the *varnas* according to merits and actions should take place at the sixteenth year of girls and twenty-fifth year of boys'. Moreover, he considered that marriages should 'take place in the same varnas and the *varna* should be based on merits, profession and temperament'. It means that not only Dayananda adds one more criterion to the definition of castes the profession but also that endogamy, which is a pillar of the caste system, needed to be enforced. Dayananda did not fight caste taboos either. For instance, he considered that a Brahmin needed only to eat food prepared by caste fellows because 'The nature of genital fluids made in a Brahman's body due to special kind of fooding is different from that made in chandalas body on account of bad diet. The body of the candalas is full of rotten particles due to rotten diet'. He was obviously a clear proponent of sanskritisation and the Arya Samaj exerted a strong influence in this direction over the lower castes of North India. The first anti-Brahmin movement of North India was probably the Arya Samaj. But in contrast to what happened in Western and Southern India, this movement made a very ambivalent impact since it promoted sanskritisation. The activities of the arya samajists among the Yadavs of the Gangetic plains are a case in point.

Logically enough, the most obvious implication of the Arya Samaj in the North Indian countryside lay in the sanskritisation of the Jats, as evident from the ideology of the All India Jat Mahasabha which was founded in 1905 as 'an offshoot of the Arya Samaj'. On the one hand this caste association, as so many others, asked for a special treatment from the Government; on the other hand it claimed that Jats were Kshatriyas. Arya Samajists exhorted the Jats to give up the consumption of alcohol and meat and recommended that severe restriction should be 'imposed on the movement of women'. The schools established with the association's support had often telling names such as the Jat Vedic School founded in Rohtak in 1913 and generally taught Sanskrit in order to enable the Jats to teach Sanskrit and therefore occupy 'a profession which for centuries was the exclusive monopoly of the Brahmin'. The Arya Samajists propagated the same kind of ideology among the Yadavs.

The Arya Samaj *updeshaks* continuously canvassed for the adoption of the sacred thread by the Yadavs. Their campaigns were especially successful in Uttar Pradesh and Bihar. The Yadav rulers of Rewari, Rao Yudhishter Singh, true to his role as protector of the cows founded a Goraksha Sabha in conjunction with the Arya Samaj – which had started to create such *sabhas* all over North India. The arya samajists also enrolled the Yadavs in the cow protection movement. This movement, initiated in 1893 and relaunched at different points of time in the first two decades of the century, attracted many Yadavs who were anxious to emulate the upper castes. In the Bhojpuri region, Gyan Pandey, who emphasised 'the special role of the Ahirs' in this movement points out that 'we have evidence here of a relatively independent force that added a good deal of power to cow-protection activities [...] marginally 'clean' castes who aspired to full 'cleanliness' by emphasising the purity of their faith and the strictness of ritual adherence to it on the issue of cow-slaughter'. Such a process can hardly be presented as 'a relatively independent force'. Both phenomena may not be mutually exclusive, however. The same Ahirs who took part in the cow-protection movement and could also petition the Bihar Census Commissioner for being recognised a Kshatriya origin also refused to do *beggar* for the upper castes. Revisiting the notion of sanskritisation, Srinivas himself points out that it 'embodies a strong element of protest against the high castes: 'We dare you to stop us emulating you seems to be the spirit underlying emulation'. A specialist of the Yadavs, M.S.A. Rao also questions the opposition between sanskritised movements and egalitarian movements:

> ... the backward classes attempt to acquire, simultaneously goods and services belonging to religious, educational, economic and political fields. That is, they claim higher ritual status, right of entry into caste Hindu temples, or establish a set of institutions parallel to the Brahmanical ones. They claim higher educational benefits, employment opportunities and political representation. From the point of view of the social movement approach all these demands belong to the same structural plane as expressions of egalitarianism.

While the difference between sanskritisation and other low castes' movements needs not to be exaggerated, there are still differences and it is very difficult to follow Rao when he pretends that 'the Yadavs were not imitating the 'twice-born castes'' when they were donning the sacred thread, but were challenging their monopoly over this privilege'. They tried to upgrade themselves while recognising the symbols of the Brahmins as superior-thesis the sanskritisation perspective. This approach does not necessarily imply a sense of equality since the caste in question may try to be recognised as higher in order to look down at the others which were on the same level. The first history of the Yadavs was written by R.V. Khedekar's father, was taken up by his son and published in 1959 under the title *The Divine Heritage of the Yadavs.* The book situates the origins of the Yadavs in the Abhiras and then the ruling dynasties mentioned as Yadavs in the Mahabharata and the Puranas. The descendants of Krishna naturally form the core group of this heritage. But dynasties regarded as Jats and Marathas, like those o f Kolhapur, Barada and Bharatpur are also included in this historical reconstitution. This openness could have been part of an attempt at federating different castes but in fact, the Yadav 'historians' admit that these groups have succeeded and try to highlight the superiority of *their* caste. The ethnic dimension of their 'narrative' is therefore narrower than that of Phule or Dravidians. They try to demonstrate that Abhiras were Aryan origin. Lucio Michelutti shows that in the wake of Khedekar, K.C. Yadav and then J.N.S. Yadav base their claim on inscriptions which may suggest that the Ahiras were the main ruling dinasty of North India as early as the second century Before Christ.

This largely mythical history enabled Yadav intellectuals to invent a golden age.

Khedekar pretends that 'Even in the vedic age the Yadavs were upholders of the Republican ideals of Government', under the aegis o f Krishna himself. More importantly, he stresses the Aryan origins of his caste:

> The Yadavs were those 'ancient Aryans who were the custodians o f this Bharat Varsha and who possessed the highest virtues which attracted God to be incarnated amongst them, to play with them, to sing the sweet melody of the Bhagavad Gita in order to bring peace and prosperity in the world. Without the help of the Yadav, Shri-Krishna could not have done anything'.

This narrative certainly aims at giving the Yadavs an ethnic identity, but this ethnicisation process is embedded in the sanskritisation logic. In contrast to the lower castes leaders of Maharashtra and South India who tried to invent a Bahujan or a Dravidian identity which presented the Shudras and Untouchables as the originals inhabitants of the country *against* the Aryans, the Yadavs claim that they *are* Aryans in order to exhauce their status *within* caste society. W.R. Pinch cites 'Yadav-Kshatriya historians who, in the 1930s, held that Yadavs were 'the ancient citizens of the land of the Aryans'.

The All India Yadav Mahasabha, through which Khedekar federated regional associations based in Punjab, Uttar Pradesh and Bihar in followed the sanskritisation path under the guidance of Rao Balbir Singh, the ruler of Rewari who still played a prominent role in the Yadav movement. Interestingly, he was elected to the Punjab assembly in 1937 on a Hindu Mahasabha ticket. The programme of the AIYM is easy to summarise. It advocated vegetarianism and teetotalism. It militated in favour of the adoption of the name 'Yadav' all over India and so far as material interests were concerned, it incited the Yadavs to embrace new professional careers and put pressure on the British to make the army recruit Yadavs as officers.

While the AIYM helped the Yadavs to get united, in 1945 dissidents founded a rival caste association, the All India Yadav Sangh whose activities were even more sanskritised it took part in the 1966 anti-cow slaughter movement for instance. The main weakness of the Yadavs was their incapacity to make alliances with other castes of similar rank, like the Kurmis, who suffered from the same problem themselves!

The Kurmis are also concentrated in Bihar and UP where they represented respectively 3.6 and 3.5% of the population in 1931. The Kurmis generally work as cultivators and are looked at as middle caste peasants but they claim to be Kshatriyas. The ground for this 'kshatriyaisation' process was prepared by the Ramanandi *sampraday* which, as other sectarian movements, 'welcomed shudras as equal members of the monastic community'. By the last decades of the XIXth century, Kurmi leaders were the first among the low castes to fashion caste stories emphasising 'an ancient past of kshatriya distinction that had long since deteriorated into present-day shudra dishonour'. These stories, which were gradually propagated by printed bulletins, relied on the Vaishnava mythology as spelled out by the Ramanandi order. Kurmis were presented as descending from Ram's two sons, Kush and Lav the Kushwahas also claim that Kush was their ancestor but interestingly not attempt at merging these two groups ever took shape.

The first Kurmi caste association was founded in 1894 in Lucknow to protest against the British decision to reduce the recruitment of Kurmis in the police. The Kurmis of Awadh then created a Kurmi Sabha and declared that other castes like the Patidars the Kapus (from Andhra Pradesh), the Vokkaligas the Reddys, the Naidus and the Marathas were also Kurmis. The association gained momentum in 1901, during the census operations when it claimed that Kurmis were Kshatriyas. The All India Kurmi Kshatriya Mahasabha, which was officially registered in Patna in 1910, combined the defence of the caste secular interests and sanskritisation.

Kurmis and Yadavs, even though they occupied similar social positions failed to get united. The first attempt was made in Bihar in the 1930s. It involved the Yadavs, the Kurmis and the Koeris, a caste o f agriculturists representing 4.1% of the state population. Members o f those three castes joined hands in 1930 to contest the local district board elections. They lost badly but in 1934 formed the Triveni Sangh, a political party named after the confluence of three rivers, in Allahabad. In 1936 about one million members had allegedly paid the fouranna fee. However, at the same time, in 1935, the Congress formed the Backward Class Federation 'to counter what they viewed as the dangerous class features of the Triveni Sangh and Kisan Sabha movements'. Congressmen deprived the low caste movement from some of its leaders by co-opting Kurmi leaders and Yadavs. And then they refused to give tickets to Triveni Sangh candidates. The party suffered from a serious setback during the 1937 elections but in the few places where it won like Arrah and Piro Shahabad district upper caste landlords retaliated violently. The Triveni Sangh and the Kisan Sabha also failed to make an alliance because of the traditional antagonism between the low castes represented by the former and the Bhumihars who dominated the latter.

Many years later, the Kurmis tried to play a pivotal role in a similar arrangement. During the 30th session of the All India Kurmi Kshatriya Sabha, some of the delegates suggested that the word 'Kshatriya' should be removed from the name of the association and a resolution was passed to discourage the sanskritisation process. In the same way, it was decided to constitute a caste federation with the Koeris. The Kurmis leaders were not planning to create a new caste through intermarriage, but a union they called 'Raghav Samaj'—after one of the names of the Lord Ram —a choice they justified by presenting the Kurmis and the Koeris as descending respectively from Lav and Kush, two sons of Ram. While the sessions of the Sabha were often presided over by Marathas, Patidars etc., in the 1970s about 30% of the executive bureau members were from Bihar. The attempt to federate the Koeris and Kurmis was rather inconclusive, no doubt because of difference in their status and economic activities.

The failure of the Yadavs, Kurmis and Koeris to form caste federations in North India can be explained from different points of view. One explanation lay in the fact that the Yadavas 'consider themselves to be natural leaders of backward classes'; their leaders even argued that their caste fought against injustice during the Dwapara Yug under the leadership of Krishna and that they should now show the way in the battle against the upper castes exploitation. This approach did not enable them to forge stable caste federations. This ethos prevented the low castes from developing a common, ethnic as well as 'federated' identity like in the West or in the South. The same kind of reasoning can be made about the untouchables' movement.

The North Indian Untouchables and the limited ethnicisation of caste The Untouchables of North India were also exposed to the influence of the Arya Samaj at the turn of the XXth century.

Briggs emphasises that 'During 1911, preceding the Census enumeration, both the Arya Samaj and the Mohammedan communities made special efforts to enrol Chamars, especially those who were Christians'. This competition was part of the politics of numbers. It concerned a small minority since in 1911 there were only 1,551 Arya Samajist Chamars in the United Provinces, but most of the Jatav leaders were exposed to it. Their name, in itself is very revealing. The Arya Samaj missions were responsible for propagating these views. They were especially successful through their schools among the sons of Agra Chamars who had become rich thanks to leather trade. Manikchand Jatavaveer (1897-1956), one of the founders of the Jatav Mahasabha in 1917 was a teacher in a school of Agra run by the Arya Samaj. Sunderlal Sagar another co-founder of the Sabha in Agra was even versed in Sanskrit so much so that he was called Pandit. A Ahir co-founder of the caste association, Swami Prabhutanand Vyas was an Arya Samaj monk. They all preached moral reform, vegetarianism, teetotalism and temperance for achieving a cleaner status. That was also the first inclination of Swami Achhutanand who was to become the most important Scheduled Caste leader o f the United Provinces in the 1920s-1930s.

A Chamar, Swami Achutanand was born in a village of Farukkabad district in the United Provinces. His father was a foot soldier and his uncle a subedar in the army of British India – like Ambedkar's, his family benefited from the government's policy of recruiting untouchables in the military personnel. He was attracted by the itinerant life of Hindu ascetics while he was still very young. He worked as an *updeshak* of the movement, under the name of Hariharnanda, from 1905 till 1912, mainly in Shuddi Sabhas which were in charge of 'purifying' untouchables. But then he revolted against the Arya Samaj and spends five years working at exposing the organisation under his new name, Swami Achutanand. In a violent indictment o f the Arya Samaj, he declared once : 'This sect has been constructed in order to save the Brahmin religion from the attacks of the Christians and Muslims. Its profession of purification are a grand and a clever verbal gimmick of the *varna* system'. He ridiculed the Arya Samaj schemes o f inter caste marriages, asking the leaders of the organisation why they do not arrange for such marriages also with twice-borns if they were true reformers. In a conference he organised in Allahabad in 1930 he attacked the Arya Samajist reinterpretation of the *varna* system in the following terms :

> Earlier, caste and *varna* were based on birth. Now, they are being said to be derived from the talents and achievements of a person as preached by the Arya Samaj. If this is true then left the *dwij* [twice-born] marry their sons with our simple and homely daughters for the next generation as to vindicate this truth.

Swami Achutanand enunciated the outlines of his Adi-Hindu philosophy for the first time in 1917 twenty years after Thass in a collection of poems and couplets. According to him, the Untouchables were the first inhabitants of India and the rightful owners of this land. The Aryans came from outside, 'as refugees' who, by resorting to tactics and strategies, captured power and subordinated the autochthonous people: 'They did not win over our own ruler by their good and noble deeds but by clever manoeuvres and later called them demons and Asuru and Satan. They destroyed our culture and civilisation and made us untouchables and outcastes in the heart of our own society.'

Swami Achutanand maintains that the Adi-Hindus had their roots in the Indus Valley civilisation in the region of Harrapa and Mohendjo Daro. He explained the difference between Shudras and Untouchables by arguing that with the coming of the Aryans those sections of the defeated people who accepted the *varna* system became *Shudras* and those who did not became Untouchables. The Adi-Hindu philosophy was well designed for promoting the unity of the Shudras, the Untouchables and the Tribals since it endowed those three groups with a common-cultural and ethnic background : once upon a time, they were parts and parcels of the same people. Swami Achutanand – like Ambedkar – did not pay any real attention to the Adivasis but he did try to unite the two other groups in a political perspective : 'If these two categories were to come together and make an organisation then they would count for 20 crores [200 millions] and become the most important majority group in society and could make a government of their own...' Swami Achutanand adopted the same expression – Bahujan Samaj – as Phule. However, the organisation he launched in 1919 was called the All India Achut Caste Reform Sabha. According to his biographer, the first Adi-Hindu council was started in Andhra, then in Delhi in 1922, in Madras and in Punjab. In Lucknow and in Poona, a journal named *Adi-Hindu* was started and, in Punjab, another newspaper *Adidas* was also launched for publicising the ideas of Swami Achutanand.

The Adi-Hindu movement gained momentum in 1922, when Swami Achutanand protested against Gandhi's Non Cooperation Movement and especially his boycott of the Prince of Wales' visit. Swami Achutanand emphasised that the Congress was an organisation of 'twice born Brahmans who are as foreign to India as are the British'. He said he was favourable to the visit of the Prince of Wales and the British appreciated : when Lothian Committee organised its hearings in Lucknow, he was called upon to give a testimony about the Untouchables' conditions. Later on, in the early 1930s, he asked the British for the introduction of separate electorates.

The Congress leaders took exception of his pro-British stands. He was accused of being a Christian in disguise and an agent of the British paid for dividing the Hindu community. But in fact, the congressmen's hostility came from his emancipatory discourse and the way he was mobilising the Untouchables against the caste system. His strong criticism of the Manusmriti was especially resented. In reaction, the Arya Samaj started an All India Shraddhanand Dalitodwar Sabha whose objective was to break up the Adi-Hindu movement. With the help of G.D. Birla, M. M. Malaviya also started an All India Achutodwar Sabha, which organised meetings between 1924 and 1927. Later on it merged with the Congress – backed All India Dalit Varg Sabha.

There were direct confrontations between Swami Achutanand and Congress leaders in several occasions. Once, during the Mahakumbh Mela of Allahabad, the Arya Samaj organised an All India Dalit Liberation Conference under the auspices of Purushottamdas Tandon, a conservative Congressman, one of Malaviya's lieutenants in UP politics. In this forum, Tandon spoke about the Hindu mythology and how the Nishads found liberation by washing the feet of Ram and worshipped him. One stated that all dalits can sell food items at the railways stations. The other one that the washing clothes and making shoes was the vocational task of the Adi-Hindus and that any twice-born Hindu engaging in this matter should marry his children amongst these castes and share their food. The later resolution amounted at consolidating the caste system.

Swami Achutanand's attitude towards the caste system remained ambivalent indeed. For instance, in the Adi-Hindu Sabhas the caste and sub-castes were all represented : instead of trying to eradicate them, Swami Achutanand recognised castes amongst the Untouchables. More importantly, his egalitarian discourse was largely framed in a religious mould drawing its inspiration from the *bhakti* tradition. Swami Achutanand, even after leaving the Arya Samaj remained a sadhu. He was given his official name, 108th Swami Achutanand in revealing circumstances. In the late 1920s he organised in Delhi, outside the Red Fort, the foundation meeting of a Jati Sudhar Achut Sabha when he challenged any Brahmin to *shastrarth* for the interpretation of the classical Hindu text and epics. It was certainly on their part a shrewd way to co-opt him. He obviously resisted this attempt but did adopt the style of many Dalit saints before him. He draw his inspiration partly from the *bhakti* idiom. According to C.P. Jigyansu, 'His style of address was poetic and musical, similar to the

Bhakti leaders of the 16th or 17th century, but his discourse was radical and biting'. This is a very apt way at describing the ambivalence of Swami Achutanand. His biographer pertinently emphasised that the 'Adi-Hindu agitation had started in a religious mould'. Indeed, after severing his links with the Arya Samaj, Swami Achutanand studied the writings of the Sikh Gurus, Kabir, Dadudayal, Namdev and Redam Sahib. Singing, chanting formed an essential part of his meetings. This old style of discourse is very particular to the cultures o f the oral tradition where songs, poems and other narratives formed an essential ideological component of the preachings'. This modus operandi stood in stark contrast with Ambedkar's westernised style. While Swami Achutanand supported Ambedkar he might have been uneased by his condemnation of the bhakti. Furthermore, Swami Achutanand organised some of his meetings during religious functions. In 1931, he held a conference on the preachings of Kabir in the heart of brahmanical orthodoxy, the Allahabad Maherkumbha Mela. Basically, Swami Achutanand discovered social equality in religion :

> 'Our religion is not Brahminism but Sant Dharma or Sufi way of life. Our religion does not believe in discrimination or differences between humans. For all humans are equal and have equal rights'.

This quotation is a good summary of the thought of Swami Achutanand. He emphasises that the Untouchables are the original inhabitants of India and that, correlatively, they are the torchbearers o f the most ancient religion. This creed, however, recalls the *bhakti* cults since it emphasises the worship of saints and equality before God. Ambedkar always criticised the *bhakti* cults because they delinked equality before God from social equality – and he accused Gandhi to do the same.

Nandini Gooptu convincingly argues that the Adi Hindu movement arose in the wake of the resurgence of *bhakti* cults among the Untouchables in the late XIXth century early XXth century. Worshipping Kabir and Ravidas then became widespread among urban untouchables migrants in U.P, and ceased to be practised only by insular religious orders : new temples and statues were built, festivals and pilgrimages organised. India. If '*bhakti* was resurrected as a caste-based religious expression solely of the untouchables', it could not be practised 'as a form of denial of caste distinctions'.

Indeed, N. Gooptu admits that 'the criticism of the caste system by the Adi Hindu leaders was rather limited and had a narrow focus on the lack of rights or opportunities for the untouchables. The leaders did jettison the notions of "low" or "impure", but concentrated on proving that such stigma and disabilities should not be attached to them due to caste status. Nor did they attempt to question the concept that work was inherited. Instead they claimed that "low" work was not the true inheritance of the Untouchables. It was largely to buttress this claim that they asserted their pre Aryan ancestry as the original rulers of India, for it enabled them to argue that they should re inherit the ancient rights o f which they had been deprived'.

Far from establishing a separate identity that would situate the Untouchables out of the caste system, the Adi Hindu movement used their so-called original identity as a means for promoting their status *within* the system. And correlatively, the *bhakti* resurgence did not imply a radical questioning of their belonging to Hinduism. They questioned Brahminism by adhering to a rather popular tradition but their practise of this religious cult recalls the modus operandi of the Hindu sects which precisely derived from *bhakti* whose egalitarian impact has always been other worldly.

The movement also suffered from organisational weaknesses. While the 'informal nature of links between apex Adi Hindu organisations in the towns and local caste groups in neighbourhoods contributed to the strength and breadth of the movement', by 1924 local Adi Hindu Sabhas had been set up in only four cities of U.P. In fact the Adi-Hindu movement remained chiefly confined to Agra and Kanpur. Out of the 23 main Dalit leaders of the United Provinces in the first half of the century, almost 50% were from these two cities.

In addition to these limitations, the movement also failed to unite the Untouchables, in terms of commensality or otherwise. Its leaders tried to organise inter dining ceremonies but did not meet very enthusiastic responses. Untouchables leaders of North India could not agree either about the strategy that was to be implemented vis-avis the British.

If Government were to improve their political status by giving them honorary offices, adequate representation on local bodies and legislatures and in public services commensurate with their numerical strength, their social position would automatically improve and social injustice would become a thing of the past. For social position of the depressed classes would rise pari passu with the rise in their economic condition a thing which is inconceivable in the case of any community without advancement of its political status.

Such a discourse foreshadows or echoes one of Ambedkar's main initiations, namely that only power could enable his caste mates to emancipate themselves. However, all the Jatavs did not share these views. In fact this movement was impeded by the activism of the Dalit leaders who stuck to the sanskritisation approach. It was especially affected by the competition of the Depressed Classes League that was founded at Lucknow in 1935 by R.L. Biswas with Jagjivan Ram as General Secretary and P.N. Rajbhoj as Secretary. The moving spirit behind this association at least one of its chief architects Dharam Prakash, was a staunch arya samajist who opposed Ambedkar's moves in favour o f conversion and was elected to the Constituent Assembly, and then to the Rajya Sabha, on a Congress ticket.

In the 1930s, a similar division opposed the proponents of joint electorates with reserved seats, such as Bohre Khem Chand the president of the All India Shri Jatava Mahasabha and those who supported Ambedkar's demand regarding separate electorates, such as the United Provinces Adi-Hindu. Association. This cleavage more or less coincided with the one opposing the proponents of sankritisation and those who were more favourably inclined towards an egalitarian, ambedkarite strategy, the important point being here that the former tended to dominate the Jatav movement till the 1930s. After the publication of the White Paper which was to be the basis of the 1935 Government o f India Act, the Agra based Jatav Conference sent a memorandum to the Deputy Secretary to the Government of India where it was said :

> The Jatavs are the descendents of Yadu, the founder of Jadav [sic] tribe, from which the great Hero of Maha Bharat, Lord Krishna, came. But this position of superiority could not remain intact. Our community fell down from that great height to this degraded status in the Hindu fold [...] our present position is the outcome of the age-long inhumane oppressions of Brahminism or the Kshatriyas. We, Kshatriyas of the past, are labouring under various sorts of disabilities, restrictions and religious injunctions imposed on us by

> the Orthodox Hindus. But we are at loss to understand the exclusion of our Jatav community from the list o f the Scheduled Castes given in the White Paper. The result of this horrible negligence would, no doubt, be the sacrifice of the interests of our community.

Such a discourse suggests that the Jatav movement was still under the influence of sanskritisation. Owen Lynch points out that 'The Jatavs were not attempting to destroy the caste system; rather they were attempting to rise within it in a valid, though not licit, way'.

The influence of Ambedkar made a strong impact on the Jatav movement in the 1940s so much so that the Maharashtrian scenario with Dalit acquiring a separate Buddhist identity could be used to avoid the trap of sanskritisation. Even those who did not convert themselves to Buddhism regarded the Untouchables as descending from the original Buddhists and, therefore, prided themselves of being the original Indians: 'Buddhist identity has replaced Sanskrit Kshatriya identity'. Also, for the Jatavs, 'political participation' became a 'functional alternative' to sanskritisation, in the sense that they tried to achieve social mobility through access to power. This empowerment process was fostered by the British policies of positive discrimination and gradual democratisation since they both incited the caste to transform itself into a pressure group and to assert itself as a collective body. However, such a change was confined to the Jatavs of Agra. Except the president of the Scheduled Caste Federation of the United Provinces, Piarelall Kureel who was a Kureel from Unnao district, most of the supporters of Ambedkar were Jatav's from Agra movement. A similar evolution only took place with the Noniya who abandoned the Arya Samaj for political action and the Mallahs Babu Ramcharanji who had founded the All India Nishad Maha Sabha in 1920 joined the Adi-Hindu movement in 1925 and became president of the Adi-Hindu Sabha in 1927. In 1933 the All India Nishada Sabha claimed that 'the Mallahs are the descendants of the ancient Nishadas and Chandalas of the Vedic age and they themselves and the Hindus in general regard them as such up to the present time'.

In many cases sanskritisation on the basis of arya samajist influences or not remained prevalent. In the 1911 and 1921 censuses, some 26 low castes claimed the status of the twice-born castes. Certainly, sanskritisation and social mobility were not mutually exclusive but the former reflected the pervasiveness of the value system of the caste hierarchy anyway.

In 1935, after the publication of the government of India Act, the All India Dhobi Association protested against the exclusion of their caste from the Scheduled Castes which had been decided under pressures from other associations such as the Arya Samaj oriented United Provinces Razak. Association which pursued the sanskritisation path. The President of the latter organisation, for whom Dhobis were Kshatriyas, considered that giving his caste fellows the status of Untouchables would be 'a stigma on character and ability, an obstruction to self-advancement and improvement'. Similar conflicts happened in the case of the Khatiks, an Untouchable caste of meat cutters.

The Bundelkhand Prantia Kori Sabha, which claimed 20,000 members passed a resolution in 1936 to support the view that 'the Cores of India have always been classified amongst the touchable castes with the right to Samskaras' and that in the Manusmriti they are 'held to be born of a Kshatriya in a Vaishya mother'.

Similarly, the salt manufacturers of North India, the Noniyas, who belong to the lower orders of the shudras, did not emancipate themselves from the sanskritisation pattern till the 1960s-70s. In 1898 rich notable of the caste established an association claiming for the Noniyas the status of Cauhan Rajputs.

The 'New Cauhans' undertook to ritually don the sacred thread, something the upper castes strongly objected for sometimes. For William Rowe, the 'Cauhan Movement' provided the Noniyas 'a mechanism which allowed them to reduce the discrepancy between their contrasting positions in the ritual and economic hierarchies' but this movement 'does not challenge but rather upholds the traditional stratification system'. Interestingly, in the early 1960s, the 'new Cauhans' still considered the RPI 'as "the dirtiest party in Indi. However, the youngest generation was dissociating itself from sanskritisation and get more politicises. Like in Madras and Bombay twenty years ago when the Montage – Chennmsford reforms had fostered the organisation and politicisation of the lower castes, the Untouchables mobilised in the context of the 1935 Government of India Acts. The above examples suggest that the proponents o f sanskritisation remained strong and hindered the efforts made by others for uniting the caste against the brahminical order. Secondly, when castes reached this kind of unity they did not succeed in forging federations.

References

Munshi, Kaivan and Mark R. Rosensweig, "Traditional Institutions Meet the Modern World: Caste, Gender, and Schooling Choice in a Globalising Economy." *American Economic Review* 96(4):1225-1252, September 2006.

Miguel, Edward, "Tribe or Nation? Nation Building and Public Goods in Kenya versus Tansania," *World Politics,* 2004, 56 (3), 327-362

Omvedt, Gail, *Dalits and the Democratic Revolution: Dr. Ambedkar and the Dalit Movement in Colonial India,* Sage Publications, Delhi, 1994

Pandian, J., "Political Emblems of Caste Identity: An Interpretation of Tamil Caste Titles," *Anthropological Quarterly,* Vol. 56. No. 4, Pp: 190-197, October 1983.

Rao, Vijayendra and Michael Walton, "Culture and Public Action: Relationality, Equality of Agency and Development," Chapter 1 in (V. Rao and M. Walton – eds.) *Culture and Public Action,* Stanford University Press, Stanford, 2004.

Srinivas, MN, *Social Change in Modern India,* University of California Press, Berkely, 1966.

4

Caste and Identity Politics

Identity politics has become a prominent subject in the Indian politics in the past few years. Rise of low castes, religious identities, linguistic groups and ethnic conflicts have contributed to the significance of identity politics in India. The discourse on Identity, many scholars feel, is distinctly a modern phenomenon. Crag Calhoun aptly describes the situation when he argues that it is in the modern times we encounter intensified efforts at consolidating individual and categorical identities and reinforce self-sameness. This is primarily a modern phenomenon because some scholars feel that emphasis on identity based on a central organising principle of ethnicity, religion, language, gender, sexual preferences, or caste positions, etc, are a sort of "compelling remedy for anonymity" in an otherwise impersonal modern world. It is thus said to be a "pattern of belonging, a search for comfort, an approach to community." However, the complex social changes and the imbrications of various forces, factors and events in this modern world have rendered such production and recognition of identities problematic. Cascarilla succinctly elucidates this by observing, "the modern subject is defined by its insertion into a series of separate value-spheres, each one of which tends to exclude or attempts to assert its priority over the rest", thereby rendering identity-schemes problematic. Nonetheless, the concerns with individual and collective identity that simultaneously seeks to emphasise differences and attempt to establish commonality with others similarly distinguished, have become a universal venture.

Identity politics is said to "signify a wide range of political activity and theorising founded in the shared experiences of injustice of members of certain social groups". As a political activity it is thus considered to signify a body of political projects that attempts a "recovery from exclusion and denigration" of groups hitherto marginalised on the basis of differences based on their '*selfhood*' determining characteristics like ethnicity, gender, sexual preferences, caste positions, etc.

Identity politics thus attempts to attain empowerment, representation and recognition of social groups by asserting the very same markers that distinguished and differentiated them from the others and utilise those markers as an assertion of selfhood and identity based on *difference* rather than *equality*. Contrastingly placed, it is to imply that adherents of identity politics essentials certain markers that fix the identities of social groups around an ensemble of definition absolutes. The proponents of identity politics thus, assign the primacy of some "essence" or a set of core features shared only by members of the collectivity and no others and accepts individual persons as singular, integral, altogether harmonious and unproblematic identities. These core markers are different from associations markers like those of the workers who are defined more by their common interests rather than by certain core essential naturally '*given*' identity attributes of the groups engaged in identity politics. Though many would argue that "worker" was an identity deserving legitimacy and as a group, its movements can be referred to as identity Politics, but probably the term "identity politics" as a body of political projects implied to in contemporary discourses refers to certain essential, local and particular categorical identities rather than any universalisation ideals or agenda.

The strongest criticism against Identity Politics is that it often challenged by the very same markers upon which the sense of self or community is sought to be built. It is despite the fact that identity politics is engaged in numerous aspects of oppression and powerlessness, reclaiming and transforming negative scripts used by dominant groups into powerful instruments for building positive images of self and community. In other words the markers that supposedly defines the community are fixed to the extent that they harden and release a process of in-group essentialism that often denies internal dialogicality within and without the group and itself becomes a new form of closure and oppression.

Identity Politics as a field of study can be said to have gained intellectual legitimacy since the second half of the twentieth century between 1950s and 1960s in the United States when large scale political movements of the second wave-feminists, Black Civil Rights, Gay and Lesbian Liberation movements and movements of various Indigenous groups in the U.S. And other parts of the world were being justified and legitimated on the basis of claims about injustices done to their respective social groups. However, as scholars like Heyes point out that although "'Identity Politics' can draw on intellectual precursors from Mary Wollstonecraft to Frants Fanon, writing that actually uses this specific phrase is limited almost exclusively to the last 15 years.

In India we find that despite adoption of a liberal democratic polity after independence, communities and collective identities have remained powerful and continue to claim recognition. In fact, Beteille has shown that the Indian polity has consistently tried to negotiate the allegiance to a liberal spirit and the concerns and consciousness of community. According to Bikhu Parekh this process has recognised a wide array of autonomous and largely self-governing communities.

It was probably this claim for and granting of recognition of particular identities by the post-independence state of India that led many scholars to believe that a material basis for the enunciation of identity claims has been provided by the post-independent state and its structures and institutions. Thus, we find identity politics of various hues abound in India, the most spectacular however, are those based on language, religion, caste, ethnicity or tribal identity. But having said this it would be wrong on our part to assume that each of these identity markers operate autonomously, independent of the overlapping influence of the other makers. In other words a homogenous linguistic group may be divided by caste affiliations that may be sub-divided by religious orientations or all may be subsumed under a broader ethnic claim.

Caste-based discrimination and oppression have been a pernicious feature of Indian society and in the post-independence period its imbrications with politics have not only made it possible for hitherto oppressed caste-groups to be accorded political freedom and recognition but has also raised consciousness about its potential as a political capital. In fact Dipankar Gupta has poignantly exposed this contradiction when he elaborates the differences between Ambedkar and Mandal Commission's view of caste. While the former designed the policy of reservations or protective discrimination to remove untouchability as an institution from Indian social life and polity, the latter considered caste as an important political resource. Actually, the Mandal commission can be considered the intellectual inspiration in transforming caste-based identity to an asset that may be used as a basis for securing political and economic gains. Though it can also be said that the upper castes by virtue of their predominant position were already occupying positions of strengths in the political and economic system, and when the Mandal heightened the consciousness of the 'Dalits' by recognisisng their disadvantage of caste-identity as an advantage the confrontation ensues. The origin of confrontational identity politics based on caste may be said to have its origin on the issue of providing the oppressed caste groups with state support in the form of protective discrimination. This group-identity based on caste that has been reinforced by the emergence of political consciousness around caste identities is institutionalised by the caste-based political parties that profess to uphold and protect the interests of specific identities including the castes.

Caste has become an important determinant in Indian society and politics, the new lesson of organised politics and consciousness of caste affiliations learnt by the hitherto despised caste groups have transformed the contours of Indian politics where shifting caste-class alliances are being encountered. The net effect of these mobilisations along caste-identities have resulted not only in the empowerment of newly emerging groups but has increased the intensity of confrontational politics and possibly leading to a growing crisis of governability.

Another form of identity politics is that effected through the construction of a community on the shared bond of religion. In India, Hinduism, Islam, Sikhism, Christianity, and Soroastrianism are some of the major religions practised by the people. Numerically the Hindus are considered to be the majority, which inspires many Hindu loyalist groups like the RSS or the Siva Sena and political parties like the BJP (Bharatiya Janata Party) or the Hindu Mahasabha to claim that India is a Hindu State. These claims generate homogenising myths about India and its history. These claims are countered by other religious groups who foresee the possibility of losing autonomy of practise of their religious and cultural life under such homogenising claims. This initiates contestations that have often resulted in communal riots.

Historically, the Hindu revivalist movement of the 19 century is considered to be the period that saw the demarcation of two separate cultures on religious basis—the Hindus and the Muslims that deepened further because of the partition. This division which has become institutionalised in the form of a communal ideology has become a major challenge for India's secular social fabric and democratic polity. The rise of Hindu national assertiveness, politics of representational government, persistence of communal perceptions, and competition for the socioeconomic resources are considered some of the reasons for the generation of communal ideologies and their transformation into major riots.

Identity schemes based on religion have become a major source of conflict not only in the international context but since the early 1990s it has also become a challenge for Indian democracy and secularism. The rise of majoritarian assertiveness is considered to have become institutionalised after the BJP, that along with its 'Hindu' constituents gave political cohesiveness to a consolidating Hindu consciousness, formed a coalition ministry in March 1998. However, like all identity schemes the forging of a religious community glosses over internal differences within a particular religion to generate the "we are all of the same kind" emotion.

In post-independence India the majoritarian assertion has generated its own antithesis in the form of minority religions assertiveness and a resulting confrontational politics that undermines the syncretised dimensions of the civil society in India. The process through which this religious assertiveness is being increasingly institutionalised by a 'methodical rewriting of history' has the potential to reformulate India's national identity along communal trajectories.

Identity claims based on the perception of a collectivity bound together by language may be said to have its origin in the pre-independence politics of the Congress that had promised reorganisation of states in the post-independent period on linguistic basis. But it was the "JVP" Committee's concession that if public sentiment was "insistent and overwhelming", the formation of Andhra from the Telugu-speaking region of the then Madras could be conceded which as Michael Brecher mentions was the "opening wedge for the bitter struggle over states reorganisation which was to dominate Indian Politics from 1953 to 1956". But the problem has been that none of the created or claimed states are mono-ethnic in composition and some even have numerically and politically powerful minorities. This has resulted in a cascading set of claims that continue to threaten the territorial limits of existing states and disputes over boundaries between linguistic states have continued to stir conflicts, as for instance the simmering tensions between Maharastra and Karnataka over the district of Belgaum or even the claims of the Nagas to parts of Manipur.

The linguistic divisions have been complicated by the lack of a uniform language policy for the entire country. Since in each state the dominant regional language is often used as the medium of instruction and social communication, the consequent affinity and allegiance that develops towards one's own language gets expressed even outside one's state of origin. Thus language becomes an important premise on which group identities are organised and establishes the conditions for defining the 'in-group' and 'out-group'.

Though it is generally felt that linguistic states provide freedom and autonomy for collectivities within a heterogeneous society, critics argue that linguistic states have reinforced regionalism and has provided a platform for the articulation of a phenomenal number of identity claims in a country that has 1,652 'mother tongues' and only fourteen recognised languages around which states have been reorganised.

You will study in detail about the ethnicity in unit 26 of the book 2 of this course. There are two ways in which the concept of ethnic identity is used; one, it insiders the formation of identity on the basis of single attribute language, religion, caste, region, etc; two, it considers the formation of identity on the basis, of multiple attributes cumulatively. However, it is the second way formation of identity on the basis of more than one characteristics culture, customs, region, religion or caste, which is considered as the most common way of formation of the ethnic identity. The relations between more than one ethnic identities can be both harmonious and conflictual. Whenever there is competetion among the ethnic identities on the real or imaginary basis, it expressed in the form of autonomy movements, demand for session or ethnic riots.

Identity has become an important phenomenon in the modern politics. The identification of a members of the group on the basis of sharing common attributes on the basis of all or some of the attributes, language, gender, language, religion, culture, ethnicity etc. Indicates the existence or formation of identity. The mobilisation on the basis of these markers is called identity politics. Identity politics gained legitimacy in the 1950s and 1960s in the United States.

4.1. Caste and Identity Issues

India is quite undeniably the most stratified society in the world. Over and above huge income disparities, there are caste, religious, and community differences that are deeply engraved into everyday social relations. No doubt, the nature of caste and community interactions has changed over time, but considerations along scripture lines still remain important markers both at the public and private domains.

Although tribes and religious distinctions exist in other societies as well, what sets India apart is the prevalence of the caste order. There are really no phonetically differences between castes, Bitot's presumed that Hindus have specific coded substances in them that set them apart from one another. Commingling of substances led to becoming polluted, and therefore social relations had to be finely calibrated to make sure that people did not compromise their inherent and inalienable substances by being in close physical proximity with members of different castes.

Even this is not that difficult to comprehend. Physical separation is a dominant diacritic of racism: Indeed everyday interactions at the level of community, religion, and linguistic affiliation often partake of this prejudice. But what makes caste stand apart from other forms of stratification is that in this case there are elaborate and ritualised rules that ordain not just how distinctions should be maintained, but also prescribe sanctions should the norms be violated.

This too, one might take as a quantitative exaggeration of a principle that is not unknown in other societies. Perhaps, it is an extreme form of stratification with cognate likenesses in racism, religious separation, and so on. In which case, the problem of comprehending caste is not difficult as all one has to do is to enlarge the scale and deepen the grooves of scripture prejudice. This is primarily because of the popular belief that castes that are considered impure according to the Brahmanism hierarchy, nevertheless participate willingly in their own degradation

The most systematic and influential proponent of this position can be found in Louis Dumont's *Homo Hierarchicus*. It was not as if Dumont was saying anything that has not been said before. Butin the course of his exposition on caste as a state of mind, he gave the term "hierarchy" a technical and sophisticated meaning. According to Dumont, a pure hierarchy allows for economics and politics only surreptitiously, but only in the interstitial levels. Otherwise, the hierarchy stands firm as its two poles stand in opposition to each other. At one extreme of this hierarchy is the Brahman (or the most pure), and at the other stands the untouchables (who are positively polluting). The castes in between are encompassed by this pure hierarchy, which is obsessively ranked on the purity/pollution principle.

There have been others before Dumont, such as Boggle Ghurye Leach Muriate and subsequently, Beck Milliner and Moffat among others, who would concur with Dumont's general position although they did not quite articulate their views in quite the same way. But the fact that castes were ranked in an undisputed hierarchy was unquestioningly accepted by all. And as castes were often linked to occupations, these too were ranked along the purity/pollution principle If Leach could argue that competition between castes was unthinkable, then it was primarily because, in his scheme of things, each caste knew its place and abided by the overarching hierarchical order. The difference that Dumont made is that he provided the theoretical underpinning to all this by insisting that a pure hierarchy is a state of mind to which all those in the caste system willingly acquiesce. As all castes are included within this all encompassing pure hierarchy, each caste ideologically participates in upholding the system as a whole.

As long as caste is seen through this optic, it is not at all surprising that the phenomenon should appear so unique and exotic, almost defying universalisation categorisation. It would be difficult to find a parallel in any other society where the subjugated people supposedly endorse the moral order that so thoroughly denigrates them. A single all embracing, all acquiescing, hierarchy was, of course, expressed with the expected hyperboles in Brahmanism texts such as the Yagnavalkyasmriti and Manusmriti, but it was the nineteenth century Ontologists who were the modern propagators of this point of view and gave it wider respectability. Sadly, social anthropologists, who could have corrected this notion with their field observations, also succumbed to this position. So strong was the persuasive power of exotica! As Beteille once rather trenchantly observed, many anthropologists often miss the larger analytical picture as they are constantly searching for differences and unique totalities.

Contemporary evidence indicates that caste identities cannot be strait-jacket within an unrelenting hierarchical grid where the status of the pure and the impure are empirically and unproblematically firm in their interactional nexus. In fact, this feature was noticed long ago by Senart, Bougle, and Blunt. For example, Senart argued that castes should be seen as units, and one should not rush into arranging them in a hierarchy. Even Bougle, who otherwise believed that hierarchy was an important characteristic of caste, nevertheless forcefully demonstrated that castes also mutually repel one another. That these two formulations were mutually contradictory did not strike Bougle with any degree of analytical force Blunt was perhaps the most incisive of them all when he observed that "if the caste system was devised with the object of preserving 'the purity of belief and ceremonial usage,' it has been a singular failure". And yet, the dominant Brahmanism view so dominated the intellectuals that it was Dumont's understanding of caste that swept Blunt, Bougle, and Senart under the carpet.

The fact is that the caste order is characterised by contesting notions of hierarchy and that is why we find competitive assertions of caste identity. Nor is it that status concerns in these multiple hierarchies are always linked to purity and pollution issues. They may also be associated with power and wealth, as among the merchant Jain castes, much more directly than what caste purists would have us believe. A general insensitivity toward this aspect of caste has led to the over valuation of the Brahmanism version of hierarchy, both in scholarly works and in popular imaginations. This has also contributed to the general intellectual puzzlement as to how one should conceptualise the relationship between caste and politics because here we have tension and competition in place of ideological acquiescence.

If castes do not contest their positions in the hierarchy, then where does the symbolic energy to compete for power in the political arena come from? Each caste should be content with its lot, and its members should calmly accept the superiority of those who are placed above them in terms of purity rankings. Indeed, Leach once said that when castes begin to compete, then they no longer function as caste. The truth, however, is that the caste system sans competition and conflict never really existed on the ground. There are different rankings in different locales depending upon who has the power and the wherewithal to make a particular ranking system, or hierarchy, work to their advantage. In some cases, the Brahmans were able to realise their favoured hierarchy in practice; in other cases, it was the Jats, or the Rajputs, or the Marathas, or the Marrows, or the Lingayats, and so on. This is why it is important to factor in the notion of caste identity; otherwise tensions within the caste order will never be fully understood.

4.2. Reconceptualising Caste

The study of caste and politics can be analytically justified only when we accept that castes are, first and foremost, discrete entities with deep pockets of ideological heritage. As they are discrete phenomenas, it is both logically and empirically true that there should be multiple hierarchies as each caste always overvalues itself. The element of caste competition is, therefore, a characteristic of the caste order and not a later addition. This implies that the caste system, as a system, worked primarily because it was enforced by power and not by ideological acquiescence. Only when we are armed with this perspective are we conceptually prepared to study the relationship between caste and politics. First, the relationships between castes were played out within the confines of the closed natural economy of the village. This left no room for manoeuvre for the subaltern communities and castes. Second, in precolonial times, caste hierarchies were contested and renegotiated episodically following the Philippines of a war or a major social upheaval. As such instances were rare, it gave rise to the illusion that castes have never competed and have been politically inactive.

The tranquillity that this vision of the pure hierarchy inspired should have been shattered irreparably when certain castes began to clamour for a higher status following the census operations conducted by the colonial regime. According to Homely, during the 1911 census enumeration, a number of castes objected to being placed at inferior levels in the hierarchy or wanted to be known differently from the traditional term assigned to them. Such petitions came fast and thick because the impression had gone around at that time that the census was not just about putting down numbers but also about assigning rank and prestige. Around this time caste associations, or sabhas, began to proliferate to press for higher status both in census records as well as in everyday interactions. Some enlightened Rajas, such as the ruler of Tranvancore, also helped in this regard by elevating certain castes. The Baroda prince gave scholarships to bright students from "low" caste families. Dr. B.R. Ambedkar, the legendary leader of the Scheduled Castes and one of the founding figures of independent India's Constitution, was one such beneficiary.

British authorities intervened in the caste order in three significant ways. First, it gave the Brahmans extraordinary precedence by taking their advice on what was the correct custom. This gave Brahmans in certain regions, particularly in South India and Maharashtra a lot of supralocal influence of the kind they did not enjoy hitherto. Resentment against this growing Brahman dominance resulted in anti-Brahman movements in South India and Maharashtra from the latter years of the nineteenth century. There are two mainstream political parties in Tamil Nadu that can legitimately claim to be descendants of the original anti-Brahman Dravida Kasagham movement. Also in North India, traditional peasant castes that were classified as lowly shudras, according to Brahmanism ranking, were forming their own associations to press for their rightful status under British rule.

Second, the Morally-Minto reforms of 1909 introduced separate electorates that gave a fillip to non-Brahman castes in their quest for self-respect. They now began to organise themselves as "Depressed Classes." This gained momentum from 1917 onward, and various Depressed Caste Associations began in different parts of India. In fact, the concern for the lower castes and untouchables was evident in the colonial administration from the 1880s onward. This was initially with special reference to education, so that the poor would find a ladder to climb from "the gutter to the university". Nevertheless, such a policy also demanded the enumeration of backward classes. This process began from 1883 onward, and the list of castes included in it began to grow rapidly. As the backward class rubric also included the untouchables, there was a move initiated in Madras in 1917 to separate them for the rest for special treatment.

Third, British presence also made a difference as a number of laws were enacted to lessen the weight of untouchability that the so-called polluting castes had to bear. For example, the Madras Government passed the Removal of Disabilities Act in 1938; this was soon followed by Mysore in 1943. There after, between 1943 and 1947 a number of states enacted similar laws to free those traditionally deemed as low castes from the incubus of traditional disprivilleges. The Yadavs, Kurmis, and Koeris of North India formed the Triveni Sangh to contest the 1935 elections. Though they lost that round to the Congress, the Triveni Sangh held and gradually increased its size. It incorporated other castes from similar backgrounds into its fold to form the Backward Class Federation. The members of the Backward Caste Federation were generally tenants and small cultivators, and they used their organisation to fight for their economic interests against the landlord classes, many of whom were close to the Congress.

Recent studies, therefore, clearly demonstrate that it is not as if castes are warming up to power considerations only after India became independent. The process of questioning established hierarchies through means other than war began with the establishment of British suzerainty in India. Caste and politics were always related, but the relationship was manifested differently at different periods of time. The establishment of democracy in independent India has introduced one major change in the way caste and politics interact, and that is by making all castes legally equal. This combination between law and economic change has allowed castes that were hitherto considered low to take the fight to the traditional superior communities and even to thumb their noses at established symbolic and ritual systems. As Beteille rightly remarks, outside the domain of the family, caste is most active at the level of politics in contemporary Indian society. If this aspect of caste was not noticed in the past, then it was primarily because political upheavals of the medieval age were few and far between.

Quite clearly, castes were never outside politics; only the connection is much more transparent today. Whereas in the past ambitious castes had to "wade through slaughter to a throne," caste tensions today are a daily grind. Further, unlike colonial times, castes in contemporary India are not concerned about official rankings. Caste identities have evolved to a much higher level, and it is now a question of self over others and not self in relation to others. Thus, no matter which casteisin question, its involvement in politics is primarily to stake a claim to jobs, educational opportunities, as well as to positions of power in government bodies in direct competition against other castes. Unlike the agitation regarding the census operations in 1911 and later, caste assertions today are not just to feel good in an attributions way but to make it good in a highly competitive environment that disregards the interactional setting that the pure caste hierarchy recommends.

The break down of the traditional caste system and the emergence of caste identities that energise contemporary caste politics can be explained in a variety of ways. Winner believed that the repeated ideological exhortations of the Congress party brought an end to "the self-imposed barrier to protests by caste, that is, the acceptance of their place in the hierarchy". It may be recalled that India's struggle against British colonialism was lead by the Congress, and quite naturally this party also controlled the government uninterruptedly for 20 years after independence. According to Weiner, the charisma of Congress leaders, combined with the success of the freedom movement, led to the downgrading of the moral basis of castes. According to Kaviraj this resulted in a "democracy of castes in place of a 'hierarchy'". Although it is certainly true that the political representation and the impact of the Congress have played a significant role, they need to be placed in the context of the significant shifts in the structural plates of agrarian India. As the power of the erstwhile big landlords waned, the middle farmers and the former untouchables grew in stature and became politically more assertive.

4.3. Political Ascendance of Peasant Castes

In the years following independence, the traditional upper castes continued to rule inmost parts of India. For example, until 1977, upper castes continued to hold prominent elected positions in Uttar Pradesh, the most populous state in the Indian union. Until 1962, as many as 63% of ruling Congress members of the Legislative Assembly came from elite castes. Soon, however, traditional peasant castes such as Ahirs, Kurmis, Koeri, Lodh Rajputs, and Jats began to dominate the political escape of northern India. In the southern state of Tamilnadu, the Vanniyars and Thevars have become assertive, and in Karnataka, control was wrested in the mid-1950s from the traditional rural elite within the Congress party by the Vokkaligas and Linkages. In the North Indian Hindi-speaking belt, upper caste members of parliament fell below 50% for the first time in 1977. The challenge to the established Congress was mounted in Uttar Pradesh rather effectively in the late 1960s by a coalition of peasant castes led by Charan Singh. In Bihar, also, there was a significant decline of upper caste members of the legislative assembly after 1977

In Bihar and Uttar Pradesh, the Yadav caste has gained a great degree of political salience. In Uttar Pradesh, the Samajwadi party is headed by Maulayam Singh Yadav, and in Bihar, the Rashtriya Janata Dal has Laloo Prasad Yadav at its helm. It may also be noted that Maulayam Yadav is today the chief minister of Uttar Pradesh and Laloo Prasad Yadav's wife, Rabri Devi, is chief minister of Bihar. It is not always the case, however, that other peasant castes such as the Kurmis and Koeris always rally behind either the Janata Dal or the Samajwadi party. According to Jaffrelot, Kurmis are not as widely represented in these parties as the Yadavs are. In 1996, only three percent of Samajwadi party members of the legislative assembly were Kurmis. In Bihar, the numbers were higher but still not more than around eight percent of MLAs were from the Rashtriya Janata Dal..

The decline of the traditional elite castes in Indian politics has been discussed quite frequently in academic literature. Rudolph & Hoeber characterised the newly ascendant peasant castes as "bullock capitalists" who challenged the hegemony of the traditional Kshatriya castes, such as the Rajputs and Bhumiyar. These peasant castes constitute 34% of the population but control about 51% of land, more than any other agrarian class. As a category they are closer to "yeoman farmers" than to kulaks. Hence, the appellation "bullock capitalists" is an apposite term for their economic operation is a mix of "capitalist, preindustrial, and noncapitalist features"

The political emergence of these bullock capitalists coincides with the emergence of the backward class movement in large parts of India. To put the matter in perspective, it needs to be recalled that feudal landlordism, or samindari, as the Indian variant was known, was abolished after independence in India. This seriously undercut the economic and power base of the traditional rural elite, many of whose members also had an established urban foothold. Although there were attempts by this class to conceal the extent of their holdings by registering their possessions in the name of fictitious owners, the writing was on the wall.

In 1963, Srinivas wrote that landownership was "a crucial factor in establishing dominance. Generally, the pattern of landownership in rural India is such that the bulk of the arable land is concentrated in the hands of a relatively small number of big owners as against a large number who either own very little land or no land at all". The picture has obviously changed a great deal since the 1960s. The bullock capitalists of Rudolph & Hoeber are small owners of land, and yet they exercise considerable political power in contemporary India as can be gauged from the successes of Samajwadi party and Rashtriya Janata Dal in Uttar Pradesh and Bihar, respectively.

It is not as if these peasant castes have suddenly become much richer. The more crucial fact is that the patrons of the past have become poorer. They can no longer wield the kind of power or influence they used to take for granted. Naturally, the idea of vote banks in the control of dominant factions does not quite apply today. According to Sharma, the new dominants of rural India are not necessarily those who are economically at the top. They must, of course, have a viable economic standing, but they should also have sufficient numbers as well as political connections. Karanth puts this idea across rather nicely when he says that "it is not always necessary for a caste to have all the attributes of dominance but one or two are enough to ensure a modicum of dominance". Indeed, a modicum of dominance is more prevalent today than decisive dominance because very few castes can simultaneously claim unchallenged superiority at the economic, political, and cultural level.

The morphological features of contemporary agrarian structure inhibit cumulative inequalities and decisive dominance. It needs to be remembered that 85% of land holding in India are below five acres and

63% below three acres. Given this ground level situation, owner cultivators can hardly be expected to behave like the power wielders of yore. In addition, a large number of rural people are seeking rural non-farm employment. Today, 44.5% of rural net domestic product is non-natural-. The 50th round of the National Sample Survey held during 1993–1994 shows that 32.9% of rural households were outside agriculture. By the 57th round of the NSS during 2002–2003, the percentage increased to 35.2%. In states such as Punjab, Jammu and Kashmir, Kerala, and Haryana, the number of non-agricultural households in rural India is above 50%. This has not only led to rural exodus, but even for those who stay back in the village, it is not agriculture that solely contributes to their earnings. The poorer villagers participate in a host of occupations that require a narrow band width of skills, ranging from construction labour, to coolie, to rickshaw puller, to vegetable seller. Of course, for all of them getting a regular urban job has the highest value.

All of this suggests a picture of rural stratification that cannot uphold the earlier prestige that was accorded to the landed elite in a noncompetitive caste hierarchy. It is obvious that if the earlier hierarchy held, with all its idiosyncratic nuances, it was primarily because it was buttressed by the economic power of the agrarian rich. As that is no longer the dominant feature in rural India, castes compete out in the open. The fact of caste competition in politics should not lead us to believe that this is a restatement of the caste system. The obverse side of this collapse is the assertion of caste identities. Castes that could not project what they had always believed for fear of reprisal can now boldly assert their pride and status claims.

Numerous field studies also demonstrate that conflicts between castes are rarely resolved at the village level. In the past, the village panchayat used to mediate tensions of various kinds, but, as Karanth demonstrates, the caste panchayat, or council, has lost its importance. Seaway finds that in Bihar tensions between castes are not adjudicated at the local level. In some cases, the tensions remain unresolved; in other instances, the matter is taken to court where the decision it is not always satisfactory. In one instance, Sahay recalls from his field notes, "members of the Chamar caste were beaten up by the Brahmins. The case was not settled at the village level. The chamars went to the police and to the court for justice. When they realised that the court was not going to punish the Brahmins immediately, they beat some of the Brahmins up and withdrew the case from the court"

It has been frequently pointed out that caste politics is not to end caste but to "use caste as an instrument for social change". Democratic politics has brought about aggressive caste assertion, but this has not resulted in contesting the category of caste as such. As Sheath points out, the vertical consolidation of caste along the purity hierarchy has been replaced by a "horizontalisation". Political alliances in this horizontal scheme of caste relations are not enduring, and they are "open-ended entities". They are made keeping in mind the coalescence of secular interests, and they fade away when a better and more appropriate bargain is struck with other castes and caste clusters. For example, alliances such as KHAM and AJGAR had their best days in the 1980s and are now defunct.

4.4. Emergence of Dalit Politics

The Constitution of independent India not only abolished untouchability but also made provisions to reserve jobs and seats in government undertakings and educational institutions, respectively, for Scheduled Castes and Scheduled Tribes. With independence, and the abolition of untouchability, the untouchables became known as Scheduled Castes because they were listed for special privileges in the Schedule of the Constitution. Untouchability had diverse manifestations in different parts of India, so it was far from obvious as to which castes should be included in the Schedule of the Constitution

It is not just the owner cultivators or bullock capitalists, who are aggressively using caste as a vehicle of self-assertion, but so also are those who were earlier considered to be untouchables in the traditional Hindu caste hierarchy. This phenomenon too has an India-wide character from Tamilnadu in the south, to northern states such as Uttar Pradesh. The Republican party in Maharashtra and the Bahujan Samaj party in Uttar Pradesh are the two most widely acknowledged political organisations forwarding the aspirations of the former untouchables.

The Republican party was founded by the legendary Babasaheb Ambedkar in 1957. He later led his people to renounce Hinduism and embrace Buddhism instead. It is true that most of the votaries of the Republican party of India belong to the Mahar caste because other formerly untouchable castes of the region, such as the Mangs, Matangs, and Chambers, have stayed away from it. In fact, they often veer toward supporting the Bharaiya Janata party which is, ironically, a right-wing Hindu organisation. This is because many members of these other castes believe that the RPI is a vehicle of upward mobility for the Mahars alone.

Nevertheless, Babasaheb Ambedkar's shadow looms large even today in the politics of the former untouchables. They resent the term "Harijan" that Gandhi used for them as they consider it too patronising. They would rather be known as "Dalits," or the oppressed. Ambedkar was tl.e first to use this term to denote the Scheduled Castes for its obvious combative edge. Ambedkar, today, has been deified among the Buddhist Mahars of Maharashtra and has a similar iconic status to Buddha in many Mahar families. Ambedkar's death anniversary in 1981 provided the occasion for Kanshi Ram to inaugurate the Dalit Shoshit Samaj Sang-harsh Samit. In its attempt to attract as wide a range as possible, the DS-4 also called out to Muslims to help fight the privileges of the traditional elite castes.

In 1984, this time in celebration of Ambedkar's birthday, the DS-4 transformed itself into the Bahujan Samaj party. Since then, it has been a vital force in North India. It may not have won the elections outright in the several polls that it has faced, but by clever political manoeuvring, it has managed to propel Mayawati as the Chief Minister in U.P. On two occasions with the most unlikely political allies. The first time Mayawati's ascendance was supported by the Congress and then later by the Hindu right-wing Bharatiya Janata party.

Neither do the Dalits constitute a homogenous group. They contest for superiority among themselves. Middle class Dalits are more concerned about identity and often project themselves as indigenous people, Buddhists, and or another group. But the poor Dalit marginal farmer and landless labourers are more concerned about questions of economic exploitation, but these issues are not adequately attended to by their middle class leaders. For instance, Bureau found that Buddhism had not made a significant impact upon rural Mahar Dalits. Strict observance of Buddhist norms and a singular identification with Buddhism were more common among urban Mahars. According to Vera, no Dalit leader after Ambedkar paid any consistent attention to economic issues. Dalits are, however, very active when it comestovoting in elections. As Yadav notes, the turn out of Scheduled Caste voters was as high as 62.2% in the 1998 elections.

Although the Constitution also provides for reservations for Scheduled Tribes (STs), their situation is in many ways quite different from that of the Scheduled Castes. It is difficult to arrive at a formal definition of tribes in India; many of them are in transition, and many more are already peasants and far removed from a life in the forests. In addition, there are the tribes of Northeast India, such as the Nagas and Mioses, who are not backward because they were the ruling communities in their respective regions and not under the hegemony of the Hindus in the rest of the country. But as with other tribes in India, they too worshipped gods that were not part of the Hindu pantheon. However, stratification between classes was quite marked in many of these northeastern peoples, and that is why they do not fit our usual understanding of "tribes" though they are categorised as such in the Indian Constitution. True, the term "tribe" has been a contentious one in anthropology, and instances from India only confirm its somewhat dubious status. Incidentally, as X-axis points out, those designated as tribes would rather be called "adivasis" instead. In addition, the tendency to romanticise tribes can also be highly misleading. The belief that tribes spontaneously scoreless nature and that they are primarily hunters and gatherers certainly do not hold true for the majority of STs in India

In general, tribes are considered to be deprived communities because of their geographic isolation. In the northeast, they are in a majority, but in certain belts in east and central India, they are in substantial numbers, although never over 50% of the population of those regions. This is why tribal mobilisation, such as the Jharkhand movement, as well as those in the northeast are regional in character. Scheduled Caste organisations do not have regional autonomy or control on their agenda because their members are embedded in Hindu society and dispersed all over the country.

In recent years, two states have been formed in recognition of the numerical strength of the tribal population in those regions. This does not mean that the leadership in these states is exclusively in tribal hands. This is not possible because the tribes are not in a majority in either of these two states. Yet, by carving these separationists it is hoped that greater attention will be paid to the specific claims of the tribes that live there. The most important demand that tribes make is that non-tribes should not take away their lands and the forests from which they made a living in the past. In addition, they have also stepped up their claims for more jobs in factories and other state enterprises, with particular emphasis on those organisations that have been established on what was once tribal land.

Thus, although it might seem at first sight that the politics of tribes and castes are cognate phenomenon, the two are really quite different. In fact, as X-axis argues, SCs have been more successful in getting their claims recognised in practice than have STs. This is because of the latter's geographical isolation from the larger Hindu society. As SCs were always within the interactive nexus of the caste system, they were more adept at using the levers of power than the STs. Be that as it may, the logic of caste politics is certainly very different from that of tribal politics and therefore deserves to be understood separately.

4.5. Symbolic Defiance

No caste really thinks of itself to be inherently inferior to any other caste. It is another matter that they were never really able to espouse this point of view with the facility with which they do so now primarily because the subaltern communities were locked within a closed village economy. Because agrarian economic relations and land ownership patterns have undergone major transformations in recent times, earlier dominant castes are not as powerful as they once were.

This change in agrarian class relations, coupled with the provisions in the Constitution, has allowed for the proliferation of caste associations all over the country. It is true that this process began in the early decades of the twentieth century when caste competition at the political level first began to manifest itself.. Through *gravy gathas* and *jati puranas* these associations seek to instill a sense of pride in their primordial identities without which it would be difficult to use caste identities for political aims.

It is interesting to note in this connection that the origin tales of the non-scheduled castes rarely question established norms and customs other than staking their claim as to an exalted past. There are some exceptions such as in the case of the Khandelwal Jains of

Rajasthan, who pointedly distance themselves from Kshatriya practices and consider them to be abhorrent. Otherwise, non-SCs do not, as a rule, contest Hinduism or the various practises associated with it. The Yadav association exemplifies this rather nicely and, at the same time, demonstrates how caste loyalty can be used to forward sectional interests in the name of democracy.

Yadav associations were established as early as in the opening decades of the twentieth century. In 1933, the formation of the All India Yadav Mahasabha brought together various disparate Yadava associations under one roof. The AIYM traces the history of the Yadavs to Lord Krishna, whose earthly incarnations are many but who is most widely cast in several popular lords as romantic cowherd. He also plays the role of a sagacious warrior priest in the Bhagavat Gita as a supreme ex-agate of Advaita and the laws of karma.

By relating the Yadavs to Krishna, the cowherd, the AIYM is able to portray its followers as descendents of a mighty progenitor with Kshatriya status. As Michelutti records, the AIYM believes that the Yadavs are not just "natural politicians" but they are also the best custodians of democracy. Therefore, if one is to keep democracy alive and well, then it is the Yadavs for whom one should vote.

We related above that SCs too have their own organisations, which speak of their proud past. Although many SC associations are content in claiming Brahman or Kshatriya status, those that are politically active are keen to point out their alienation from established Hindu myths, beliefs, and rituals. When Ambedkar converted to Buddhism, he made it clear in his vows that he did not consider Buddha to be an incarnation of the Hindu god Vishnu as many Hindus claim. Nor did he follow any of the rituals of Hinduism and abided strictly by the Buddhist code.

Ambedkar's conversion to Buddhism was a highly symbolic political act that helped fuse Dalit antipathy toward Hinduism and, at the same time, that enabled them to leverage their new identity to great political advantage. In recent years, the All India Confederation of Scheduled Castes and Scheduled Tribes has held many conversion ceremonies that have attracted a lot of public attention. This was clearly in evidence when a mass conversion was held of SCs who, in hundreds, embraced Buddhism in New Delhi as recently as November

3, 2001. The point of debate is the extent to which these overt demonstrations of identity in urban India are actually carried over to the Dalits of the rural hinter lands.

Dalit politics today symbolically defy Hinduism by either promoting conversions to Buddhism or by claiming that Dalits belong to the original Kshatriya orders before Vedic Hindus entered the geographical space of India. As mentioned above, Phule of the Satyashodhak Samaj in Maharashtra argued that the so-called low castes of Maharashtra were the original and real Kshatriyas before the Brahmans and then the Muslims overwhelmed them. Many SC organisations now project their culture as the origin of all cultures in Induct civilisation. These Dalit communities believe that they are the *adi* of all other cultures in the Indian subcontinent, although the Aryans, who came later, did their best to undermine this fact. This adi theme helps further the Dalit claim that social and political supremacy should rightfully belong to them and not to the Brahmans who, by deceit and treachery, have worked their way to the top. By legitimising their cultural supremacy in terms of historic priority, Dalits gain the necessary symbolic confidence in their quest for political power in contemporary politics.

Such instances of symbolic defiance are not limited to Hindus alone. Jodhka incisively highlights how the Sikh leather workers have also challenged the established norms of the mainstream Gurudwaras and their styles of worship. These Sikh leather workers now call themselves Ad-Dermis and refuse to bow down to the dictates of the dominant Jat Sikh community. The Ad-Dermis have set up their own Gurudwaras and refuse to go to those run by Jat Sikhs. It is true that SC Sikhs have often felt alienated and unwanted in local Sikh Gurudwaras, although Sikhism is officially against casteism. Ad Dharmi Gurudwaras also give the Sikh holy book the pride of place but have a bust or engraving of Ravidas, the devotional medieval low caste saint who challenged Brahmin orthodoxy. Although Ravidas' contribution is acknowledged fulsomely in the Sikh holy book, his image is not to be found in any mainstream Jat Sikh Gurudwara. Ravidas is an important figurehead among former untouchable, especially in North India, and by installing his image in the Gurudwara, the Ad Dermis were reaching out to other SCs elsewhere, even those outside Sikhism.

4.6. Politics of Reservations

When the Indian Constitution provided reservations for Scheduled Castes and Tribes, it also added that in due course of time similar legislation ought to be devised for the Other Backward Castes as well. The population of these so-called Backward Castes is difficult to estimate, and the figures range from 25% to 52% of the total population of the country. In terms of their social and economic standing, they are placed between the traditional elite castes such as Brahmans, Banias, Kayasthas, Rajputs, other lower castes, and the SC and STs.

These Backwards are now known as Other Backward Castes (OBC) and, in general, comprise largely peasant and other agrarian communities. These castes are not untouchables but are considered backward as they lack a culture of learning on account of their lowly peasant status. Thus though they did not have to bear the burden of untouchability, their depressed economic position contributed to their general cultural backwardness. In recognition of this fact, the Constitution of India recommended that the state intervene and help these communities by legislating some measures that would break this cycle of poverty and backwardness.

In pursuance of Article 340 of the Constitution, the Kalelkar Commission was set in 1955, but it could not come to any satisfactory conclusion about who should be legitimately considered as OBCs. The Mandal Commission came into existence in 1980, and it promptly came up with a long list of 3743 backward castes on the basis of social, economic, and educational backwardness. The Mandal Commission's recommendations were implemented in 1990 by the then Prime Minister V.P.Singh.

The implementation of reservations for OBCs set off a furore of protests, including a few suicides, all over the country by those who are considered to be members of forward castes. Many felt that reservations for OBCs were not warranted for two reasons. First, this would make India a caste society by law, and second, many of those who are considered as OBCs are really quite powerful and dominant in rural India, both economically and politically. The obvious reference was to Jats and Yadavs. A number of social anthropologists wrote against reservations for OBCs primarily on these grounds.

Beteille's criticism of the Mandal Commission recommendations was widely commented upon. He distinguishes between reservations for OBCs following Mandal recommendations and the reservations that were already granted in the Constitution for Scheduled Castes and Tribes. Although provisions for Scheduled Castes and Tribes were with the intention of reaching toward greater equality, reservations for OBCs were really to bring about a balance of power on the calculus of caste. The kind of deprivations that former untouchables and *adivasis* encountered for centuries can in no way be compared to the traditional condition of the OBCs. In fact, the Mandal Commission recommendations were actually giving in to a powerful rural lobby that did not really care for equality of opportunities as much as it did for equality of results. It can also be said that Mandal recommendations are not out to extirpate caste as was the aim of instituting reservations for SCs and STs, but to represent castes, and thus make this as-cryptic marker a perennial political resource to be flogged in perpetuity.

Another major justification for upholding reservations for SCs and STs came from the acknowledgment that these communities lacked viable marketable assets that would allow them to pursue a life of dignity in a democratic society. The SCs were kept away from education, could only perform menial and polluting jobs, and suffered from a variety of other deprivations. In the case of the STs, it was their physical isolation that put them at a disadvantage with respect to others in society. Reservations for these communities were therefore meant to raise their marketable skills and educational standards to compensate for their historic lack of privileges and to facilitate their participation as equal citizens Reservations, Mandal style, only helps them to convert their political and economic assets, which are currently rural, to urban jobs and related skill assets. These they could developed their own without the necessary intervention of national level reservation policies.

If one were to look closely at the criteria for social backwardness, then it would become quite apparent that the considerations that went into the reckoning of who were the OBCs were politically weighted. The Mandal Commission listed three categories of backwardness, e.g., social, economic, and educational. In all a caste can score a maximum of 22 points but needs only 11 to qualify as backward. Each of the four indicators of social backwardness carries three points, the three indicators of educational backwardness just two points each, and each of the criteria for economic backwardness, which should have been the most important, are given only one point.

The four indicators of social backwardness are performing manual labour, what other castes think of a particular caste, do the women in that caste work outside the home, and if 25% of females and 10% of males get married above the state average before the age of 17. Each of these indicators carries three points, and it is not at all difficult for a well-to-do rural caste to score on each of them, earn 12 points, and thus qualify as an OBC. Educational and economic backwardness need not come into the picture at all. All landowning peasant castes are proud to call themselves farmers who perform manual work, whether or not they actually do so. The criterion of women working outside their homes is not a good indicator either as they need not necessarily be toiling on others' fields or as coolie labour. We have already commented upon the age of marriage, and more-over given the conditions of recording marriages in India, information on this indicator is very unreliable. Therefore, it is not unreasonable to argue, as critics of Mandal have that the provisions for OBC reservations were devised keeping political considerations in mind.

It is interesting how the Mandal recom-mendations provoked anthropologists to de-bate issues such as citisenship and equity in the context of Indian society, perhaps for the first time. Policy concerns, at the all-India level, received a kind of ur-gency in several anthropological writings in, and on India, on a scale that was never witnessed before. The governing assumption in all such works is that caste identity, and not the system, underpins and informs caste politics. This point of view is gradually gaining ground among anthropologists who are now explicitly beginning to acknowledge the discrete nature of caste identities and the consequent clash of multiple hierarchies. Dumont's prestigious *Homo Hierarchicus* for long stood in the way of realising this phenomenon, but the pressure of social facts has forced anthropologists to look for a different analytical perspective.

References

Beteille, Andre. *Caste, Class and Power: Changing Patterns of Stratification in a Tanjore Village.* New Delhi. Oxford University Press. 1996.

Ghurye, G. S. *Caste, Class and Occupation*. Popular Book Depot, Bombay. 1961.

Gupta, S.K. *The Scheduled Castes in Modern Indian Politics: Their Emergence as a Political Power*. New Delhi. Munshiram Manoharlal Publishers Pvt. Ltd. 1985.

Michael, S.M., (ed.) *Untouchable: Dalits in Modern India*. Boulder. Lynne Rienner Publishers. 1999.

5

Caste Politics and Regionalism

This chapter seeks to understand politics by looking at two important axes around which politics in India—and contemporary politics, more so seems to be revolving: caste and region. Of the two, caste is more famous and has for long been recognised as a factor in explaining politics in India. 'Region' as a factor has only assumed significance in the nineties. Since after the disintegration of the 'Congress framework' of politics, observers have noted the 'regionalisation' of politics. Rise of regional and State-based parties to prominence is an expression of this regionalisation. But apart from the dramatic proliferation and rise of regional parties, less noticed and more interesting aspect of regionalisation has been related to 'all-India' parties. The Congress, Bharatiya Janata Party Communist Party of India have themselves become regionalised in terms of their strategies and practices.

Regionalisation refers to five factors. (i) Issues are/have become region specific. Although the press may continue to project issues in 'all-India' terms, these make sense only when translated into regional contexts. This applies equally to 'secular-communal' divide or to 'globalisation.' (ii) Secondly, leadership is structured regionally and ratified regionally. Parties may still project towering 'national' leaders but State level leadership is more relevant and only through this kind of leadership people relate to 'national' politics. (iii) Regionalisation further means that social forces are constituted at the regional level. Therefore, the support base of parties can be identified only at State level. Whether one can describe the base of parties at the all-India level by adding up its base at state level is somewhat doubtful. (iv) Fourthly, in electoral and mobilisational context, the set of choices exists at the

State level. People, as voters and as groups, have to choose from among the State level choices only. (v) Following from the above factors, political competition takes place at the level of region. Consequently, the outcome makes sense only at the regional level. It is in this sense that the 'theatre' of politics has shifted to States

Before turning to the question how does this regionalisation link up with caste, let us briefly explore the elements conveyed by the term 'region.' Territoriality is the most obviously conveyed element. However, the territoriality expressed by the term 'region' often has a flexibility and indeterminacy with regards to its physical boundary. In this sense, region refers to a wide range of territorial configurations: locality, sub region, State, supra-State region etc.

It is possible to think of many factors, which prop up region as a relevant factor in politics. But the point is that territoriality needs to be translated as a political factor. Language, culture, economy, etc. Provide a base to territoriality in order to sustain in politics. It may be argued that caste is not only yet another base, but one, which potentially combines other factors in providing a base to region to operate as a factor in politics. Thus, we can imagine a complex relationship between caste and region — a relationship of interdependence: caste expresses through region becomes politically sustainable on the basis of caste; is bound up by territoriality and in constituting the social space, caste takes the form of a region.

We hope to understand the politics in post-congress phase by exploring the tension and relation between caste and region. The post-congress politics is often characterised by coalitions. However, an alliance of regional parties does not seem to be a possibility. On the other hand, caste emerged in the 1990s as a possible framework within which politics would be organised. However, it now appears that politics of backward castes seems to be stagnating. Thirdly, expressions of regionalism are vocal in some part but muted in others. Fourthly, apart from region and caste, another contending framework of politics has emerged Hindutva. It has shown signs of accommodating both region and caste.

Cast as a system of vertical division, sustains on the basis of localisation. Caste hierarchy may invoke the ideologies of *chaturvarnya* and of purity-pollution. But the hierarchy makes sense operationally, only when it is concretised in a local situation. Studies concentrating on *Jati* by sociologists and social anthropologists, have always pointed out how hierarchical ranking of *Jati* makes sense in the context of village or small localities. Similarly, cultural, ritual life of members of *Jati* is organised around village or locality. It is only in comparison to some other caste within a locality that the higher or lower status of caste can be experienced. A statement that 'carpenters dine with ironsmiths' does not carry any meaning unless it is specified as to where this entertaining took place. In other words, *Jati* as a unit of social relations, ritual status and cultural universe is firmly based within the framework of well-defined territorial boundaries. As much as vertical, horizontal separateness of a caste, too, has a locality as a point of reference.

Most castes are not only specific to a certain State but also specific to a particular area. This means that a caste, which has a concentrated existence in one area, may also constitute numerically large or significant group in that area. In a study of north India, Skywards barge has shown how caste concentration takes place at village and district level. He shows that more than fifty percent of Ludhiana's population is Jat, and Chamars and Majahabis have separate pockets in Punjab. The same applies to UP, Bihar, Orissa, etc. He argues that both in the case of peasant castes and Dalits, exclusivity seems to be the rule. This means that if in one village, Jats are the largest group; other peasant castes would almost be nonexistent. Similarly, in districts where Majahabis are numerous, other Dalit castes are rarely seen. In the case of peasant castes, the regional base is considerably expansive while non-peasant castes are often confined to smaller pockets. This pattern is evident in State after State: In Tamil Nadu Vanniyars belong to North and South Arcot, Salem and Chingleput; Thevars in Ramnad Nadars earlier belonged to Tirunelveli. Similarly, Ishava sub castes belonged to different parts of Kerala – Tiyyars to North, Ishavas to central parts and Tandans to south. The Vokkaligas of Karnataka are concentrated in the Mysore region, Constituting around 29 percent of the population of Mysor State. In Maharashtra Agris are concentrated in one district of Konkan-Raigad, Leva Patils in Jalgaon district of North Maharashtra, Vanjaris in Nasik, Ahmednagar and Beed district. Iravati Karve and Dandekar have given a detailed sketch of the residential pockets of different castes of Maharashtra. The

Mails of Rajasthan belong to Jodhpur region, and most smaller castes are concentrated in specific areas. The case of Jats of Western UP is too famous to require a mention. In Bihar, Bhumihars have a concentrated strength in the south while Rajputs have in the western parts. Kammas belong to Andhra region and Reddis to Rayalseema. One can keep multiplying this list of examples. M.N. Srinivas observed in 1957 "this kind of relationship between a caste and a region is widespread in India…". More specifically, as Washbrook observes in the context of TN, most endogamous Jatis extended over no more than a few adjacent villages

This association of many castes with specific territorial 'pockets' has produced two political results. One is the rise of 'locally dominant' castes. Srinivas' early use of the term 'dominant caste' was specifically with reference to a small locality or village or group of villages: In his 1955 essay 'The social system of a Mysore Village' Srinivas mentions that "The concept of the dominant caste is important for understanding intercaste relations in any local area.". Elaborating on the concept in 1957, he uses the phrase 'locally' dominant and then adds, "Occasionally a caste is dominant in a group of neighbouring villages if not over a district or two, and in such cases, local dominance is linked with regional dominance.". As far as 'local dominance'' is concerned, there seems to be a direct link between domination and numerical preponderance. Large size of population, though, has one other implication. Often, a caste has numerical advantage when it also has a high degree of control over resources - at the village level, land. Thus, economic power and size combine to produce patterns of local domination. If one carefully follows Srinivas' account of locally dominant caste in Mysore, two things can be drawn from it: a) this political effect of caste-region interface is an outcome of local hierarchy based on caste and b) Just as dominance of one caste the subordination of other castes is a result of 'localisation'. Castes, which are 'trapped' by circumstances into that locality, face subordination.

5.1. Construction of Regionally Dominant Castes

Localised concentration leads to localised domination and possibilities of some representation. One the other hand, throughout the twentieth century, certain Jatis evolved into castes spread over a large territory. This gave rise to the regionally dominant castes. From mid-fifties onwards, politics in most states centered around one regionally dominant caste(s). In most cases, middle level castes sought to contest the ritual superiority, material ascendance and political domination of 'upper' castes - mostly Brahmans, and in the north, Kayasthas and Thakurs. In the first half of twentieth century, the middle-caste protests took the form of non-Brahman movements in Maharashtra and in the south. In the second half of twentieth century, the middle castes extended their claims to state power at the regional level.

The non-Brahman movements in Maharashtra and south were concerned with creating 'regional' non-Brahman identities. In Maharashtra, the invocation of Shivaji and Maratha rule by the non-Brahman movement was crucial in bringing various peasant castes together. The movement also facilitated the emergence of Maratha politics on a larger scale geographically. In Tamil Nadu, the non-Brahman movement was built upon the collapse of caste and region. The Brahmans were excluded from Dravid identity. In Karnataka, the Vokkaliga 'Caste' came into being by the fusion of various peasant Jatis such as Morasui, Hallikar, Halu, Nonabad, and so on. In Gujarat, Kanabis of different areas came together in 1931 to constitute themselves as 'Patidars', although, Saurashtra Kanabis are still looked down upon by Gujarat Patidars. Also, the Leva and Kadvi divisions of Patidars are supposed to refer to sub-regional differences. Yet, from 1931 onwards, the 'Patidar' identity has evolved as a regional or State level identity. Similarly, despite internal tensions, Kshatriyas of Gujarat have been organising themselves as one group. Rajputs, who are in the forefront of the Kshatriya mobilisation, are regionally differentiated. Gujarat Rajputs being mostly tenants or landless, sought to align with Kolis and Bariyas (also landless) as Kshatriyas. Saurashtra Rajputs being landowners resisted the claims of non-Rajputs to Kshatriya status. However, over the years, the Kshatriya group of castes in Gujarat as a whole has provided a counterpoint to Patidar politics. The Kshatriya Sabha took an initiative in bringing together Rajputs and Kolis and shaping their politics. The Jats are probably the most regionally structured caste. Various Khaps of Jats span specified villages and a meeting of all Khaps, the Sarvakhap meets to discuss common matters. But alongside Khaps, Jats of western UP as well as adjoining Haryana are also organised through the all India Jat Mahasabha, which always extended support to Charan Singh.

It can be argued that both the rise of non-Brahman movement and rise of middle caste as dominant caste in many States follow a similar pattern. A protest against castes ranking high in the hierarchy gives an impetus to these processes. But these processes gain momentum when small, localised, endogamous Jatis overcome their localisation by seeking either in mythology or history a link with a larger territorial unit. This development is accompanied by formation of territorial or even 'all-India' associations -Mahasabhas or Mahasanghas - of the newly evolved caste group. A moderately reformist posture follows vis-a-vis intra-caste practices, particularly marriage practices. Since the process is ideologically rooted in opposition to upper castes, the claims of such 'castes' relate to share in power, opportunities for material uplift and amelioration of tradition-inflicted disabilities. Central to this whole process is the journey from locality to region. Once a caste crosses the threshold of locality, the possibilities of realising political claims become very real. A geographical expanse allows the concerned caste to make claims on representational basis besides the basis of caste injustice. In fact, most dominant castes, as also proponents of non-Brahman movement, claim that the heritage of that region belongs to them; they are the true and authentic bearers of symbols associated with the particular region; they represent the culture of that region; the non-Brahmans are true Dravids, the Marathas are bearers of the symbol of Shivaji, Patidars exemplify the essence of Gujarati culture or Jats represent the true Kisans.

5.2. Linguistic States

If a caste claims that it represents the regional culture better than others, if follows that there will be a strong connection between such dominant castes and regionalist movements. These States constitute a region not only in just a geographical-administrative sense, but in sociocultural and political sense also. Hence the link between dominant castes and States.

One can come across many examples of different patterns of relations between caste and regional identity. These include assertions by upper castes, convenient collaboration between upper and middle castes, the rise of contending middle castes, exclusion of upper castes, etc. Probably the latest example would be Uttaranchal where caste played an indirect role. When the union government decided to implement the policy of reservations for OBCs, stiff opposition came from upper castes of Uttaranchal. It was argued that this region did not have OBCs – at least not in large numbers. From the point of anti-reservation movement, the issues of separate identity of hill people distinct from plains people, came to the forefront. Without much exaggeration, it could be said that formation of Uttaranchal is an instance of upper caste assertion where 'regional' distinctiveness was indirectly claimed on the basis of different caste composition of the population. When the Oriya speaking territory was part of Bengal, Brahmans and Karans came together to shape Oriya opposition to Bengali domination. In 1912, this same social force invoked Oriya nationalism to protest against Orissa's annexation to Bihar. Since the creation of Orissa State, the upper castes have generally retained their hold over the State's politics, culture and economy.

As far as collaboration between upper and middle castes is concerned, Maharashtra can serve as a very good example. Although the non-Brahman movement had considerably villainised Brahmans, the Samyukta Maharashtra Movement saw the Brahmans and sections of Marathas collaborating and mobilising the masses on the basis of regionalist sentiments. This collaboration had a major long-term effect. While formation of Maharashtra State ushered the Marathas into position of power, the sharpness of non-Brahmanism was almost lost. The Brahmans, of course, were not in a position to make a comeback to politics, but nor were they hounded out of politics in particular or the public domain in general. On the contrary, Brahmans continued to dominate culture, education, media, under the benign auspices of 'Maharashtra Dharma'. More tangentially, the regional assertion led by Brahmans and Marathas displaced the main focus of non-Brahman movement, considerably weakening anti-caste discourse. Instead, Maratha domination became legitimised in the name of non-Maratha lower castes, identified in the sixties as Bahujan Samaj– the contemporary OBCs.

Just as the Gujarati-Marwari baniya was the cause of Marathi Brahmans and Marathas coming together, the prominence of Tamil Brahmans resulted into the unity of Telugu Brahmans and non-

Brahman castes of Andhra. Although initially the non-Brahman Telugus joined Justice Party, they were not enamoured by the anti-Brahman rhetoric. This weakened the non-Brahman movement in Andhra. It has also been argued that cooption of elite Reddys into the congress facilitated a less acrimonious relationship between Brahmans and Reddys.. The examples of Maharashtra and Andhra show that regionalism can intervene in the competition between upper castes and middle castes. Secondly, these examples suggest that regionalism can help a smooth transfer of State level political apparatus to middle castes. Often, in this 'smooth' transfer, radicalism as a basis of political claims is lost and claims of lower castes get a short shrift through symbolic gestures and tokenism.

Starting off from limited collaboration between upper and middle castes, Maharashtra and Andhra Pradesh witnessed the rise and assertion of middle castes. A similar assertion was witnessed in UP once the Jats of western UP became politically organised. The Jat assertion took the form of a demand for 'backward' status. From this, Charan Singh also attempted to project himself as representative of backwards. However, following Jats' association with land, their leaders, Charan Singh earlier and Tikait later, harped on a farmer identity as the identity of Jats in particular but of Gujjars as well. Interestingly, during Takait's farmers' agitation, at one stage, activists of Bharatiya Kisan Union proposed that they should ask for a separate state for western UP. Thus, the caste of Jats is an example of middle caste assertion at the regional level. Politics of Haryana is another instance of Jat assertion at State level while in Rajasthan; the Jat assertion took the form of a concerted effort to claim backward status. The Jats of Rajasthan deviated from pro-congress politics to vote for BJP in 1999 for the sole purpose of getting their backward status recognised. The Jat Mahasabha decided to vole for BJP once Vajpayee promised to concede their demand.

Many States have witnessed keen competition between two castes or caste clusters. In instances of such competition, the contending castes usually belong to a middle status. In Rajasthan, the competition between the Jats and Rajputs has been rather neatly transformed into a bipolar party situation. Gujarat and Karnataka are the other two examples of contending middlc castes but politics there is not organised so neatly. The Patidar caste also gained control over resources and sought to displace the Brahmans and baniyas from political power. However, Gujarat politics is characterised by congress efforts to attract Kshatriyas, Swatantra Party's efforts to forge an alliance of Patidars and kshatriyas, Patidar alliance with Brahmans and Banias in opposition to reservation and growing affection among Kshatriyas towards the congress. These developments have led to the emergence of BJP as a Patidar force in the nineties. Karnataka witnessed a tussle between Vokkaligas and Lingayats right from the time of creation of a Kannada speaking State. Therefore, two Kannada speaking States were demanded. This has been recorded by the State Reorganisation commission. Thus, here is an example of a large caste cluster opposing a unified linguistic State for fear of loosing its numerical advantage. Vokkaligas dominated Mysore politics between 1947 and 1956. Since 1956, although Lingayats did get an upper hand, political dominance was shared by these two contending caste clusters till 1972. It was noted by Ambedkar that linguistic States would only lead to consolidation of the 'upper' castes, jeopardising the interests of scheduled castes. In Punjab, for instance, the scheduled castes were not very supportive of the demand for a separate State of Punjab by reorganising the State on linguistic communal lines. Even Sikh untouchables kept away from that demand fearing that a reorganised Punjab would facilitate domination of Jat Sikhs.

Tamil Nadu manifests a pattern of caste region relationship, which is distinct from other States in many respects. It did not throw up any single dominant caste although Vellalas and Nadars benefited the most from the Dravid non-Brahman movement. Secondly, the non-Brahman movement dealt with the issue of regional identity right from the beginning in the second decade of twentieth century. Non-Brahmanism was identified with Dravidianism. While attempting to unite all non-Brahman castes on the Dravid platform, the Dravid movement refused to recognise Brahmans as part of Dravid society. Just as this movement sought to effect a fusion of many non-Brahman castes, it also aspired to build a 'Southern' identity opposed to 'north'. In 1937 the movement led by Periyar waged an anti-Hindi agitation. The logical culmination of anti-Hindi, anti-north Dravidian non-Brahmanism was reached in 1939 when Justice Party demanded 'independent' Dravids than. Thus, caste-region interaction in Tamil

Nadu strengthened an exclusionary regional nationalism. However, this exclusion did not last long. Once the regional claims were realised through formation of Madras State and non-Brahman claims were translated into an exten,ive policy of reservations, Brahmans were incorporated as members into the Tamil society. Brahmans are accommodated as ideologise and legitimises of the regional legacy of Dravid movement. It is indeed ironical that a strong non-Brahman movement, through its regionalism allowed a re-entry of the Brahman caste both into the elite and into the political arena in general. In the nineties, the political assertion of the Vanniyars marked the political scene in Tamil Nadu. However, Vanniyars have a long history of separate political organisation. In spite of the efforts of non-Brahman movement to bring together all non-Brahman castes, Vanniyars were organised through Tamil Nad Toilers' Party and Common weal party. Although DMK supported the latter in 1952 with a view to defeating Congress, Kamraj was successful in bringing both Vanniyar parties into congress fold. Another backward caste, the Thevars, backed the forward bloc for a long time. These details suggest that in spite of very vocal non-Brahman movement, Tamil politics did not throw up any single middle caste around which State politics could be organised. Probably, this peculiar situation led to sustained recourse to militant regional nationalism, particularly by the Dravid parties. However, as Washbrook observes, this Dravidianism 'neutralised many of the caste based issues of conflict that dominated Tamil Nadu politics in the first half of the twentieth century'. Perhaps, those contradictions, which Dravidianism sought to push under the carpet of regionalism, have resurfaced in Tamil Nadu with Dalit – OBC conflicts and Hinduisation of some backward castes. In the absence of any particular caste group as central to politics, Tamil politics took on an exclusionary character: exclusion of Brahmans, Aryans, North Indians and less explicitly, exclusion of even Adi Dravids.

5.3. Caste-region Association

Demography, agrarian relations, political economy of post-independence period combined to produce the strong linkages between region and caste. In particular, the different patterns of caste relations gave substance to region as a political category in States like

Andhra Pradesh, Tamil Nadu and Karnataka. These developments established the feature of region specific dominant castes in most parts of India. Both these ruptures in the established pattern of caste-region equation came as opposition to upper as well as newly dominant castes in various regions. In the interplay of caste and region, Dalits and OBCs were / are often excluded or marginalised.

At the intellectual level, Ambedkar was the first to grasp the implications of 'linguistic States' in terms of the consequent marginalisation of Dalits. But even before the issue of linguistic States came up, Ambedkar had realised the need to mobilise Dalits at an all-India level if they were to stake claims to political power. Thus, in the 1940s, abandoning the Independent labour party, he formed the Scheduled Castes Federation. On the one hand, through SCF, he sought to intervene in the negotiations for India's freedom and wrest minimum share in power. On the other hand, the SCF was also visualised as a major opposition to the upper caste dominated Congress in the period immediately after independence. The failure of the SCF notwithstanding, it is important to note that Ambedkar saw the unfolding of a process of conflict between SCs and upper castes and also believed that a united all-India instrument of SCs can alone take on the task of contesting upper caste claims. Although he once again veered to a more broad based party in the form of Republican party of India this party came to be identified as Dalit party and could not sustain the all-India claims which Ambedkar had always insisted upon. In the mid-eighties, Kanshi Ram formed the Bahujan Samaj Party. This party is seen primarily as the party of Dalits. In this sense, BSP manifests an all-India ambition and an awareness that upper caste domination has to be fought at the all-India level. Thus, initial lead by Ambedkar and more contemporarily the formation of BSP, challenge the caste-region nexus. They seek to problematise the caste question at the national level and force a solution through intervention in national politics. The former believes that only in a period of instability can Dalits force their entry into the network that controls national state apparatus. Therefore, unity of Dalits at all-India level and unity between Dalits and other disadvantaged castes are seen as strategies for shifting power away from Brahmanical sections of society towards the Bahujan Samaj.

In the mid-sixties, Lohia argued that 'backward castes' constitute a majority and they should be given a fair share in power. This was reminiscent of the arguments of non-Brahman movement in the south and in Maharashtra. Although backward caste politics gradually emerged in UP and Bihar, it was only in the nineties that it became an issue at an all-India level. After the agitation against reservations in Gujarat and Bihar in the late seventies and early eighties, the agitation in many north Indian States on the issue of reservations for backward castes underlined the simmering conflict between what Lohia had described as forwards and backwards. This resulted into large-scale mobilisation of backward castes dramatically catapulting protagonists of backward castes into positions of power.

These developments had two effects. Firstly, the political discourse in the country as a whole, changed considerably. 'Social justice' became the central term around which this discourse was constructed. Such a construction facilitated the entry of caste question onto the all-India political scene rather than remaining State-specific. Backwardness of certain castes and consequent political disadvantage was no more seen in State-specific contexts; instead it was conceived as a phenomenon following from Brahmanical Hindutva and domination of national politics by upper castes. As such, taking over power at Delhi was seen as the remedy. Secondly, 'OBC' claims were quickly recognised by the various political parties. In particular, the BJP exhibited remarkable adaptability by introducing changes in the social composition of its key workers in Maharashtra, Madhya Pradesh and UP. Most other parties, too, underwent the process of 'Mandalisation', the Congress probably being the slowest and most reluctant, However, even the Congress manifested awareness of this factor in Rajasthan, Gujarat, Madhya Pradesh, etc. In other words, OBC politics did not throw up any all-India instrument instead; it forced certain changes in political parties and in politics in general. Social composition of many legislatures changed during the decade of 1990 to 2000. At least at the formal level, parties conceded the claims of OBCs in terms of share in power. Politics of backward castes became an all-India phenomenon.

In the case of Dalit politics, one can witness a steady fragmentation in the post-Ambedkar period. This fragmentation takes place at three levels: party factionalism, State-specific distinction and intra-Dalit fragmentation. The RPI could never project itself as a united party of Dalits. Various rival RPI parties emerged competing with each other. The absence of a single effective political instrument resulted into the fragmentation of Dalit votes also. On the other hand, concrete political issues faced by Dalits took a State specific turn. In Maharashtra, for instance, the issue of 'renaming' a university after Dr. Ambedkar remained an emotive issue for Dalits for over a decade. In States like Bihar, atrocities by various middle castes became the main concern of Dalits. In Tamil Nadu, frustration with Dravid politics, non-accommodation in the regional identity and conflicts with lower OBC has been shaping Dalit politics at State level. Such State-specific situations are inevitable because of differences of levels of Dalit consciousness and differences in the political economy at State level. This means that the arena of conflict and the response by Dalits varies from State to State. The main adversaries of Dalits are also not necessarily common across States. The voting preferences of Dalits are also likewise shaped at State level. Dalits of Rajasthan, Gujarat, MP, Maharashtra tend to vote in favour of Congress Dalits of W. Bengal and Kerala prefer the left fronts in those States. In UP, the BSP has established itself as the main party of Dalits. In Bihar the BJP led alliance gets more Dalit votes than RJD of Laloo Yadav, probably because of the JD faction led by Ramvilas Paswan who allied with BJP. Similarly, in Karnataka also, the BJP alliance gets more Dalit votes than the Congress.

A further complication regarding the Dalit situation needs to be noted. While ideologies of Dalit politics prefer to project 'Dalit' as one social force, even at State level, Dalits do not constitute a unified social force. For various reasons, the State-specific reasons not the least, internal stratification among Dalits of different States in a reality. In Maharashtra, the Mahar Dalits are seen as politically advanced, the Matang and Chamar Dalits resist the 'Mahar domination'. The Mala-Madiga dispute in Andhra Pradesh reached such a proportion that the State government decided to divide reservation between these two communities. The Dalits of Bihar other than the Paswans do not look upon Ramvilas Paswan as their leader. In Karnataka, the large group of Madigas demand that the reservations for Dalits should be split; giving a fixed quota to Holeyas and other Dalits which will allow Madigas to enjoy 90 percent of the reservations. Further, in one instance of violent conflict between Holeyas and the dominant land owing groups, other Dalits did not come forward in support of the Holeyas. In UP, Jatavs are seen as politically powerful and getting all advantages. The Balmikis and Pasis feel deprived. In West Bengal, the Namsudras and Rajbanshis have their 'pockets' in Faridpur, Khulna, Jessore and in north Bengal districts of Cooch Behar, Jalpaiguri, Dinajpur, respectively. These two communities are seen as taking advantage of the reservations. All these details suggest the difficulty in organising an all India Dalit politics, Only by intervening in the State level political process; Dalits stand any chance of affecting politics.

The case of OBCs is not very different. To begin with, the 'OBC' category, though a convenient short hand for a large mass, is not very definitive. It includes, formally, castes included by governments in the State lists of other backward classes. As such, the question, 'Who are the OBCs?' is itself a controversial one. Inclusion or exclusion in the OBC list is often a matter of politics for those castes who have attained enough political skills. It is a common experience that castes would press for inclusion in the list of OBCs – Jats in Rajasthan, Vokkaligas and Lingayats in Karnataka are two famous examples. Needless to say, all these factors develop in the backdrop of State specific situations. Except on general issue of reservations all OBCs cannot be mobilised on an all-India level. Therefore, in the nineties, on the heels of Mandal controversy, many OBC organisations rallied round the issues of reservations. However, when it came to organising the nuts and bolts of OBC politics, the State specific situations asserted themselves. Thus, Janata Dal, which sought to bask in the glory of its pro-Mandal stand, witnessed internal bickering: the Orissa unit under Biju Patnaik distanced itself from the Mandal platform while the Karnataka unit under Hegde made its displeasure about 'Mandalisation' known to national leadership. Both State units felt it unnecessary to have V.P. Singh as a campaigner.

Much mobilisation on the Mandal platform took place in UP and Bihar. The politics of backward castes did not articulate in a substantial manner in Orissa and Andhra Pradesh. It did not have much relevance to Tamil Nadu since that State has had a long history of non-Brahman politics. In Karnataka, Congress under Devraj Urs had earlier mobilised the OBCs. Therefore, in the nineties, the Mandal platform did not evoke much enthusiasm there. This leaves the States of Uttar

Pradesh and Bihar as the main theatre of OBC politics. In a sense, the so-called all-India claims on behalf of OBC politics are based on politics in north India where the caste issue has emerged onto the political scene rather late. Thus the phenomenon of OBC politics is much more relevant to UP and Bihar than to other States.

The internal stratification among 'OBCs' is another matter where State specific issues come to the forefront. As noted above, identification of certain castes as OBCs, is itself State specific. This is borne out by the case of Jats and more effectively, by the case of Lingayats of Karnataka. The State government went on appointing commission after commission in order to resolve the issue of whether Lingayats are backward or not. Even when the issue of identification is resolved, the question of share of different castes / caste groups continues to pose a challenge. In the field of reservations, most States seem to be veering to the strategy of classifying OBCs into two or three groups and assuring them separate 'quotas' of reserved seats. Besides reservations, the question of 'share' involves claims over power. Various backward castes not only want to be 'included' in the apparatus of power, they hope to use power to their advantage and if possible, gain controlling share in power. Negatively put, backward castes push for exclusion of the upper castes so that complexion and content of power would change substantively. These claims bring a double conflict into focus. On the one hand there is a conflict between the already established dominant caste and the aspiring caste / caste group. The constellations of these conflicts are again State specific because the ideological battle line of upper vs. Backward translates differently in each state. In Maharashtra, for example, when Maratha domination is sought to be challenged, Kunbis, who are included in the list of OBCs, would pose a problem. The 'Maratha' caste cluster includes Kunbis. Thus, the battle is between the dominant caste and a section of OBCs vs. Other OBCs. In Karnataka, the OBCs compete with Lingayats who themselves have been claiming inclusion in the list of OBCs. Political economy of each State produces patterns of dominance in accordance to which these battle lines get defined. The other conflict involves the aspiring castes themselves. When the Brahmanical castes were displaced, on the whole, only one caste sought to replace them at the State level. With democratisation penetrating larger sections in the contemporary period, a peculiar development has taken place. Just as the established dominant caste is about to be displaced, more than one claimants emerge to stake claims over power. This does not allow any single caste to stabilise in power. The Yadavs of UP and Bihar, who claimed in the nineties that they were leading the OBC revolution, have been challenged by non-Yadavs in both the States. Both these conflicts are reflected in the party preferences of OBCs. Backward castes in different States vote differently and within a State, they are often divided among different parties.

These claims and counterclaims have, in fact, further regionalised politics during the nineties. The unprecedented rise of regional parties in the nineties has been singularly unsolicited with 'regionalism.'

The discussion so far suggests that the two 'ruptures' have been in fact, ideological formulations, which seek to challenge upper and middle caste domination by unifying all lower castes. This formulation has not been able to assert itself as a concrete principle around which politics is organised. The objective caste situation varies from the presupposition that all 'lower' castes have same experience of political exclusion / marginalisation. Also, the subjective identification of various castes with politics of 'lower' castes varies both caste wise and State wise. As a result, instead of being able to rupture caste-region nexus, both Dalit politics and OBC politics have themselves yielded to this nexus and become regionalised.

State as a sociolinguistic region is a very convenient unit for caste to operate. Although many instances can be shown where small castes intervene in local political process, effective role of caste can be detected at the State level only. At the same time, castes cannot assume all-India identities and caste alliances cannot be easily forged at the all-India level. The political salience of caste increased only after castes transcended the 'local' identities and by forging new 'mega' caste identities became significant players at 'regional' level. However, this process probably stops at the regional level. Efforts of Kurmis to forge an alliance with Cannabis and Kunbis did not succeed. Even in the case of Jats, though the Jat Mahasabha exists, Jat politics in Punjab, Rajasthan, Haryana and western UP cannot be clubbed together. Thus, patterns of caste politics cannot be replicated in different regions nor can they become all-India in their reach or spread. In this sense, caste as a factor in modern politics, has become well entrenched or rooted at the regional / State level.

The relevance of caste at the regional level flows from the following four factors:

a) Social relations of hierarchy are identifiable at the regional level, some times even sub-regional level. The fact that somebody is a Brahman simply places that person in an ambiguous position of superiority outside the region where that person belongs; but in the region where S/he belongs, a fine tuning will be made depending upon whether that person is a Chitpavan or not. To take a concrete example, being a 'Maratha' carries meaning only in the context of Maharashtrian society. The Marathas will be simultaneously seen as farmers, warriors, ex-land lords, etc. Rather than their ritual status either as Kshatriyas or shudras, the historically constructed and materially experienced identity as 'powerful' will be quickly brought into focus. Regional associations also allow myths and prejudices/stereotypes operate as markers of ranking. These do not make sense outside of that region. Therefore for most castes, a hierarchical ranking is relevant only in specific region. Social relations based on these assumptions of hierarchy shape social attitudes about claims of power by different castes, giving way to competition or caste conflict. All the same, Brahmans accepted—though unwillingly—Maratha entry into the political arena. In contrast, the claims of Dalits are not so silently accepted. Conflicts at the village level take place when Dalits in a village try to capture the village panchayat.

b) Historically, many middle castes and some times even lower castes seek upward mobility in their ritual / social status. Studies of caste point out that this happens when a caste achieves material strength. It must be noted that the process of gaining upward mobility is strictly region-based. It is not so merely because one particular caste in one region attains material strength. It is also because, the claims are made regionally and accepted/legitimised regionally. Such 'mobile' castes even change their caste names and this is accepted in the given region. Transformations from Kunbi to Maratha or

Kanabi to Patidar are of course famous. Similarly, the mobility of Nadars of Tamil Nadu has been well documented. Other examples include the awadhias, mahatos, jhanuks taking up Kurmi identity, gwalas, gopes, becoming Yadavs, Padayachis of Tamil Nadu becoming Vanniyar Kshatriyas, etc. Such mobility facilitates horizontal unity among castes.

c) In the course of competition among castes, regionalism or sub-regionalism can be very easily invoked. Regionalism servers either of the two purposes. It can project one caste/ caste group as inheritor, protector or representative of regional identity and pride. This way, an assault on that caste or caste group is easily seen / shown as assault on regional pride and self-respect. Implicitly, this also means that advancement of the interests of that caste constitutes regional advancement and therefore, the demands of the caste group can be transformed into demands for regional development. To be sure, regionalist politics is shaped by many factors. What we are suggesting here is that once caste and region are identified, the interests of caste can be projected as regional interests.

d) Apart from the ideology of Regionalism, region can provide yet another advantage to the 'dominant' castes. Every dominant caste seeks to legitimise its dominant position on the basis of some ideological argument. Region as the social unit having a common cultural-linguistic context automatically forms a basis from which justification of domination can be adduced. Alternatively, arguments by the dominant caste make sense within the region. Thus, Jats' claim of being Kisans or Haryana Jats' claims for a martial tradition appeal the people in those respective regions rather than outside the regions. Similarly, Lingayats' claims of reformism in the orthodox Brahmancal Hinduism become relevant only in the Kannada speaking region. The ideology of 'Maharashtra Dharma' justifying the Brahman-Maratha leadership or the Bhadralok ideology of elite domination also has similar region-specific appeals. In the 'dominant caste thesis', the emphasis on numerical strength has deflected attention from both the contents of domination and the ways

> of attaining domination. Mere numerical strength would not lead to domination; claims of 'high' status usually accompany numerical strength. But a high ritual status is not the only 'ideological' component. 'Dominant' castes employ a more complex set of ideological arguments in order to win the 'dominant' position and we argue that region provides a helpful playground for working out these arguments.

It follows from this that any counter hegemonic assaults on the dominant caste would emanate from a similarly regionally situated arguments. In Tamil Nadu, the non-Brahman movement sought to delegitimise the Brahmans by suggesting that Brahmans are not true Dravids. But more forcefully, Phuley brings in the imagery of non-Brahmans as 'natives' by virtue of their association with agricultural activity. If both, the claims of domination and challenges to them, are regionally situated, region becomes a theatre of caste conflicts and configuration caste with political and economic dimensions.

Given the mutually reinforcing relationship of caste and region in contemporary Indian politics, it is argued here that challenges to concrete instances of caste domination can meaningfully rise at the regional level. This would further strengthen the links between caste and region. These links produce region/State-specific configurations of caste, which fit the region's political economy. In the light of this argument certain trends may be noticed. These trends indicate the possible ways in which caste is likely to be constructed in Indian politics.

In his introduction to 'Caste in Indian Politics', Rajni Kothari, long ago, pointed out the process of caste polarisation. He further said, as one polarisation is resolved in favour of one caste or caste category, new polarisation emerge...'. In many parts of the country, instead of neat polarisation, 'more complicated and fragmented constellations of power' emerged. Thus, in the arena of caste politics, on the one hand new 'dominant castes' have emerged on the scene; at least many new 'ascendant' castes have come to the forefront. On the other hand new equations have emerged. The most noted one is the BJP led equation of upper castes and lower OBCs in Uttar Pradesh. In Maharashtra, the Charmakars and Matangs have been veering away from Congress and RPI, preferring the Shiv Sena and BJP. The Bahujan Mahasangh in Maharashtra has been trying to forge an alliance of Dalits and OBCs.

These new equations do not necessarily follow a similar pattern across the States. But one common factor needs to be noted. In the emerging alliances traditional boundaries of ritual status are seldom followed. Alliances would be formed depending upon the perceptions about which caste / caste group monopolises resources. Beside, the choice of allies is often ad hoc, contingent upon who are perceived as adversaries. Underneath this contingent nature of alliances, there seems to be a consideration of two factors. One is consideration of material factors. Castes/caste groups tend to ally when their material interests do not clash - or in fact compliment - each other. When an alliance is likely to obtain some power for the caste such an alliance becomes acceptable. Both these considerations go beyond simple alliances based on ritual status - alliances are not made simply because castes occupy a common status as Shudras or Dalits.

Secondly, and partly following from the above, there is a disintegration of caste 'blocs' of Dalits and OBCs. We have discussed this point. Not only such blocs do not materialise at all-India level, they seem to be disintegrating even at the level of States. The trend seems to be moving in the direction of 'ethnicisation' of caste. One factor contributing to this process seems to be the pressure of modern reformist discourse delegitimising vertical structure of caste hierarchy. In this background, caste survives, if not as upper-lower then, as 'different' groups having different culture, ritual, 'histories', etc. Thus, caste becomes a 'community'. But ethnicisation of caste has other reasons as well. One is that small castes still find no place in calculations for electoral purposes. They may be relevant in constructing caste 'blocs' but do not receive the benefits either politically or materially. It is not necessary for us here to accept this logic but that seems to be a factor influencing the process of formation of single caste organisations. Such organisations function simultaneously as sociocultural associations, pressure groups pursuing immediate material concerns of the caste and vehicles of caste elates for riding into the power structure. Although it is tempting to look at such caste organisations as a political resource, they imply localisation of caste. Such localised ethnicisation is bound to entrap castes both into local boundaries and issues of culture, identity, history rather than of material advance and structures of domination.

Thirdly, after reaching a high point through 'Mandlisation', caste appears to be reaching a dead end in terms of its mobilisational potential. At one stage caste interests were advanced through regional mobilisation. In the next phase, mobilisation took place on the issues of reservations for OBCs (in Bihar, Gujarat) followed up by the Mandal issues and claims of the leaders of OBCs for power sharing. The nineties have witnessed acceptance of OBC reservations as State policy. These developments have meant that the space to be occupied by caste issue is bound to shrink except for further competition among OBCs for greater share in power. At the local level, provision enabling reservations to SCs, STs and OBCs in local government bodies, has ensured that no effective mobilisation can take place and no party will take interest in such mobilisation. This does not imply that caste has lost relevance but that as an organising principle of politics, caste may have reached its limits. Like region earlier, caste may have to search for catalysts that will revitalise the emotive and mobilisation capacity of caste as a sphere of politics.

This obviously raises doubt about the democratising potential of caste as a sphere. The caste-region nexus meant that just as domination of a caste or caste group would get established, it will be challenged by rival groups or by newly emerging lower sections. However, if our assessment that caste alliances are ad hoc and less mobilisational is correct, then the arena of caste politics is likely to lose the potential to democratise Indian polity. Further, throughout the nineties, the emphasis seemed to be on the 'presence' in positions of power. The twin thrust of controlling state power and diverting it to an agenda favouring the 'Dalit-Bahujans' was lost in the nineties. These developments have deprived the arena of caste politics of democratising possibilities. These issues obviously go much beyond the question of caste-region nexus. But they also point towards the challenges faced by a core sphere of Indian politics: the sphere of caste politics.

References

Balgopal K. A Tangled Web : Subdivision of SC Reservations in AP, *Economic and Political Weekly,* March 25-31. 2000.

Betteile Andre. *Society and Politics in India,* Delhi, OUP. 1992.

Frankel Francine R. and M.S.A. Rao (eds.) *Dominance and State Power in Modern India,* Vol. I, Delhi, OUP. 1989.

Francine R. and M.S.A. Rao (eds.). *Dominance and State Power in Modern India,* Vol. II, Delhi, OUP. 1990.

Jenkins Rob. Where the BJP Survived : Rajasthan Assembly Election, 1993, *Economic and Political Weekly,* March 12. 1994.

Palshikar Suhas. *Politics of Marginalised Groups,* (Report submitted to UGC), Dept. of Politics and Public Admn., University of Pune. 2000.

6

Caste Politics in Maharashatra

Over the last two decades, studies of the Maratha polity have moved away from frameworks wherein the Marathas were viewed as either predatory hordes of men from low-caste and nomadic communities relentless in their pursuit of revenue extraction or Hindu warrior-nationalists pitting their "Maratha" volar and manliness against Islam and the Mughal Empire. Revisionist hysterography on the Marathas has long roots, for example, in the writings of the liberal economic nationalist, Mahadev Govind Ranade, who proposed a genealogy for Indian nationalism through Maratha history in *The Rise of Maratha Power* and in S.N. Sen's *The Military System of the Marathas* which traced overlaps between Mughal and Maratha military regimes. While these works challenged the depiction of Maratha history as the unfolding of Hindu history, they nonetheless suffered from the malaise of claiming the Marathas for a contemporary anticolonial nationalism. However, recent studies have focused on those sociopolitical aspects that distinguished Maratha state formation: sophisticated structures of revenue contracts and col-lection, monetisation of services, a market in patrimonial tenures, expansion of agriculture from the Deccan heartland into the frontier regions of middle India in the interest of settled revenue collection, and finally, an elaborate legal-bureaucratic regime distinguished by a system of fines and punishments. This Maratha polity accords with developments in various parts of the subcontinent between the sixteenth and eighteenth centuries, when new groups—Jats, Rajputs, Marathas—arose out of the contexts of military service and tenurial holdings under the Mughals

"Maratha" was an expansive category that was intimately related to early modern patterns of labour mobilisation for land and military markets, and included a range of persons whose bids for political and economic power had succeeded, from the lowly *kunbi* peas-ant-cultivator to the ninety-six elite Maratha families, the *shahannavkuli,* who claimed a genealogical link with the Rajputs. *Thus, state formation in the Deccan region was characterised both by the increased salience of the category Maratha in signifying emergent patterns of power, and by a growing number of persons laying claim to Maratha as identity.* Entry into the category Maratha was possible through marriage, political-economic control over land, and over time, through the fabrication of genealogical affinity with the *varna-jati* combination of the Kshatriya-Rajput. The Maratha polity transformed in the eighteenth century into what the historian Hiroshi Fukasawa has termed a "Brahminical" state ruled by Chitpavan Brahmins, the Peshwai. It suffices here to note that the state-society linkages of the Peshwai produced a unique collective memory of Brahmins' political domination and not merely their ritual authority. This situation and the tripartite caste structure of the Deccan enabled an unusual critique of caste oppression.

The consolidation of a Maratha polity was symbolically marked by Shivaji's coronation as Chatrapati in 1674. By then, the Deccan was characterised by a sedentariness populace, monetisation of the economy, and a highly organised regime of revenue collection, though Maratha user-aunty was initially achieved through practices of social banditry and guerilla warfare. Significantly, Maratha dominance provoked challenges to Brahminical authority conducted within ritual idioms. The most famous illustration of the pattern is Shivaji's coronation as Chatrapati, or lord of the *chhatra,* a large parasol or canopy placed over Hindu gods and kings to signify grandeur and dignity. The controversy over Shivaji's claims to Kshatriya lineage—he came from a family of *patils* near Pune who acquired power through military service to the Nisam Shah of Ahemdnagar—arose when a section of Deccan Brahmins rejected the possibility of allowing Shivaji to be coronated with Vedic rites reserved for twice-born Kshatriyas. Though Brahmin authority sanctified temporal claims, it was powerful only when supported by idioms and practices of sovereignty. The belatedness of Shivaji's coronation and its ritual recognition of Shivaji's consolidation of real power over the Deccan are noteworthy. Even more important are the multiple signification of the term "Maratha" and growing conflict around efforts to align Maratha *jati* with Kshatriya *varna*.

Brahmins continued to deny the Basle royal family's claim to Vedic rites and thus rejected their identity as twice-born Kshatriyas. Instead, they argued that the Bhosles were Shudras entitled to rites performed according to the Puranas. Symbolic insults to Maratha identity gained traction across the nineteenth century as the Chitpavan Brahmin community gained political visibility as a consequence of the Brahmin *peshwa,* or prime minister's increased centrality in political affairs. The declining political fortunes of the Bhosle family popularised the growing perception among upwardly mobile Maratha-*kunbis*, that a repetitive structure of Brahmin insult and non-Brahmin humiliation was *the* governing logic of history. Indeed Brahmins had long maintained that the genocide of Kshatriyas by the Brahmin Parashurama, the sixth incarnation of the Lord Vishnu, as related in the Dasavatara, or the ten incarnations of Lord Vishnu, was proof that there were only three castes in the Kali Yuga: Brahmins, Shudras, and untouchables. Thus the Vedokta controversy between Pratap singh and the Chitpavan Brahmins of Poona between 1820 and 1830, and again in 1900 between Shahu Chatrapati of Kolhapur and his *rajopadhyaya* resuscitated the long-standing battle over Maratha demands for recognition as Kshatriyas in the face of Brahmin efforts to reiterate their Shudra identity. Shahu's response was distinctive, however, and it is a symptom of the extent to which conflicts between Brahmins and non-Brahmins defined the sociopolitical landscape: in 1913, he challenged Brahmins' exclusive control over scriptural knowledge and ritual performance by establishing a school to train non-Brahmin priests, and by 1921 he had established an alternative locus of Kshatriya ritual authority.

By then the Deccan had undergone significant political transformation, and both Brahmin and Maratha responses were mediated through a powerful new presence, the East India Company. The Peshwai ended when East India Company forces defeated Peshwa Bajirao II in 1818. From then, the colonial state increasingly played a significant role in defining the meaning and social experience of the term "Maratha"; produced a set of affective attachments and institutional investments in history and identity, and enabled the rise of a newly salient, oppositional term, "non-Brahmin." Ironically, colonial intervention accelerated two seemingly contradictory processes: the secularisation of caste *and* its novel association with Hindu religion. The colonial government abdicated direct responsibility for adjudicating issues of ritual status, religious rights, and community standing, though these were important realms of state intervention under the Old Regime. While this produced new openings for challenging caste discipline and Brahminical norms, the mediation of Brahminical knowledge played an important role in colonial knowledge formation. Power was no longer exercised through explicitly hierarchical registers, but through binary distinctions between "religious" and "political" arenas that respected neither social experience nor popular categorisation.

For non-Brahmin communities, colonial modernity had a twofold effect. It produced new investments in history and caste identity, and it provoked affinity with a new range of modern institutions spaces through which social mobility for the downtrodden and exploited might be accomplished. Colonial infrastructure, and its multiple and dispersed effects in the form of a colonial "sensorium," was inextricably linked to new experiences of the self and enabled radical egalitarian ideology to percolate through caste radicals' discourse, from ideas of self-respect and equality among intimates to a critique of the structured political-economic inequities of Brahminism.

A distinctive Mahar history was the ground from which other claims to social inclusion emerged and on which differences from non-Brahmins set a divergent trajectory for Dalit politicisation. In drawing on a racial theory of conquest to explain the subjugation of non-Aryan Kshatriyas, the Shudras and *atishudras,* by Aryan Brahmin invaders, Jotirao Phule transvalued colonial-national fascination with theories of Aryan conquest to argue that a permanent and irreconcilable hostility between Brahmin and non-Brahmin had characterised caste society from its inception. Phule never used the term "Hindu" in his writings, lest it appear that he was describing a consensual religious cultural formation. However, by the time Phule was writing the terms "Arya" and "Aryan" had come to symbolise a set of associations between language and territory and between territory and religion, enabling a particular vision of the national-archaic: the civilisation history of India was now aligned with a territorial bounded, geographically distinctive protonational space, Bharat or Bharatvarsha.

Reversing European narratives about the divergent civilisations status and material development of Indians and Europeans, both Hindu reformer Bal Gangadhar Tilak and Arya Samaj leader Dayanand Saraswati positioned Aryan society as coeval with Vedic religion, even as they posited Bharat as the home of modern-day Hindus who had exported their religious values to the European world long ago. Even the downtrodden communities had a place in this reconstituted Vedic past: because their degraded lifestyles were a consequence of forgetting their Aryan identity, they could be redeemed through *shuddhi.* Indeed, the desire to reconstitute a glorious Aryan past in India's present was evident across the board. Phule's conception of *history as caste conflict,* however, recuperated a non-Aryan Kshatriya past for Maharashtra's downtrodden. Arguing that the word "Kshatriya" originated in the Sanskrit *kshetra* he imaginatively linked agricultural labour with military service, fields of cultivation with battlefields, and the humble peasant-cultivator with a past of military prowess. Then he went even further, asserting an exceptional role for the downtrodden, the Mahars and Mangs, who had offered the strongest resistance to the Aryan-Brahmin invaders. Interpreting the term "Mahar" as Mahaari Phule argued that the Mahars had twenty-one times freed their Dravidian brothers from conquest by Aryan Brahmins but were finally defeated through chicanery and cunning. Subsequently, the Brahmins, Phule's pejorative term for these ritual specialists, composed sacred texts to justify their ill treatment of vanquished Dravidian Kshatriyas: "So that would never lift their hand against the Brahmins had a black thread tied around their necks, and prohibited even their Shudra brethren from touching them. He started the practice of calling these Mahaari Kshatriyas by the names ati-Shudra, Mahar, any aj, Mang, and Chandal."

As punishment for resistance, the Mahars were defined as untouchables and banished from society, condemned to poverty, feeding on dead carcasses and wearing the black thread as a symbol of servitude. A *paddy* written by the president of the Bombay Shri Somavanshi Mitra Samaj, Pandit Kondiram, who was influenced by

Phule, drew on this imagery to communicate the continued effects of past horrors. They dressed in clothes taken from corpses, wore iron jewellery, ate from broken clay pots, and owned only "dogs and asses; rats and mice. They were dispossessed, shadowy figures reduced to begging and eating food unfit even for animals.

Kondiram ended with the powerful image of Mahar children sitting on a dung heap, their bodies covered with ash, sores on their eyes, rags covering their buttocks, their stomachs "sunken and empty." Kondiram's imagery echoed the detailed prohibitions of texts such as the Manusmriti, which relegated untouchables to the very edge of human society, near graveyards and on dung heaps. While Pandit Kondiram, like Phule, agreed that the *shudra-atishudras* were Dravidian Kshatriyas, he presents here a very specific set of images of Mahars' destitution. Though Phule had argued that the *shudra-atishudras* were a political collective, he had also held Brahmins responsible for creating divisions among them. Coached by wily Brahmins to "hate the Mahars and Mangs," Shudras had forgotten that the untouchable communities were once brave Kshatriyas.

Early Dalit activists such as Gopal Baba Valangkar and Shivram Janba Kamble drew on Phule's recuperation of a militant history for the Dalit communities. Both, however, hitched a martial Mahar identity as Dravidian Kshatriyas to a new goal—a claim to continued employment in the British Army. Army service and its suspension deeply affected the first generation of Dalit publicists who had experienced social mobility and relatively little discrimination in the military. The significance of military service for Mahar Dalit is best understood by examining Valangkar, whose experience in the army, combined with immersion in Phule's Satyashodak ideology, resulted in a systematic Dalit critique of caste injustice. He was an active member of the Satyashodak Samaj while in the military. In 1886, he retired as army *havaldar* and went to Dapoli in the Ratnagiri district of the Konkan to become a schoolmaster. Dapoli was a unique settlement of Mahar and Chamber military pens. ners. In the Ratnagiri district, 2,180 Mahars were on the military rolls, 1,150 of whom were listed as pensioners. In fact, Mahars were described as "owning much land" in Dipole.

By 1892, however, Mahars were collateral damage of a decision by the British government to stop recruiting untouchables. They were victims of the "martial races theory" adopted by the British Army after the Mutiny to justify reorganisation of the military along caste lines by excluding Dalits and Brahmins who were regarded as weak, effeminate, and incapable of martial courage.

If the British army justified military exclusion, Mahar Dalits mobilised Phule's concept of history as race war to emphasise their martial identity. Educated up to the Normal School examination in Poona's Shri Ganesh School, Valangkar was deeply influenced by Phule's critique of Brahmin hegemony and the radical egalitarianism of Satyashodak thinking. Subhedar R. S. Ghadge, a military pensioner who later became a member of the Poona branch of Vithal Ramji Shinde's Nirashrit Sahayyak Mandal recalled that when he was stationed in Poona along with Valangkar, they heard Jotirao Phule lecturing the Mahar regiment about the bravery of the Chambhars, Mahars, and Mangs who had valiantly fought the Aryan Brahmins in ancient times. Another member of the Satyashodak Samaj, Govind Ganpat Kale, recalled that Phule was a frequent visitor to Valangkar's home in the Maharwada in Bhavani Peth and that Phule often tested members of the Samaj by seating them in the same *pangthi* as Valangkar, while food was served. While the Samaj might have tolerated such experiments in Phule's lifetime, Valangkar himself became a victim of caste prejudice a few years later. In 1895, five years after Phule's death, the Samaj decided to ban Dalits from their meetings.

Valangkar's activism manifested both significant continuities with and new departures from Satyashodak thinking. In 1888, Valangkar wrote a *Vinanti Patra* in which he offered an extensive critique of caste exclusion in the form of a series of questions regarding the divine rationale for *jati* and *varna* distinctions, and for the practice of un touchability. Elaborating upon Phule's account of the defeat of the Shudra-*atishudras,* Valangkar argued for a repetitive structure to the outcasting of the untouchable communities after their original defeat by Aryan Brahmins, and he historicised Dalits' social stigmatisation to the *peshwa* period, when lower castes and untouchables had faced severe religious exclusion and social violence. Again during the Peshwai, the lower-caste and untouchable communities had found themselves subject to severe caste discipline under a Brahminical state. As in Phule's account, the abject position of the Dalit was historically produced through the foundations conflict between Aryan Brahmins and the autochthonous Dravidian communities of western India. In Valangkar's account, however, ordinary conflict was overlaid with an argument that specified a key element of Dalits' degradation, their eating of carrion. This became a recurrent theme in Valangkar's explanations of Dalit stigma, which drew on the real-life experiences of Mahar communities.

In addition to founding the first Dalit organisation in the Bombay Presidency, the Anarya Dosh Pariharak Mandali (ADPM), Valangkar was a frequent contributor to the newspapers *Sudharak* and *Din Bandhu*. In the 1890s, he toured western India performing *kirtans* against the ill treatment of the Dalit communities. When he was nominated to the Mahad Local Board in 1895, caste Hindus and Muslims boycotted the board's meetings. This provoked a series of reports in the *Din Bandhu* criticising Valangkar's treatment. Ironically, this incident occurred in the same year that the Poona branch of the Satyashodak Samaj decided to ban untouchables from their meetings.

Valangkar was adept at the organisational practices of the Satya-shodak Samaj, but he was also familiar with the workings of colonial institutions such as the school, the army, and finally, the colonial bureaucracy. When faced with evidence of social exclusion and stigmatisation specific to the untouchable communities, Valangkar responded by seeking colonial intervention to safeguard Dalits' historical rights. In July 1894, Valangkar drafted a petition on behalf of the ADPM to the Bombay government demanding equal employment and civil rights for the untouchable communities. None of these petitions received a positive response. However, the petition became a crucial forum for writing Mahar Dalit history and for self-representation. In this genre, Dalits positioned themselves as supplicants and pleaded that historical wrongs to proud warriors required redress, while drawing on new discourses of social inclusion and civic equality to make their case.

Phule's historical conflict between Brahmin and non-Brahmin produced the *shudra-atishudra* as a revolutionary subject. Like the Dalit to come, *shudra-atishudra* named a community that did not exist it signalled a potentiality, but also defined that group historically by valorising their military prowess and indignity while challenging their defeat at the hands of wily *that* Brahmins. The power of Phule's narrative lay not only in the refusal of Brahminical hegemony but also in the claim to self-representation by the *bahujan samaj* of the downtrodden and toiling c .stes, now valued as key political actors against alien interlopers. They were the Rakshasas, the protectors of the land, who, once vanquished, appeared in Hindu mythology as *asuras,* or demons. History was a counter to historical forgetting, an antidote against religious superstition and ideological indoctrination. Valangkar took up the narrative of *shudra-atishudra* bravery and military valor and the critique of Brahmin chicanery and cunning. Unlike his notable predecessor, Joti-rao Phule, whose investment in Enlightenment rationality and human-ism was combined with efforts to reinterpret Hindu popular culture, es-pecially the Puranic tradition, Valangkar turned to the Rg Veda and the Bhagavad Gita, and argued that they put forth competing views on the origins of untouchability: the former relied on a model of descent codified in the Manusmriti, while the Gita were based on a theory of *karma,* or doing. Valangkar's argument regarding a key contradiction between caste as religious transcendental and caste as derived from a theory of action gave the practice of untouchability a more specific history, even as it allowed Valangkar to challenge religious ethics from *within* the scriptural tradition. This was distinct from Phule's rationalist humanism, belief in a formless Universal Creator, and his efforts to propagate his Sarvajanik Satya Dharma each of which verged on atheism.

If Valangkar's critique was enabled by forms of anticaste critique popularised by the Satyashodak Samaj, the Samaj's expulsion of its Dalit members in 1895 was an early sign of fissures within this imagined community of the *shudra-atishudra.* By the early decades of the twentieth century, anti-Brahminism had transformed into political non-Brahminism with a focus on converting the demographic predominance of the non-Brahmin into political power. Currently, the once expansive, incorporative Maratha identity associated with anti-Brahminism became an exclusive identity tied to the realisation of ritual Kshatriya status, or to forms of peasant populism. As non-Brahmins poured into the Congress, Dalits' conflicts with the Congress were increasingly inflected with a Dalit/non-Brahmin antagonism. Crucially, emerging distinctions between Dalits and non-Brahmins were played out on the field of intimate life and familial relations, gender and genealogy. The regulation of sexuality, in particular, was an important axis for the politicisation of caste identity.

6.1. Dimensions of Caste Politics

Hindu scriptures, especially the Manusmriti, defined both lower castes and women as impure, polluting, and subject to detailed regulation. It is not surprising that Phule and Valangkar equated the flights of these groups. Phule's earliest reform efforts addressed both lower castes and women: he opened school for untouchable students in 1852 and home for upper-caste widows in 1854.

Enforced widowhood, an important target of caste radicals' critique, focused on the inhuman treatment of the widow, who was to insured, subject to severe sartorial codes, prohibited from wearing jewellery, and forced to observe dietary restrictions to control her passions. Sexual anxieties about the widow were long-standing, but Hindu reformers' and caste radicals' renewed focus on the treatment of widows coincided with the colonial state's efforts to reform the Hindu joint family.

Caste radicals were distinctive and vociferous in emphasising the importance of caste respectability and sexual purity to the reproduction of Brahminical patriarchy. Thus, when Phule and his wife, Savitribai, opened a home in1854 for upper-caste widows who faced intimate violence ranging from physical abuse to impregnation, they were criticising a Brahminical order that sanctioned such practices, even as they were challenging upper castes' capacity to protect "their women." Tarabai Shinde extended their critique in *Stri-Purush Tulana* written in 1882 in response to the conviction of an upper-caste widow, Vijayalakshmi, of infanticide. Shinde attacked the hypocritical stance of criminalising women rather than challenging the sexual excesses of men and argued that all men, not merely Brah-mins, were implicated in the ill treatment of women. He compared the tonsure of widows with cows going to the slaughterhouse and argued that widows were deeply susceptible to sexual advances by "ascetics, mendicants, and priests" who congregated at holy places to take advantage of them. Indeed, an established trope in anticaste polemic was Brahminism's ideological reduction of women and the lower castes to beasts of burden: their sentience and physicality were inversely related to their value as persons.

Because enforced widowhood exposed the structuring relationship between caste hegemony and control over female sexuality, the practice provided the occasion for early critiques of the caste order and of Brahminical mores in particular. A dialogue between a widow and her father in a Satyashodak *jalsa* uses the widow's physical disfiguration to stage a broader critique of enforced widow hood and to challenge its growing acceptance among non-Brahmin communities where *pat* had previously predominated.

In the first decades of the twentieth century, Satyashodak *jalsas* were the main vehicles for spreading the Samaj's message to the rural populace. Traditional *tamashas,* renowned for their word play and sexual innuendo interspersed with song, typically began with an invocation to Lord Ganapati. The stories centered on the theme of Lord Krishna's dalliances with his *gopis.* Instead, the Satyashodak *jalsa* invoked the *gana* as leaders. Satyaji's dialogue with Brahmin women on the irrationality of Hindu ritual, discussions about the exploitation of the peasantry, and critiques of the Brahmin-moneylender were popular. The use of coarse and insulting language was standard. Bhimrao Mahamuni from Otur is credited with having staged the first *jalsa* with the support of Shahu Chatrapathi and Krishnarao Bhalekar. Ramachandra Ghadge started his famous *jalsa* troupe in 1915. Colonial reports indicate the extent to which the Satyashodak Samaj relied on the *jalsa* and other popular cultural forms. By 1929, more than twenty-nine troupes were performing in southern Maharashtra. By 1932, however, the Bombay government noted a marked decrease of the performance of Satyashodak *jalsas,* but attested to their continued cultural significance:

> "The Satyashodak Samaj hit on tamashas as a means of propaganda amongst illiterate rustics and the points they make are probably coarse, but though the Brahmans have complained to me of the coarseness of the attacks made on them in these tamashas by the Satya Samaj, I have never yet been able to get a statement of any particular words they con-sider offensive. What happens, apparently, is that songs are sung containing offensive stories from sacred books and these are represented as Brahman morality."

Satyashodak activists experimented with new social forms and counter cultural strategies to challenge Brahmin hegemony and exploitation of female suffering. Like the jalsa, another important effort centered on politicising Hindu marriage as the hinge between intimate and public political life, and as the site where ideologies of caste purity and gender respectability were articulated *as caste power*. Thus the Satyashodak marriage eliminated the need for a Brahmin priest and emphasised self-respect and equality within marriage. This challenge to the social reproduction of caste through religious exploitation of the non-Brahmin communities, and the sexual regulation of women, inspired Ambedkar, who urged Dalits to perform Satyashodak marriage. He even presided over one in Vidarbha in 1927. Similarly, Self-Respect marriages in south India in the movement's heyday took the politicisation of marriage to new heights. Self-Respecters, especially their leader, Periyar, or E. V. Ramasamy Naicker, urged activists to perform intercaste and widow remarriages and celebrated them in movie halls and theaters, where they were performed at ritually inauspicious times.

The political import of the Satyashodak marriage is reflected by a legal case from to our in Poona district, a site of radical Satyashodak activism. A Brahmin *joshi* demanded his traditional fees for performing a marriage even though the Satyashodak marriage had eliminated his role. On appeal to the Bombay High Court, Balaji Patil argued that his fellow caste members had performed his daughter's wedding in keeping with ancestral tradition. His legal representative recognised the novelty of the Satyashodak marriage, however, and argued: "The marriages were performed without any prescribed ceremonies, and no priest as such, was employed. There was no *ganeshpujan*. There was nothing beyond the placing of garlands on the necks of the bride and bridegroom. There was no distribution of fees; therefore the village joshis cannot claim any fees. *There is a separate ritual for the Sudras of the defendants caste. That ritual was not performed.*" The 1888 judgment by Justices Sargent and Candy supported the Satyashodaks' argument that because the wedding of Patil's daughter was not performed as a recognisable non-Brahmin or Shudra marriage, the *joshi* was ineligible for fees. By refusing to sacralise marriage *on the Brahmin's terms,* the Satyashodak marriage positioned itself as an explicit challenge to the social reproduction of caste through the sexual regulation of women. This was of a piece with challenges to Brahmin sacerdotal power and ritually "pure" status in important rationalist texts such as *Svayam-upright* and *Gharache*

Upright that empowered non-Brahmin communities to perform religious rituals with-out Brahmin intervention.

Though caste radicals were preoccupied with challenging caste ideology by rethinking marriage and sexuality, they were by no means immune to the extension of novel patriarchal practices into their own households. In the last quarter of the nineteenth century, enhanced regulation of women became a mechanism to resolve anxieties about social status among upwardly mobile, politicised Marathas. This partial segregation of women involved withdrawing their labour and physical presence from public space and became a status marker for Maratha families claiming elite Kshatriya status. Meanwhile, Dalit publicists and reformers underlined the susceptibility of Dalit women to sexual violation according to "custom" and focused on enforced sexual servitude through women' ritual dedication. Even as Dalit publicists launched a severe critique of the interdependence of sexual compulsion and the material deprivation of Dalit communities, their efforts to modify Dalit intimate relationships also enhanced the authority of male Dalit reformers.

The contradictory effects of the social reform of gender by caste radicals can be explained by the fact that Dalit and non-Brahmin political subject-formation increasingly involved the politicisation of Dalit and lower-caste men through the reform of family and female subjects. Earlier, colonial paradigms of social reform had intersected with. Brahminical models of caste and sexual purity to produce egomaniac ideologies of domesticity, female enfranchisement, and companionate marriage. In the first decades of the twentieth century, however, non-Brahmin critiques of the gendered character of caste were muted by emergent forms of caste conflict that increasingly framed the modernisation of gender as dependent on the reconstitution of caste masculinity.

An important consequence of the discrete, if mutually entailed, trajectories of gender reform and the politicisation of caste by anticaste radicals was that the subject of non-Brahmin and, later, Dalit politics was imagined as male.

By the early decades of the twentieth century, Jotirao Phule's resonant narrative of Brahmin invasion and political usurpation was redirected to serve an argument regarding the impure, miscegenated origins of the Chit-pavan Brahmins. Maratha masculinity was directly engaged in the re-sulting narratives, while Dalits were rendered marginal to the conflict. The emphasis on Dalit and Maratha masculinity was the result of caste radicals' initial emphasis on the importance of gender and sexuality in the constitution of the community of caste. Their divergent trajectories can be explained, however, through caste radicalism's intersections with the institutional contexts of colonial modernity and the discursive logics of an emergent cultural nationalism.

In Maharashtra, it was said that there were only Brahmins and Shudras in the Kaliyuga. This indicated a Brahmin-centric view of the degradation of the all intermediate castes to Shudra status. Constant conflicts over Shudra status were in evidence from the 1700s, if not earlier, and became especially virulent by 1830 with regard to Chitpavan Brahmins' determination to downgrade the Kayastha Probus to Shudra status. But who were the Chitpavan Brahmins? Phule had framed them as aliens and interlopers. Valangkar embellished Phule's account: the Konkani Chitpavan Brahmins were Semitic people who had fled the Babary coast, were shipwrecked off the Malabar coast, married low-caste women from the Konkan region, and became a caste of fisher-men. Valangkar went further to explain the distinctions between Mahar and Maratha. He described the Mahars as *varnas* of mixed *jatis* who shared the line-age of other Dravidian Kshatriyas—Surya, Chandra, Shes, and Yadu. If Valangkar distinguished the Marathas from other Dravidian Kshatriyas, it is because this was a pronounced theme of Maratha genealogies produced in the early decades of the twentieth century, which sought to redefine Marathas' status as *Aryans* and as Kshatriyas.

Dalits *and* Marathas past felt compelled, however, to engage with the Chitpavan Brahmins' genealogy related in the Sahyadrikhand, a caste origin myth that referenced an act of genocide in the Dasavatara to explain the disappearance of Kshatriyas from the Deccan. In the Dasavatara, the axe-wielding Brahmin Parashurama, an incarnation of Vishnu, is said to have exterminated all Kshatriyas during the Treta Yuga, in retaliation for his father's murder. To extirpate his sins, Parashurama tried to perform penance. Unable to find Brahmins in the Konkan, he created the Chitpavan Brahmins by purifying a group of sixty fishermen at a funeral pyre. The Chitpavans were rendered pure *(pavana)* through funereal ashes *(chitta)*.

If this genealogy rendered Chitpavan Brahmins of dubious distinction, it created an even more compromising account of non-Brahmins. The Shudra-Kshatriyas of Kaliyuga, it was said, were the product of illicit in-tercaste unions between Brahmin sages, *rishis,* and enslaved Kshatriya women. The term "Shudra," in both popular discourse and legal texts, conjured the dishonor of impure origins, a bastard identity born out of bondage, sexual degradation, and servitude. No less than B.R. Ambedkar was impelled by this account of sexual violence to argue that, " every case, the Kshatriyas are shown to have undergone an abject surrender.. The surrender of the Kshatriyas was so to say purchased by them by offering their women to the victorious brahmins. Who can take such dirty, filthy, abominable and vainglorious stories of reconciliation as true historical facts? Only a supporter of Brahminism can do so. Indeed, Maratha assertions in the early twentieth century challenged this foundation narrative of sexual violence and caste miscegenation by addressing the *Brahmin's* miscegenation identity.

In order to align themselves with region and nation, Marathas asserted that they were the original inhabitants of Maharashtra and thus true nationalists. To make their case they drew on colonial racial typologies inflected by regional caste conflicts and made sometimes confusing and inconsistent distinctions between Aryans and Dravidians, and Hindus and Brahmins. By the turn of the century, Maratha purity had become a sensitive issue for Maratha activists and elite Maratha families alike. The latter distinguished themselves from Marathas of uncertain status, referred to by a range of terms—*cauda, akkarmashe* and *kharchi* —and sought to legitimise status through ritual incorporation into varna hierarchy. Marriage advertisements seeking pure alliances between elite, wealthy Maratha families began to appear in the pages of the Kolhapur newspaper *Vijayi Maratha* and the more conservative, Belgaum-based *Rashtraveer*.

Such practices were doubly inflected by the desire to challenge Brahmin hegemony and to claim for Marathas a distinctive Kshatriya identity by aligning *jati* with *varna* status. The net result was a shift away from Phule's tradition of radical egalitarianism and critique of religious orthodoxy toward an embrace of Aryan identity for Kshatriya Marathas, now increasingly represented as Hindus with full access to Vedic rituals in contrast to Brahmins, who were portrayed as being of questionable origin. Notable exceptions to this tendency are Mukundrao Patil, editor of the *Din Mitra*, who repeatedly urged an expansive identity for non-Brahmin castes as non-Aryan Hindus ranged against Brahmin domination; and the non-Brahmin activists Keshavrao Jedhe and Dinkarrao Javalkar.

Maratha assertions of pure Kshatriya origin positioned them asAryan originators of Hindu scriptures with a first claim to Vedic authority, and Maratha polemicists urged non-Brahmins totake up the thread ceremony and other Vedic rituals to assert their superiority over Brahmins. This erased the illegitimacy Phule had attributed to the scriptures as signs of Brahmin cunning and made for the Maratha Kshatriyas a central place *within* Hindu history. It also left intact the narrative of the defeat and humiliation of the Dravidian Shudra.

The reconstitution of the Maratha self was thus inherently unstable. At one level it constituted a challenge to Brahmin power across the *longue durée*. However by positing a direct correspondence between the uneven political regimes that produced Maratha as a resonant caste identity in western India and the ritually exclusive *varna* status of Kshatriyas, Maratha assertion relied on a genealogy that denied salience for Phule's imagined collectivity of *shudra-atishudras*. As debates over caste identity intersected with narratives of sexual violence and structural analyses of the sexual reproduction of caste, complex political tensions between Brahmins, non-Brahmins, and untouchable were also staged. Between 1922 and 1926, an aggressively masculinised counter discourse became a major node of conflict for non-Brahmin challenges to Brahmin superiority.

Ganpati and Shivaji *melas* started in the 1890s by radical Hindu nationalist Bal Gangadhar Tilak had countered Muharram processions by politicising public space and religion through everyday cultural symbols and historical figures associated with intimate practices of Hindu religiosity. The *melas* included street marches, singing, and the staging of plays that created a context for displays of anticolonial rhetoric and patriotic fervour.

In turn, Chatrapati *melas* counterstaged Maratha masculinity. Participants wore warrior costumes, carried spears and javelins, sang *mela* songs criticising Brahmin hegemony, and asserted the true national patriotism of non-Brahmins. The Peshwas were blamed for losing Maharashtra to the British. Insults were common. By 1924, nightly fricassees between Tilakites and non-Brahmin activists brought the *melas* under extensive police surveillance and caused the banning of many songs and publications by both sides. The liberal organ, *Servant of India,* noted that the Chatrapati *melas* showed that could beat the originators of the festival on their own ground, that is, in the employment of indecent language.

This aggressively masculinised non-Brahmin political culture exacer-bated caste antagonism through a sexual politics. Popular pamphlets made sexual innuendos about Brahmin women and represented widows as symbols of Brahmin tyranny. They cast aspersions on the sexual purity of Brahmin communities, characterising them as the illicit offspring of Maratha men and Brahmin women. Brahmins were routinely described as *dasiputras* in polemical texts, thus reversing the Brahmins' narrative of the Marathas as Shudras and the offspring of *dasis*. Indeed, Brahmins complained that one of the taunts employed by the activists was, "the Chatrapati *mela* has come; Brahmin women better run."

Gender and genealogy were discursively central to this emergent non-Brahmin public sphere. Non-Brahmin activists emphasised the history of concubinage and Brahmin men's sexual exploitation of lower-caste women through popular-cultural representations of the Peshwai as a period of sexual debauchery. To suggest that Brahmins were foreigners and the offspring of caste miscegenation threatened the Brahmins' claim to caste purity and, therefore, to ritual authority. Government censorship of "inflammatory" or "obscene" texts illustrates the growing significance of a public sphere of print and performance in exacerbating Brahmin/non-Brahmin conflict in Poona, hotbed of Titillate activism.

Let us begin with publication of *Deshache Dushman* in 1925, with an introduction by Keshavrao Bagade. The controversy over the text was preceded by demands that same year that the Poona municipality honour Phule with a statue. The deep-rooted resistance of Brahmins and conservative non-Brahmins—including Phule's relative, Belabour Phule—who accused Phule of being a Christian convert who destroyed Hindu religion, intensified friction and set the stage for a spirited response. The Oriental Translator described the book as "written in the most intemperate and objectionable language; in places the violent fury of the writer has so carried him away that his whirling words are barel, intelligible."

Deshache Dushman branded Brahmin leaders as traitors sprung from a stock of foreign invaders of low status and questionable origins. The authors argued that Brahmins were well known for using any means to assert their superiority. Tilak and Vishnu Shastri Chiplunkar—the latter famous for his vitriolic criticism of Phule and the social reformer Gopal Hari Deshmukh, or Lokahitawadi, in his 1874 *Nibandhamala*—were referred to as enemies of the country "born from the vomit of Brahmans" Chitpavan Brahmins were generally described as "Satan," "cobras," "sons of prostitutes," and "mother goers." Indeed the litany of complaints against Brahmin patriotism comprised an account of Brahmin treachery, sexual licentiousness, and female exploitation. Shivaji's protection of Brahmin women from the depredation of Muslim men was mentioned in conjunction with Brahmin hypocrisy about the behaviour of their women—"the That mind thinks religion is destroyed when a Shudra is crowned king but cannot comprehend when a Brahmin woman comes jumping from the bed of a Shudra. Brahmins, it was noted, had the vile tendency to "suspect their mother's chastity," "shave women," and to allow widows to throw their illegitimate children on "crossroads eight times a week." At the same time, the Brahmin priest "who calls the non-Brahmins Shudras an enemy is a bad mash ducat who casts evil glances at their women." Equating Brahminism with slavery, the text noted, "it is a sin to give alms to a Brahmin who smokes ganja, drinks wine and ascends the staircase of houses of ill repute. To get marriage solemnised by Brahmins is tantamount to polluting an auspicious occasion writing the horoscope of a future slave generation."

The controversy over *Deshache Dushman* was heightened by a set of parallel publications that challenged Brahmin hegemony and its ritual and material enslavement of non-Brahmins. R.N. Lad, the editor of *Masur,* and Annabhau Chavan, writer of "The Marriage Ritual of the Bhats According to the Shastras, or Their Foolish Foolishness," were sentenced to nine months rigorous imprisonment for promoting communal enmity. In his piece of June 5, 1926, which described a marriage ceremony that took place in Masur on May 25, Chavan issued a challenge to "the extremely foolish, wicked, mean Bhats in Masur, the daredevil donkeys, the That sons of prostitutes, who seek the evil of the benefactor, who give the form of untruth to truth, and truth to untruth, the cruel Bhats who put the barber's rasor on the heads of their mothers and sisters." Chavan argued that Brahmins refused to tolerate the reforms of the Satyashodak Samaj because it challenged them directly. He described Brahmin priests as Go-laks, or the illegitimate offspring of "shaved widows," and warned of dire consequences if they cheated non-Brahmins or clamored for "more Dakshina" in the future.

Antagonism between Brahmins and non-Brahmins was at an all-time high in Pune in August 1926 when a young Maratha man named Hari Narayan Dhana-vade was accused of attempting to molest an eighteen-year-old Brahmin woman named Dwarakabai. An inflammatory newspaper article reported that a witness had seen "the accused in the act of moving his face towards her" when he was dragged away from his victim. Dhanavade maintained that he had been standing in a doorway, far from the incident, when he was set upon by thirty to thirty-five Brahmin youth.

Tilak's *Mahratta* editorials: "It is an insult to the womanhood of Maharashtra. To the Brahmans we have only to say one word. If they wish to live in honour then they must face the crisis with courage, manliness and bravery. They must take every step to defend the honour of their sisters and daughters. The newspaper noted the increased frequency of such incidents in the prior six years in southern Maharashtra, where a concerted campaign to boycott Brahmins had been taking place. The *Vijayi Maratha* challenged this view and noted that "public rudeness to women was originally inculcated by the Tilakites and Brahman Ganapati melas and Titillate and Brahman anti-feminist movements," and that there was an "old tradition" of "composing abusive song against educated women" and "reviling them at will." The paper went on to note that it was non-Brahmin men who had protected Brahmin women when they were abused and set upon by Brahmin men for supporting the Patel Bill.

In the first decades of the twentieth century, a set of mutually constitutive if deeply contradictory sociopolitical processes were at work: emergent forms of upper-caste female mobility and domestic modernity; the heightened centrality of Maratha genealogy and of

Kshatriya status for upwardly mobile non-Brahmin families; a long-standing critique of Brahmin hegemony and Hindu history; and finally, a burgeoning anti-colonial movement that sought political unity among disparate castes and classes and that took distinctive regional shape. Chatterjee's argument describes the logic of anticolonial nationalism as *derivative* of colonial categories and *reactive* to the colonisers discourse about the colonised, so that cultural nationalists could value the domestic intimate even as they sought to transform gendered relations within the family. Chatterjee's account addresses the affective centrality of the domestic sphere for nationalist thought, but fails to take note of the political ambiguity that surrounded this figure. Given the centrality of gender and sexual regulation to the discursive hegemony of Brahminism in western India, the Brahmin woman had long personified elements of non-Brahmin critique, even as she became the rallying point for a renewed politics of Brahminism.

In contrast to this public, explicitly confrontational, masculinity politics, Dalit reformers' masculinity was predicated on the reform of gender within their community and the defence of community honour against the disdain of outsiders. In 1908, the *Somavanshiya Mitra* published a letter from Shivubai Vallad Lakshman Jadhav-Sonkamble, who identified herself as a *murali*. *Muralis* were young girls from the Mahar, Mang, *kunbi*, and so-called nomadic communities who were married off to the god Khandoba at his temple in Jejuri in fulfillment of a vow. *Muralis* wore a *mangalsutra* of seven cowrie shells and, although human marriages were denied them, as nominal wives of the god they were obligated to provide sexual services to men. *Murali* dedication was among a range of regionally distinctive practices involving women of all statuses, which came to be glossed by the colonial state as ritual "prostitution." The lives of dedicated women, however, were more complex. Many re-mained with one partner all their lives. As temple servants, others acquired property in the form of tax-free *inam* lands. Women from Dalit and nomadic communities were historically associated with the traditions of courtly performance, especially the erotic *lavani*. By the twentieth century, they were more closely associated with *tamasha* performance, now depicted as a lewd and raunchy popular cultural form.

The legendary Pavalabai was dedicated as a *murali,* though her ex-quisite beauty and performative skills brought her to the attention of the famous Brahmin *tamasgir* Patthe Bapurao, born Sridhar Kulkarni. Pavalabi joined Patthe's troupe and became his companion. Though she was a famous performer, Pavalabai's career mirrored the reduced significance of traditional popular culture to an emergent Dalit politics and the growing presence of a reformist critique of female sexuality.

Shivubai's letter was written against this backdrop of male reformers working to abolish stigmatising practices, especially ritual dedication and sexual servitude. She responded to a letter written by a Mahar *panch* castigating *muralis* as social evils whose sexual promiscuity was ruining Dalit men and their families. Shivubai objected that she was forced to do her job by the men of her community. She noted that many women converted to Islam and Christianity to avoid prostituting themselves. Shivubai's indictment of the men who perpetuated the practice was distinctive. Her point was overwhelmed, however, by multiple and overlapping efforts to criminals the practice.

The practice of *murali* dedication was strongest near Jejuri and in southern Maharashtra, where it was associated with a distinctive inheritance practice among the Mahar and Talwar communities. In 1906, the collector of Bijapur argued that "the prevalence of the practice of dedicating girls to prostitution among the Mahars is partly attributed to the fact that the male issue of prostitute daughters are allowed to succeed to a Mahar watan" when a man dies without male offspring. Bomanji argued that even if the practice was customary, "this recognition of illegitimate children should be stopped. " On February 27, 1857, the collector of Dharwad had "brought to notice the law of inheritance prevailing among Mahars and other low castes that a man dying without male offspring could leave property to a daughter only if she was a 'professional prostitute.'" The collector noted that though it was practiced among "groups comparatively unimportant in numbers and social position," the "loathsome custom" encouraged women to lead a life of "privileged profligacy." Government Resolution no. 6788, passed on January 22, 1858 barred ownership through illegitimately. Locally, however, the practice was clearly condoned. A complex case from 1873, involving a Talwarki *watan* in the name of "Vianki Talwar," brought up questions of whether a prostitute's adopted son, or her prostitute sister's biological son should inherit her estate. In this case, as with all other cases originating in the Dharwar district, it was decided that inheritance should skip the prostitute and go directly to her male illegitimate offspring. Thus the depiction of the practice of ritual dedication as a form of sexual servitude was only partially true: *murali* reform gathered steam after female inheritance was stigmatised and Mahar and Talwar men had become beneficiaries of governing paradigms that privileged patrilineal inheritance.

By the 1890s, various missionary groups had taken up the issue and suggested punishing parents and priests who enforced the tradition and recommended the transfer of dedicated women to orphanages. N.G. Chandavarkar, a social reformer, famous justice of the Bombay High Court and a member of the Society for the Protection of Children, made similar recommendations. The figures for dedication in southern Maharashtra for the period 1905– 9, when the *murali* controversy reached its height, was as follows: 836 in Belgaum, 911 in Bijapur, and 876 in Dharwar district. The Bombay government's inquiry into the practice encompassed more than four hundred pages of testimony by district magistrates in Bombay, extensive debate on whether *murali* dedication could be criminalised, as well as far-reaching transformations of Hindu law to prevent illegitimate from inheriting— whether male offspring of *muralis* or *dasiputras* customarily entitled to a half share from a Shudra father's estate. The opinion of Dalit male reformers was not solicited, let alone the *muralis*.

Though sidelines by the government, Dalit reformers like Kamble applauded the effort and lobbied for community support. More significant, if rarely noted, is the fact that public attention to the practice of *muralis'* dedication shifted power within the community toward the viewpoint of male Dalit reformers and publicists. The degradation of Dalit women became a powerful issue around which they mobilised to demand gendered respectability through the abolition of customary practice. Debates over ritual dedication— now recast as prostitution—became crucial to the reconstitution of Dalit masculinity even as it secured the social power of publicists, pedagogues, and community spokesmen.

Shivubai's letter launched a furious debate in and beyond the *Soma-vanshiya Mitra*. Efforts were made in Jejuri to educate families against dedicating their daughters. Shivram Janba Kamble held a meeting in Jejuri where he made a speech against the practice. *Muralis* like Shivu-bai held fathers responsible for pushing their daughters into the practice and criticised male customers for creating a market for *muralis*' sexual labour. But men castigated *muralis* for seducing them and breaking up families, thereby assuming *muralis*' "consent" to their dedication. This was tricky given the normal age of dedication and its representation as customary practice. And yet, *muralis* were blamed for perpetuating a practice that stigmatised the entire community.

Increasingly, Dalit reformers—like missionaries—suggested criminalising *murali* dedication. A 1909 reformers' petition demanded the registration of *muralis* and the prosecution of parents who performed new dedications. This produced a climate among Mahars that was responsive to criminalisation of the practice. By then, the Bombay government had reached a consensus that criminalism the practice was the most direct means of curtailing it.

Although some *muralis* supported criminalising the practice of dedication, their primary focus was on redefining their position within the Dalit community. In addition to prosecuting *muralis,* Dalit reformers like Kamble also promoted *murali* marriage and sexual monogamy as the route to gendered respectability. Shivubai argued that marrying *mu-ralis* acknowledged men's responsibility for the practice, even as it en-hanced *muralis*' self-respect and community standing. In fact, on April 18, 1909, the *Somavanshiya Mitra* noted that Shivubai had married the social reformer, Ganpatrao Hanumantrao Gaikwad.Marriage offered protection in a context where men were actively involved in acquiring, dedicating, and frequenting *muralis*.

As the reform of the traditional practice of *murali* dedication came to be allied with the reform of the Dalit intimate, sexual monogamy and the production of family became appealing alternatives for Dalit men and womento whom this held out a recognisable model of respectability. Sex-ual respectability was achieved, however, through the stigmatisation of "custom" and ritual servitude or dedication.

The fraught position of female subjectivity "between community and state" is an enduring binarism in South Asian historiography. An adroit colonial move allied women with caste and religious communities and simultaneously castigated communities for reproducing female backwardness and preventing female emancipation. As the relationship between women and community deepened, first in reaction to colonial in tervention and later as a form of nationalist glorification, the possibility of gender equality was also precluded. By the turn of the century, upper-caste nationalists had recuperated women as symbols of a modernised "tradition" and relegated them to the inner recesses of community life, arguing that women would be enfranchised from within community rather than through colonial state intervention. An issue taken up largely by Christian missionaries and later by Dalit reformers, *murali* reform was distinct from this colonial-nationalist association of women with tradition. The ill treatment of the upper-caste Hindu widow by scriptural injunctions is an apt comparison, although Dalit reformists differed in their efforts to create a set of secular associations between femininity and domesticity.

As the work of regulating Dalit women continued in more dispersed forms, the degraded status of women was seen to be closely related to the emasculation of Dalit men. Fifteen years after the *murali* issue died down, an editorial by the Dalit activist and thinker B.R. Ambedkar asked why Brahmin and upper-caste women enjoyed an exalted status as mothers when Dalit women's children were subjected to humiliation and denied basic recognition, negating all the desires that a mother might have for her child's well-being. He went on to say, "You have given birth to men, and when we are treated worse than animals, it hurts you." Importantly, however, the onus was on Dalit women to reform themselves and play a central role in modernising the community. They had to resigning the gendered habitus: "You should wear your sari in the way that upper-caste women wear their saris. You incur no expense by doing so. Similarly, the many necklaces around your neck, and the silver and tin bangles you wear from wrist to elbow is a mark of identification.... If you must wear jewellery, then get gold jewellery made. If you cannot, then don't wear jewellery. Pay attention to cleanliness!"

What did these exhortations mean for women from a stigmatised community? On one hand, like upper-caste ideologies, they symbolically associated women's status with community status. On the other hand, they emphasised the significance of clothing, jewellery, and the right to ceremonial display as aspects of self-fashioning vigorously policed by upper castes. The right to a new habitus, to good clothing, footwear, jewellery, and bodily comportment was critical to Dalit self-fashioning. Though discourses of sexuality and of female enfranchisement were caste-specific, the focus on the feminised body—how it was experienced and represented—was central to a range of political processes. Thus emergent forms of a caste-specific female subjectivity were directly implicated in the production of a social field where transformations of the non-Brahmin and Dalit habitus could occur, and they deeply affected emergent forms of caste masculinity. The politics of *caste and gender* complicated modes of political participation and of subject-formation associated with masculinisation and community modernisation. In a very real sense, however, the stage was set for a Dalit public sphere rendered male.

6.2. Identity of Mahar Dalits

As a distinctive identity for Mahar Dalits was clarified in the late nineteenth century, so too were the emerging tensions of village life intensified— conflicts between Dalit and Maratha groups over provision of services, the exploitation of caste labour, and friction between claims to Brahmin proportional representation and anti-casteism increased. The situation made escape from the village highly desirable for Dalits.

Mahar Dalits migrated to cities like Bombay and Nagpur in disproportionate numbers. According to the Indian census, between 1872 and 1881 the number of Mahars in Bombay rose 66 percent. By 1938, almost 92 percent of untouchable workers in the city were Mahars. Mahars performed unskilled labour under difficult and exploitative working conditions. They were concentrated in particular industries: more than 60 percent worked in the railways or textile mills—the railways were the first and most significant mode of Mahar employment and drew a majority of workers from the Nasty and Ratnagiri districts. Significant numbers worked for the municipality, for factories, and for public works companies such as Bombay Electric Supply and Transport (BEST). Mahar migrants from Setaria comprised the bulk of dock workers and coal miners. Urban migration and urban infrastructure provoked key transformations of Dalit selfhood. *Din Bandhu*'s commentator on urban life was clear that modern travel obliterated caste distinctions, because it was impossible to maintain caste taboos or regulate contact in public conveyances. Lower-caste use of steamboats, trains, and trams opened a new dimension where touch was rendered anonymous even as it was secularised. However, these new spaces were in constant danger of being overwhelmed by social pressure to reproduce hidebound Brahminical beliefs and practices, as Valangkar's *abhang* warned.

It is likely that Valangkar's *abhang* was publicising the Din Bandhu Sarvajanik Sabha, which was formed in 1884 by Krishnarao Bhalaker and others to counter what they considered to be a Brahmin-dominated, exclusivist Sarvajanik Sabha. Valangkar drew on a set of gendered associations between social stigma and public intercourse to challenge Dalits' civic exclusion. Like a woman naturally "shy of her husband and public gatherings" when she was menstruating, Dalits also experienced "shame" and self-revulsion. One was never to see a Mang or a Mahar in public. Valangkar's *abhang* challenged the Dalit's internalisation of pollution and proposed that without equality between Brahmin and Mahar, between the excessively fortunate and the excessively stigmatised, there could be no true "public." In the interplay between literal touch and the imaginative democratisation of the body he saw possibilities for self-fashioning and political transformation. Going further, Valangkar also suggested that only with a *caste mind* cleaned of impurities could the Sarvajanik Sabha accept the Dalit castes.

Ironically, then, the institutional spaces and amenities of colonial urbanity exacerbated the experience of the caste body by highlighting the irrationality of caste segregation. As Dalit publicists denaturalised the caste order, they also motivated caste Hindus to justify caste distinction in new ways that utilised the regulatory power of colonial institutions to produce new instruments of caste hegemony.

Access to education was a long-standing demand of Dalit publicists, as it had been for Satyashodak activists. Education was central to self-fashioning because it demystified the Brahmin trickery at the heart of the continued dehumanisation of Dalits and non-Brahmins. There was also the material fact of Brahmin preponderance in colonial administration. Conflicts over access to colonial schooling emphasised the built-in contradictions of colonial education. In 1882, the Hunter Commission asserted the government of India's commitment to untouchable education, reaffirming. Wood's Dispatch of 1854, which opened government-funded schools to all castes in response to missionary pressure. For instance, the first public schools in Poona's Purandhar district opened in 1836, but by 1839 only 17 of 759 pupils came from the untouchable communities. The numbers did not rise significantly in following years. The most famous case is of the Christian Mahar convert from Dharwar who petitioned the government in June 1856 after being denied admission into the government school. The Bombay government refused to compromise the education of the majority of caste Hindu students at a government school for the sake of "a single individual" by making caste Hindus associate with a Mahar student.

The Free Church of Scotland and the American Marathi Mission had supported Phule's Society for the Promotion of Mahars and Mangs, which established schools in Pune between 1848 and 1852. The extensive involvement of missionaries in the field of untouchable education was viewed as blurring the line between proseletysation and social service, compromising the colonial state's explicit commitment to religious non-interference after the 1857 Mutiny. Colonial officials held missionaries responsible for politicising untouchables who showed "independence and self-sufficiency," by inciting them to "claim a right" even when untouchable themselves chose not to exercise it, thus exacerbating conflict between the majority of caste Hindu students and a few untouchable students.

Conflicts over equal education in the 1880s and 1890s confirmed government fears of unrest. Such an incident had taken place in Rajangaon, in Sirur *taluka,* Pune, in October 1886, when the village *patel* and *kulkarni* twice closed down a school run by the American Marathi Mission, using violence and intimidation to prevent the seven Mahar children from attending the school run by Indian teachers. Or else, as happened in Manmad, Nasty district, in 1884–85, caste Hindus financed an English class through private funds rather than sending their children to the Anglo vernacular school run by the Church Mission Society, which also admitted untouchable students. Often, the government's anxiety to maintain the population of students attending publicly funded English schools undercut the commitment to education for untouchable. Increasingly, the colonial government faced a spate of petitions as untouchable students petitioned for civic inclusion, while the parents of caste Hindu students wished to exclude untouchables from classrooms. The Bombay Education Department had considerable leeway in deciding issues on a case-by-case basis in this contentious atmosphere. As government's general commitment to native education confronted its specific commitment to untouchables' education, a novel resolution arose: Dalit students were placed on the school's verandahat adistance from both caste Hindu classmates and the classroom, to fulfill the colonial mission of educational access.

Sitting on the verandah obstructed the untouchable students' vision and hearing and left them vulnerable to the adversities of climate. In 1916, Communist activist R.B. More attended classes on the first floor of a school in Tale, in the Mangaon district, sitting on a scaffold erected by school authorities. Reinterpreting the caste Hindu position as the majority sentiment, colonial officials made the verandah a new technology of seg relation that reproduced caste exclusion.

Diploe, the hub of early Dalit activism, was also a significant site of struggles for equal education. After the Society for the Propagation of the Gospel closed down its primary school, military pensioners petitioned the government on July 1, 1892, to enrol fourteen of their children in the municipality's primary school. After asserting that admitting Dalit children would cause caste Hindu students to leave the school, the Dipole municipality agreed to open a separate class with a separate teacher if the Mahar and Chamber pensioners could collect enough boys. B. R. The children were barred from the common water supply. The right to education, when combined with new practices of segregation, paradoxically *intensified* untouchable students' experience of stigma.

The Diploe petitioners protested on September 8, 1892, requesting that the students be included in the other classrooms. When their petition was rejected by the Diploe municipality, the petitioners approached colonial officials, who asked the municipality whether the children could be accommodated on the verandah. The municipality replied that the verandah was not large enough for all the children, but that the Dalit petitioners could pay Rs. 50 to enlarge it. Stalled, the pensioners continued up the bureaucratic line until J. Nugent, commissioner of the Southern Division, told Vishnudas Hari Barve, the chairman of the municipality, that he was required to open the school to the Dalit children. The municipality responded that equal education should occur gradually in order not to offend orthodox sensibility, and by November 1894 the municipal engineer had not yet approved verandah extension. After threatening repeal of the school's grant, Director of Public Instruction K. M. Chatfield instructed the Dalit children to maintain a safe distance from other Hindu children in the classroom. A visit to the municipal school at the end of 1894 found "the Officers' children sitting in the same class rooms along with the other boys at the distance of three or four feet and receiving instruction with the class regularly."

The Dapoli pensioners were said to be satisfied, because "they never wished that their children should mix with the other boys but they wanted that they should receive instruction along with them, separately in the same class rooms, and this is now done." Almost a decade later, in 1901, the president of the ADPM sent another petition to the Bombay government, claiming that Dalit students continued to be excluded from the school. As Dalit students tried to enter schools at the turn of the twentieth century, equal right to education was converted into the right to segregated education for untouchable students: caste restrictions were respected due to fear of boycott by caste Hindu students. The school verandah was anew mechanism of exclusion that encompassed overlapping structures of exclusion. One was based on Brahminical norms that replicated caste hierarchies. The other, grounded in liberal language, acquiesced to caste Hindus' refusal of mixed-caste schools as a matter of respect for the opinions of the majority community.

Levels of education among untouchable students continued to be abysmally low: less than 0.48 percent were literate in 1911; by 1931, that number rose to 2.9 percent. In response to segregated schooling, Mahar Dalits in Nagpur, Bombay, Poona, and Amalgamator established separate schools and hostels for Dalit students in the first two decades of the twentieth century, complementing earlier work in Vidarbha and the Central Provinces. By 1908, Vithal Ramji Shinde's DCM ran fifteen day schools, six Sunday schools, and four industrial schools in Bombay, Poona, and Ahmednagar. By 1909, the DCM had even reached into Dipole. In 1916, of 1,600 Depressed Class students, 500 were enrolled in Shinde's schools. Though they were spurred by the failure of government schools to include Dalit students, separate schooling defined a powerful strategy for refashioning the Dalit self.

The Mahar community's growing refusal to countenance socioritual stigmatisation produced new sites of contestation. Like separate education facilities, efforts to build separate temples reflect an arc of Dalit critique. The economic enfranchisement of an important group of Mahar elates in the Vidarbha region enabled the institutionalisation of a separate religious authority for Mahars. The 1877 opening of Empress Mills in Nagpur had provided a new source of livelihood for Mahar Dalits. In addition, a Mahar petty bourgeoisie of *malgusars* financed the move into an industrialising cotton economy. This educated elite maintained links with rural areas, endowing schools and hostels and playing a role in shaping early Dalit politicisation.

Born in 1864, Vithoba Raoji Moon Pande typified the new Mahar "small scale capitalist" first mentioned in an 1899 settlement report for the Nagpur district. Educated in a mission school and influenced by critiques of caste hierarchy and Hindu superstition, he took advantage of his frequent travel as a cotton trader to act as a *pracharak* for the Gorakshan Sabha which had links with the Arya Samaj. In 1906, Moon Pande established the Any a Samaj, renamed the Loyal Mahar Sabha in 1912 and presided over by his close associate, the Reverend G. D. Philips. Before he died in 1924, Moon Pande had requested nomination to the Central Provinces Legislative Council. Like Valangkar, Moon Pande's life coincided with the emergence of the Dalit public and publicists in the crucible of colonial modernity.

When Mahars were denied use of the Ambal tankat Nagpur's Ramtek temple in 1903, Moon Pande mobilised a large group of Mahars who belonged to *bhajan mandalis*. They went to the home of the temple owner, Raoji Raghuji Bhosle,who gave Mahars permission to bathe at the Ambal tank on the condition that they stop eating beef and, more generally, desist from unhygienic practices. Moon Pande appears to have supported this reform because he held meetings in villages near Nagpur to persuade Mahars to stop eating beef, even demanding that they take a public oath to that effect. Although they did so, it was clear that relations with temple authorities had reached an impasse. The Ramtek Temple Committee asked Mahars to channel a portion of the fees paid to the *pande* at the *ghats* to the Gorakshan Sabha to fund separate Mahar bathing *ghats* at the temple tank. No Mahar *ghats* were built, however.

Moon Pande responded to the Brahmins' exploitation of Mahars at the Ramtek temple by establishing a separate Mahar priesthood to minister to the community's religious needs. To counter the Gorakshan Sabha's failure to build separate Mahar *ghats,* Moon Pande asked permission from the Ramtek Temple Committee to build a separate temple for Mahars on January 24, 1905. In March 1906, he acquired land for the purpose at a high price. That same year the Any a Samaj committee took over management of the new Mahar *ghats,* established an independent Mahar priesthood, and gave Moon Pande *pandeship,* the right to perform rites and receive *dakshina* from Mahar pilgrims at the *ghats.*

By 1907–08, this parallel structure of religious authority protected Mahar pilgrims from paying extravagant sums for *shraddha* rites. Moon Pande's use of Mahars' growing economic strength to assert a positive Hindu identity went further. Along with the Reverend G. D.. Construction began on October 27, 1920, and was completed in 1924, shortly before Moon Pande's death.

Separate institutions signalled failed efforts at civic and religious equality. They also indexed the changed discursive and political contexts of Dalit self-fashioning. Unlike the establishment of separate schools, Moon Pande's temple and Mahar priesthood reproduced religious hierarchy by legitimising the priest's role. At the same time, his work underscored the growing economic strength of an emerging Mahar elite whose power as reformers within the community allowed them to challenge the Hindu hierarchy. Moon Pande's actions were radical and reformist, and indicated the ambivalences of Mahar religiosity and the limits to Hindu inclusion.

Perhaps more pointed and problematic is the matter of thirteen Mahars who entered a temple dedicated to the god Meghnath, an incarnation of Shiva, in the village of Washer in Chanda district of the Central Provinces on September 22, 1922. They "slaughtered a goat there, sprinkled its blood upon the idol, put *shendur* on the image and adorned it with flowers." Though staged as religious worship, this incident blurred distinctions between the sacred and the profane because anointing a deity with goat's blood could also be interpreted as an act of defilement. The ambivalence of the animal sacrifice arose from its signifying potential as worship and defilement. If upper-caste

Hindus interpreted animal sacrifice as desecrating the temple, it is also true that temples to Shiva, a non-Brahmin god in Maharashtra, would have allowed the practice of animal sacrifice. Was it the sacrifice of the goat or the physical presence of Dalit worshippers in the temple that challenged its sacrality? Could the right to worship encompass the right to worship differently, as well as the right of Dalits to worship in a mixed-caste temple?

6.3. Dalit Activism

By the late 1920s, conditions enabling Dalit activism were well in place. The distinctive ideological and institutional contexts in which Dalits' lives were enmeshed from the later nineteenth century facilitated an incipient discourse of rights and emergent conceptions of the Dalit self as a historical actor and a political subject. Nonconformist Christianity and imaginative alliances with radical Euro-American traditions of free thought had influenced ideas of self-respect, equality, and social justice, while the radical anti-casteism of the Satyashodak Samaj associated the stigmatised existence of Dalits and non-Brahmins with the Brahmins' ritual, economic, and social domination. Ironically, Dalits' experiences with the institutional infrastructure of colonial modernity amplified the impact of stigmatisation and exclusion.

The Dalit public that coalesced in the first decades of the twentieth century reflected the changed experience of Dalitness: by the 1920s, disparate and localised challenges to the caste order had coalesced into an explicit demand for civic rights. When three thousand people gathered in the town of Mahad on March 19, 1927, for nonviolent public action, a *satyagraha* to take water from the Chavdar tank, they were testing a resolution. Three years earlier, the Mahad municipality had granted untouchables access to the town's public water sources. Apparently, civic inclusion threatened religious orthodoxy. The priest of the temple next to the tank ran through town announcing that the *satyagrahis* were not merely taking water from the tank, but were also attempting to enter the temple. Caste Hindus attacked Dalits, many of whom were severely wounded and taken to the hospital, while others sought shelter in Muslim homes. The Chavdar water tank was ritually purified soon thereafter to rid it of the polluting touch of Dalits.

One might have anticipated that such violent resistance to Dalits' claims would bring their struggle to a close. Instead, another *satyagraha* was started on December 25, 1927. A weekly letter from Mahad's district superintendent of police noted that "and bills in connection with satyagraha of untouchables at Mahad are being distributed all over Mahad and Mangaon talukas. The argument in the handbills is that... Untouchables have a right to take water from the aforesaid tank. This right must now be established."

Ten thousand people gathered in Mahad this time. They took considerable risks in participating in the *satyagraha* and faced retaliatory violence. As Dalits asserted the right to participate in the *satyagraha,* tensions between non-Brahmins and Dalits assumed an economic dimension in rural areas where Maratha or non-Brahmin landlords directly exploited Dalit labour: "We had never imagined that these issues would be publicised so quickly. But like the waving of a magic wand begging for *bhakar* and eating dead meat has stopped in Kolaba district. But in those villages where these new programs have begun are not allowed to come and go in the village, in some places wastelands given to them have been taken away."

In a spectacular challenge to the orthodoxy of religious sanctions behind caste distinction, *satyagraha* organisers, who included caste Hindus and Dalits, agreed to burn the sacred text, the Manusmriti. A longtime Brahmin associate of B.R. Ambedkar's, G.N. Sahasrabuddhe, moved the resolution to burn the text at Mahad. Ambedkar, who had read portions of the Manusmriti with a pundit in the months before the conference, had with him a copy of those segments concerned with the punishment and social exclusion of women and Shudras. Those portions were burned in public rejection of caste hierarchy and sanctioned violence. Ambedkar acknowledged the debt to the techniques and strategies of popular nationalism, comparing this rejection of the caste order with the burning of foreign cloth by Indian nationalists to challenge colonial exploitation. Both cases were examples of spectacular refusals of oppressive sociopolitical orders.

The events of 1927 marked a significant departure in Dalit politics and inaugurated urban-centered regional association forms. The Bombay-based Bahishkrit Hitakarini Sabha was the organisational force behind the Mahad *satyagraha*. Also known as the Depressed Classes Institute, the BHS was formed on July 20, 1924, to promote education and social reform among Mahar Dalits. In Bombay, it established a free reading room, a Students' Conference, and a Mahar Hockey Club. In its early phase, the BHS undertook joint programs with organisations such as the Social Service League dominated by caste Hindu reformers. BHS activists intervened in village-level conflicts and held Bahishkrit Parishads across the Bombay-Konkan region.

Throughout the interwar years, new conceptions of public access and civic inclusion animated Dalit public action. As radicalised Dalits made bold public rights claims and launched an attack on the symbols of caste orthodoxy, they enlarged their repertoire of activism as well as their conceptual vocabulary of politics.

References

Karve Iravati and V.M. Dandekar. *Anthropometric Measures of Maharashtra,* Poona, Deccan College. 1951.

Kothari Rajni (ed.) *Caste in Indian Politics,* New Delhi, Orient Longman. 1970.

Lele Jayant K. and Rajendra Vera (eds.). *State and Society in India,* Delhi, Chanakya. 1990.

Pradhan M.C. *Political Systems of the Jats of Northern India,* London, OUP. 1966.

Roy Ramashray and Richard Sisson (eds.) *Diversity and Dominance in Indian Politics,* Vol. 2, New Delhi, Sage. 1966.

Srinivas M.N. *The Dominant Caste and Other Essays,* Delhi, U.P. 1989.

7

Caste Reservations in Education

This chapter examines the contemporary reality of schooling of children belonging to Scheduled Caste and Scheduled Tribe communities who have been historically excluded from formal education the former due to their oppression under caste feudal society and the latter due to their spatial isolation and cultural difference and subsequent marginalisation by dominant society. There are thus sharp differences between these two categories of population in terms of socioeconomic location and the nature of disabilities. However, there is also growing common ground today in terms of conditions of economic exploitation and social discrimination that arise out of the impact of iniquitous development process. Concomitantly, the categories themselves are far from homogenous in terms of class, region, religion and gender and what we face today is an intricately complex reality.

For a society that had lived for a millennium by a value system based on division and hierarchy, classically manifested in the system of caste-feudal patriarchy, the post-independent Constitutional commitment to social equality and social justice marked a watershed in its historical evolution. A synthesis of two ideologically divergent principles i.e. the principle of merit and the principle of compensation – constituted the modern Indian political discourse on equality and was operationalised in the establishment of democratic socialism and the welfare state. Along with guaranteeing equality of citizenship, the state assumed the primary responsibility for compensating for histories of discrimination, exploitation and marginalisation and providing special support to the Scheduled Castes and Scheduled Tribes. As is well known, the Scheduled Castes (henceforth SC) and Scheduled Tribes (henceforth ST) are not sociological but administrative categories of population identified by the Constitution of India for compensatory discrimination and special protection. They intend to comprise those who were at the bottom and margins respectively, of the Indian social order – vis. Caste groups who because of their low ritual and social status in the traditional social hierarchy and tribal groups because of their spatial isolation and distinctive cultures have been subject to impositions of disabilities and lack of opportunity.

Special state institutions were set up for the advancement of SC/ST and various legalisation, social policies and programmes were drafted which were geared to their economic and political development and achievement of equal social status. It has been difficult however, to identify these categories in terms of criteria laid down by the state. The 'problem' of the scheduled tribes has been a vexed one, given the various levels of social and cultural distance and varying degrees of voluntary or forced assimilation exploitation and/or displacement. In fact, it has been pointed out by Galanter that just where the line between Scheduled Tribes and non-Scheduled Tribes is to be drawn has not been clear. There are problems of overlap with caste and controversy whether a specific group is more appropriately classified as a ST or SC. Policy however treats the SC and ST groups homogeneously. Moreover it rests largely on the assumption that mainstreaming is progress, while paying lip service to preserve distinctive cultures, especially of tribals who are coerced into assimilation.

Education was perceived as crucial to processes of planned change. It was seen as the key instrument for bringing about a social order based on value of equality and social justice. Expansion and democratisation of the education system was sought, the two primary egalitarian goals of which were the universalisation of elementary education and the educational "upliftment" of disadvantaged groups. The State's special promotional efforts have undoubtedly resulted in educational progress for the SC/ST especially in regions where policy implementation combined with the dynamism of reform, and most crucially with anti-caste, dalit, tribal and religious conversion movements.

The last two decades have spelt the decline of the Welfare State under the powerful impact of global economic forces and neo-liberal economic policies. The egalitarian ethic underlying planned change and development is being rapidly decimated. The ideology of the Indian State's New Economic Policy emphasises the pre-eminence of markets and profits. In the context of an elite directed consensus on the inevitability of liberalisation and structural adjustment, the predominant problems and debates of education have undergone major shifts. Structural adjustment have provided the legitimacy and impetus for a number of educational reforms that pose a direct threat to the mission of universalising elementary education and equalising educational opportunity for SC/ST, especially those left behind. The state is withdrawing from social sectors of education and health and delegating its social commitments and responsibilities to private agencies and non-governmental organisations.

7.1. Educational Status of Scheduled Communities

7.1.1. The Scheduled Castes

The Scheduled Castes constitute around 16 per cent of the Indian population today. There are marked state and regional variations in terms of these proportions. Punjab has the highest proportion at 28 per cent. Among the larger states, (barring the North Eastern, where high tribal concentrations exist) Gujarat has the smallest percentage of SCs at 7.41%. From a sociological point of view, apart from their increasing visibility the most significant contemporary fact concerning the Scheduled Castes is their growing political assertion and identity formation as 'dalit'. As pointed out by Beteille, it is not easy to form a single consistent view of the present position of the Scheduled Castes because the regional diversity is so large and the balance between continuity and change so uncertain. Whereas in the past the social condition of the Scheduled Castes was governed strongly by the ritual opposition of purity and pollution, the calculus of democratic politics has become important today.

Urban migration, education, occupational change and religious conversion have been pursued by the scheduled castes as key strategies of socioeconomic emancipation, status change and acquisition of a new social identity. They have achieved varying degrees of success.

Anti caste and dalit movements have provided the bases for political consciousness and assertions of new self-consciousness and new self-respecting collective identities grounded in both moderate-reformist and radical ideologies. Contemporarily, the rigours of pollution, social practices of untouchability and social relations of servility vary greatly in different parts of the country. The widespread upsurge of atrocity signifies continued caste based oppression. Caste and occupation were closely interlinked in the traditional socioeconomic order, and the lowest manual and menial occupations were reserved for the SC. The link has gradually been broken but not completely. There have been shifts to caste free occupations. Changes took place with the arrival of new opportunities in rural employment and petty business as well as through education based occupational and social mobility in rural and urban contexts. However, economic exploitation and economic disadvantage and continued concentration in menial occupations continue to sustain and reinforce the degraded social position of the majority of the SC. Rural SC are predominantly landless and impoverished agricultural labour. Women are multiply subordinated.

In general the reduction of disparities and inclusion within "mainstream" urban and rural society has taken place in predominantly stigmatised, exploited and oppressive ways for vast sections of SC, particularly for those located in the relatively more tradition-bound and socio-economically "backward" states/areas. Under the post 90s impact of global processes the poorest SC have been most adversely affected and become more poverty stricken. Studies have pointed out to growing incidence of poverty, rising levels of rural unemployment, wage squeeze, rising levels of mortality and illness as well as declining levels of consumption shares, real wages and consumer monthly per capita expenditure among the SC.

7.1.2. The Scheduled Tribes

A conspicuous trait of Indian culture is the survival of tribal society and culture in the midst of a rapidly changing society. Scheduled Tribes who inhabit isolated mountainous regions were not appropriated into the agriculture based kingdoms of the plains, in the absence of easy communication and transport facilities. Kosambi identifies the spread of Brahmanism and its rigid subordination of individual to social function with the spread of a more productive agrarian order.

According to the Census of 2001, the Scheduled Tribes, constitute 8.1% of the Indian population. In absolute terms, this comes to some 83.6 million people, classified under 461 different communities. They are spread over the entire country but are most heavily concentrated in central, eastern and northeastern India. Two broad types of scheduling vis. Area based and community based exist for tribes. Areas under the Fifth Schedule belong to nine major states of western and central region extending from Maharashtra on the West to Jharkhand in the East. Vulnerable tribal population of some states are left out however, such as in West Bengal, Karnataka, Tamil Nadu and Kerala. The Sixth Schedule applies to tribal areas in states of the North East.

Unlike the relatively dispersed SC population, about 90 percent of the Scheduled Tribes are found in a few states. Orissa and Madhya Pradesh have more than 20 percent. More than 50 percent lives in parliamentary constituencies where they form the majority. They are defined partly by habitat and geographic isolation but more on the basis of social religious, linguistic and cultural distinctiveness. The ST occupy a belt stretching from the Bhil regions of western India through the Gond districts of central India, to Jharkhand and Bengal where the Mundas, Oraons and Santhals predominate. There are also pockets of Scheduled Tribe communities in the south and very small endangered communities in the Andamans. Northeast India contains a large proportion of the Scheduled Tribe population, including the different Naga sub-tribes.

Tribes represent differing levels opposing cultural principle of organising life due to varying histories of assimilation and exploitation. Colonialism marked a turning point in the history of tribals. Economic interests of the colonists required large scale acquisition of natural resources, reducing tribals to positions of economic and cultural subservience to non-tribal communities. Forced absorptions have continued to take place at the behest of the aggressive dominant economic and political forces. Analysing the post colonial situation, Desai classifies the tribes according to various stages of cultural development which gives some broad idea of the variation. Class I are the "purest of pure" ST groups. Problems of the relatively isolated Scheduled Tribe population are qualitatively different and demand different solutions; class II include those having contact with plains; class III – is the largest section in a peculiar stage of transition.

They are looked upon as – "backward" Hindus, ST only in name, having been uprooted from the tribal mode by bonded slavery. Like the Scheduled castes, the consequence of 'mainstreaming' through education and/or employment has occurred for them but largely at the lower echelons. Christian missionaries have been responsible for spreading education among tribal population in various parts of the country – a development which had diverse social and political consequences for the tribes. Importantly, political assertion, middle class entry and like the SC, is the creation of a gap between tribal elates and the rest. Class IV tribes are an old autocracy – for e.g. the powerful Bhil, wealthy Santhal and Oraon, Mundas, who won historical battles of cultural contact. North Eastern tribal society, located in the peripheral extreme eastern region came under both colonial and Christian influences. However, the magnitude of the Christian impact as a motive force to modernisation has varied between these tribal regions. On the whole, small sections of tribal groups have benefited while majority remain impoverished.

Capitalist onslaught on the tribal way of life by the Indian state and by national and global business interests have brought about further economic ruin. Large scale alienations and dispossession from land and natural resources, and displacement due to mega development projects such as big dams, power plants etc. Have pushed the tribals into conditions of stark economic deprivation. Those who once led a bountiful existence now struggle for basic livelihood. As pointed out by Chalam scores of studies show how these processes have worked in tribal dominated regions. Post 90's the flow of funds for Tribal Sub-Plans are declining, worsening the bad situation created by a faulty implementation strategy, since its inception in the Fifth Five Year Plan.

7.1.3. State Provision for Education of SC and ST

State commitment to the education of SC/ST children is contained in Articles 15(4), 45 and 46 of the Indian Constitution. Article 15(4) underscores the state's basic commitment to positive discrimination in favour of the socially and educationally backward classes and/or the SC and ST. Article 45 declares the state's endeavour to provide free and compulsory education for all children until they complete the age of 14 years. Article 46 expresses the specific aim to promote with special care the educational and economic interests of SC/ST. In its effort to offset educational and socio-historical disadvantage, the Indian state conceived a range of enabling provisions that would facilitate access to and ensure retention of SC and ST children in school. In the initial Five Year Plans, the focus was on making available basic educational facilities such as schools especially in remote areas and providing scholarships and books. Both Central and State governments took up the responsibility of special educational provision. The scope of enabling interventions expanded considerably after the Fourth Five Year Plan.

Special schemes pertaining to school education of SC/ST children currently include:

1. Free supply of textbooks and stationery at all stages of school education
2. Free uniforms to children in govt. Approved hostels and Ashrams schools, and in some states also for children in regular schools;
3. Free education at all levels;
4. Pre-matric stipends and scholarships to students at middle and/or high school stage;
5. Special scheme of pre-matric scholarships for children of castes and families engaged in unclean occupations like scavenging, tanning and flaying of animal skin;
6. Girls and boys hostels for SC/ST students and lodging facilities in hostels of backward classes including SC/ST;
7. Ashram schools for tribal children started with the intention of overcoming the difficulties of provision in remote regions and also rather patronisingly to provide an environment "educationally more conducive" than the tribal habitat.

In addition, several states have instituted schemes such as scholarships to SC students studying in private schools, merit scholarships, attendance scholarships for girls, special school attendance prises, remedial coaching classes, reimbursement of excursion expenses and provision of midday meals. The last has been recommended as an integral element in schooling by the Working group on Development and Welfare of the Scheduled Castes during the Eighth Five Year Plan.

Several studies carried out in the initial decades after independence and in particular, the landmark Report of the Commission of SC/ST of 1986-87 showed that educational progress till the mid 80's was slow and uneven.

The following section attempts to capture the current picture of school educational advance of SC and ST children in the country and the states.

7.1.4. School Participation of SC and ST Children

The examination of recent trends in enrolment, attendance and dropout for SC/ST children is hampered by absence of relevant and complete statistical data. The main sources which have been utilised are the Census, Statistical Publications of the Ministry for Human Resource Development, the NSSO, Reports of Commissioner and Commission for SC/ST. We have also drawn upon existing studies.

The situation of literacy provides a rough indication of overall educational progress as well as serves as an index of past educational opportunity. The rural female ST literacy rate has doubled since 1991 but is still the lowest at 32.4%. Sharp differences persist between the general population and SC/ST population in rural areas.

7.1.5. Education of Scheduled Castes

The growing demand for schooling and its utilisation among Scheduled Castes is reflected in the significant increase in both enrolment ratios and attendance rates. Enrolment ratios (percent enrolment of population in age-group corresponding to the standards) as is very well known, are not reliable indicators of educational progress due to considerable inflation caused by over reporting and enrolment of overage children. For the Scheduled Castes in India, the ratios stand at 111.91 percent and 61.33 per cent respectively at the primary and middle levels in 1995-96. They range from a high of 263.3 in Maharashtra to a low of 26.2 percent in Arunachal Pradesh at the primary level. At the middle level, Assam ranks first with an enrolment ratio of 176.16 per cent and Arunachal Pradesh is again last with 17 per cent. Among the larger states, where SC population percentage is significant, SC enrolment is poorest in states which are known to be overall socio-economically backward vis. UP, Bihar, Orissa etc.

Among the large states also having substantial SC population, Rajasthan, Uttar Pradesh and West Bengal emerge as poorest performers at the primary level. Their enrolment per cent does not match their percentage in the population. In the rest of the states school participation of SC is satisfactory in these terms. However, at the middle level, in as many as eight States enrolment per cent is much lower than population. Surprisingly, this list also includes Tamil Nadu.

Current school participation data for the 6-14 year age group, however, considerably deflates the scenario of impressive gains in enrolment and suggests that the task of enlisting continued educational participation continues to be enormous. Firstly, Non-attendance among Scheduled Castes is higher than among the general population rates (around 20 % in the 6-10 and 29 % in the 11-14 year age group in 1998). The corresponding percentages for the general population are 16 per cent and 23 per cent.

The percentage of non-attendance is higher in rural (19.3 %) as compared to urban urban areas (9.7 %). It is lower among rural girls as compared to rural boys (23.4 % and 15.4 % respectively). Recently however, attendance rates are believed to have risen in hitherto educationally backward states under the impact of a spate of new government schemes and programmes directed at attaining the elusive goal of universalisation of elementary education. Large gains are claimed among SC and ST groups and girl children. In Rajasthan for instance, it is claimed that the increase was to the tune of more than 20 per cent. One will have to await detailed educational data from census 2001 and NSSO to confirm these perceived trends.

The attendance rates for Rural SC boys and girls for the year 1993-94, lagged behind "other" presumably "forward" caste boys and girls in almost all states where SC population is significant. Expectedly, attendance rates are the highest in Kerala. They are lowest for boys in Bihar – only 46 per cent. Rural girls in Rajasthan are the worst off at an abysmal 21.5 per cent. Rural SC girls also have low participation rates in Andhra Pradesh, Madhya Pradesh, Orissa and Uttar Pradesh. Gender gaps within the SC are also sizeable in most states except Himachal, Kerala and Assam. It is also important to note that in some state like Punjab for instance, though SC attendance rates are higher than the national rates, the gap between SC and non-SC is quite large. The gender gap is also smaller but in certain states like Madhya Pradesh and Rajasthan it is still quite large. This is also true of Maharashtra, an advanced state as far as education of SC is concerned.

Marked disparities also exist within the Scheduled Castes for e.g. between the relatively advanced Mahar-Buddhists and Chambers on the one hand and the Mangs on the other in Maharashtra. Similarly, between Malas and Madigas in Andhra Pradesh, Pallars and Parayars in Tamil Nadu, the Ad-Dermis and Mashabis in Punjab. In Bihar the Musahars are in a state of acute educational backwardness.

The impact of poor attendance and dropout is readily visible in completion rates of elementary schooling, which are far poorer for SC as compared to higher caste groups. NFHS data show that only around 50 percent of children aged 10-14 years completed primary school and 42 percent have completed middle school in 1998-99. Caste-wise desegregation shows that Scheduled Caste children compare poorly with non scheduled caste groups. Only 43 per cent SC children completed primary schooling, and 42 per cent completed middle school in the respective age groups. Corresponding figures for the 'other' castes are much higher at 58 percent and 63 percent.

Another study points to sharp inter-state differences in completion rates of children aged 12 and 16 years. Primary school completion rates for Scheduled Castes are relatively high in Kerala (96 % for SC as compared to 100 % for the other castes). Maharashtra (79.21 %) lags behind Kerala. In Tamil Nadu the rate stands at 41.96 percent. Rajasthan (35.15 %) and Uttar Pradesh (30.52 %) are the most poorly off. However, the proportion of children who completed primary school is relatively low. West Bengal has a most shockingly low completion rate of only 19.28 percent for the SC children aged twelve. Middle school completion rates for sixteen year old SC children range from a low of 21 per cent in Bihar and 31 per cent in Rajasthan to 74 per cent in Maharashtra, 63.89 per cent in Tamil Nadu and 90.8 per cent in Kerala.

7.1.6. Education of Scheduled Tribes

Enrolment ratios for scheduled tribe children stand at 113.03 per cent and 50.04 per cent respectively at the primary and middle levels of schooling in 1995-96. They range from 184.18 per cent in Assam to 12.38 per cent in Goa at the primary level and from 104.7 per cent in Assam to 16.1 per cent in Goa at the middle level. At middle level, the rates come down substantially except in Assam, Kerala and Lakshadweep, where they are over 100 per cent. In Himachal Pradesh, Manipur, Misoram, Nagaland and West Bengal, they are much higher than the natural average of 50 per cent. Arunachal Pradesh has the lowest enrolment ratios among North Eastern states.

In all states, except in Madhya Pradesh, Orissa and Rajasthan, the situation is satisfactory. At the middle level however, Maharashtra and Gujarat join this group of states. Even in Kerala one notes that ST enrolment percent in standard VI-VIII falls short of population percent, even if slightly so! Net enrolments rates were estimated by the 1994 NCAER household survey. The gap between ST and non-ST children in the 6-14 years age group was as large as 17 per cent. Further, according to NCAER survey in rural areas, ST children had the lowest ever-enrolment rates (EER) in 1994 (68% among boys and 52% among girls) as compared to children in general (77% among boys and 65% among girls) and Other Hindus in particular (83% among boys and 71% among girls).

Rural school attendance rates of Scheduled tribe children are highest in Sikkim, Misoram, Nagaland, Andaman and Nicobar, Manipur, Meghalaya and Assam. In Andhra Pradesh, Bihar, Madhya Pradesh and Orissa the other states where ST population is significant they are lowest. For ST rural girls in these states they are 27.1, 29.8, 34.2 and 32.3 per cent respectively. In urban areas, the pattern is more or less repeated with the same states doing well and badly.

Drop out among ST continues to be high. A majority of ST children who enrol in class I drop out within a few years of entering school. Official dropout rates of tribal children from school in 1988-89 were as high as 78 per cent between classes I and VIII. Almost 65 per cent of tribal children leave school between classes I and V. Dropout rates are extremely high among girls in general (68 per cent) and tribal girls in particular (82 per cent). Classwise enrolment at the primary stage also suggest that the sharpest drop in enrolment of tribal children is between classes I and II. There exist sharp differences between the states in terms of most indications of educational progress. Intra-tribal variations in education must also prevail as suggested by literacy data. The Naga tribe of Meghalaya is the most highly literate. In Arunachal Pradesh, a huge gap in literacy is indicated between Khamiyargs and Panchan Morpa and in Orissa between Kulies (36.4 per cent) and Mankirdias (1.1 per cent). Specific studies of educational disparities between and within tribal groups need to be done.

7.1.7. Situation of Persistent Unequal Access

Several crucial points directly emerge from the brief survey reported above. Regional studies which we have not reviewed here due to constraints of space have brought out the others points. Firstly, a significant proportion of Scheduled Caste and an even greater proportion of Scheduled Tribe children continue to remain out of school. This is so even in the younger age group, indicating that accessing basic school is still a problem, especially in certain states and regions which have suffered gross neglect by the polity and State. Secondly, and on a more positive note and notwithstanding the tendency of deliberate overestimation, there is an unprecedented rise in enrolment of both Scheduled castes and Scheduled tribes, which indicate a strong desire for education. Thirdly, and a dampener on the situation is that attendance rates at both primary and middle school and completion rates are far from satisfactory. This indicates that dropout, failure are problems that afflict SC/ST children to a far greater degree than the rest and they thus continue to lag behind them in terms of educational attainment. Fourthly, there is great unevenness in the educational participation of the various states, and between regions/ pockets. In some states progress is very good for both boys and girls but in others it is very poor. In most states girls are far behind the boys. There are also sharp disparities between rural urban areas. Even in the relatively advanced states like Maharashtra, Tamil Nadu and Punjab there are marked regional, intra SC/ST and gender disparities on all educational indicators. Fifthly, though we have not done a systematic comparative analysis, Scheduled tribes appear to lag behind the Scheduled castes in most of the larger states barring of course the North East. Finally, there is a strong indication that specific regions and specific SC and ST groups face extreme and gross educational deprivation, within which the situation of girls is abominable.

It is clear that the country still struggles to ensure equitable access to SC/ST, while the resolve to universalise elementary education and equalise educational opportunity was to incorporate notions of equality of access, equality of survival and equality of learning achievement. Gender, caste, tribe and class inequalities exist in access, retention and years of completed schooling. Disparities in scholastic achievement an area where we have little systematic comparative data are even more glaring as revealed by a few micro studies. In sum, despite considerable quantitative progress, exclusion remains a depressing feature of the educational scenario of SC/ST children.

Poverty and exploitation, displacement and forced migration in search of livelihood and economic betterment are some of the consequences that arise out of forces of polarised class formation, expansion of informal economy. The SC and ST are disproportionately affected by these processes. Sociocultural practices of exclusion and discrimination continue to define the existence of the poor Scheduled Castes. Scheduled Tribes are increasingly sucked into the vortex of rural and urban exploitation and inequality. Several studies have affirmed that educational inequality (of access and achievement) has multiple bases in the contemporary structures of caste, class, gender and ethnicity evolving in interaction with political economy. They show that caste-class relations and values of cultural oppression are crucial to denial of education. There is a lack of basic material condition including situations of acute poverty. It has been quite emphatically established that a sizeable section of the population is too poor to avail of education which is far from free and entails unforgettable costs. One recent study with an all India sample has lent ample credence to the assertion that poverty and caste act as fundamental deterrents to education. The phenomenon of labouring children exists and so do situations of hunger, under/malnourishment and ill health among low caste/class and tribes. Casteism breeds low self-esteem. Dominant cultural capital, knowledge, skills of schools are lacking among the SC/ST.

Class along with caste and other forms of minority ethnicity are today a fundamental category of social exclusion. For the SC and ST caste, tribal ethnicity and class are reproduced in a variety of ways in relation to school. Traditional systems have undergone tremendous change and assumed complex forms deriving out of the ascendance of capitalist economies and labour markets and of systems of political patronage which thrive in the name of democracy. New sociopolitical forces combine with the old and mediate through community, family, culture and ideology to adversely affect dalit and tribal communities and influence educational access and participation of their children.

Gender, the oldest basic category of subordination militates against women and girls of SC and increasingly ST communities. Today Scheduled castes and tribal communities, some of whom have had histories of egalitarianism, are patriarchal. Women hold largely subordinated positions in the modern organisation of public and private labour. The role for girls in such communities is to rear children and carry out domestic labour, i.e. engagement in the reproduction of reproductive order. Girl's education this is not divorced from patriarchal structures of early marriage and motherhood and compulsory productive labour. Education is considered a male cultural resource. Informal labour market is also caste/gender segmented. Dalit women and girls are located in the dual labour market – in agricultural and caste labour in rural areas and informal low paying sector in urban areas. Combined together, the realities of reproductive (domestic) / productive (wage) labour, shape education choices of girls, which are actually choices of their families and communities. Even if the cultural atmosphere is changing now there are real limits. For women, changing caste relations have meant a bleak class reality in which there is no guarantee hence no motivation for education. Structural constraints are as yet strong and real for the SC and ST. We move now to examine the Indian schooling system and what it offers to SC/ST children.

7.2. Unequal Diffusion and Provision of Schooling

Historically, the education of both the Scheduled Castes and Scheduled Tribes has been adversely affected by the ubiquity of unequal diffusion and provision of schooling. For several decades after independence, their habitations were not adequately provided with educational facilities due to paucity of resources and the gap between the massive scale of the required operation and the political will equally of state and society. The situation improved over the years, yet inadequate provision continues to serve as the most fundamental of educational deterrents to educational participation of SC / ST children. What is most alarming is the reversal today of earlier policy of equitable provision under the impact of structural adjustment. We will examine this issue shortly.

Existing schooling conditions for SC/ST range from non-provision and under provision to the provision of the most inferior facilities, even at the basic primary level. Pre-primary education for them is even more minimal. The spread of schooling is a politico-economic process and disparities in educational access have been the direct consequence of a massively uneven diffusion of schooling. Furthermore, both the spread and organisation of the Indian education system reflect quite clearly the caste-class-tribe-gender stratified structure of society and its hierarchical ideology. The schooling system is organised in a pyramidical hierarchy in terms of quality and social composition. Urban elite schools rank at the top and rural schools especially those located in SC and ST habitations rank at the bottom in terms of quality. Low caste and tribal children are disproportionately located in the worst schools. The effective result has been continued educational deprivation and exclusion.

There are several dimensions of unequal provision and unequal quality vis:

1. Inadequate availability of schools
2. Poor implementation of school level policies of positive discrimination
3. Poor physical infrastructure of schools
4. Inadequacy of teachers and teaching
5. Poor provision of teaching learning materials

7.2.1. Inadequate Availability of Schools

Geographical location continues to be a significant predictor of whether a child will attend school, how far she will continue in school and in what type of school. Schooling within easy access has been relatively poor for the SC/ST children as compared to the general population.

Scheduled Caste families, usually live in spatially segregated clusters or habitations in multicaste villages. These residential patterns have important implications for physical and social access. School provision in predominantly Scheduled Caste habitations is much less as compared to general rural habitations. Upper-primary schooling (schools/sections) is available within an even smaller number of habitations. On the whole, higher caste habitations within larger villages are better provided. In multi caste village, hierarchical norms still govern social relations. "Social" accessibility is a problem exclusively of Scheduled Castes and of others even worse off like denotified and nomadic tribes.

Scheduled Tribe communities especially those residing in interior and inaccessible areas have had a very raw deal. As Sujatha points out, interior habitations are small in size, scattered, and sparsely populated. Most of the predominantly ST habitations are bereft of basic infrastructure facilities like transport and communication. The situation improved with the operationalisaton of the Tribal Sub-Plan and got a further boost with the formulation of NPE in 1986. Data from two surveys show that the number of habitations having schools within 1 km of habitations has increased and a higher percentage of ST population is covered. The Sixth All-India Educational Survey shows that 78 per cent of Scheduled Tribe population and 56 per cent of Scheduled Tribe habitations have been provided primary schools within the habitation. Another 11 per cent of Scheduled Tribe population and 20 per cent of Scheduled Tribe habitations have schools within less than 1 km radius. This however, has not solved the access problem because of the difficult terrain. Around one-fifth of total Scheduled Tribe population faces this problem and another 10 per cent have to commute to schools beyond distances of 2 kms.

Wider interstate variations exist in the provision of schools at the primary level. Misoram and Gujarat have the highest percentage of population and habitations covered. Bihar occupies the lowest position and in several states vis. Andhra Pradesh, Rajasthan, Orissa and Madhya Pradesh the situation is unsatisfactory with schools located more than a kilometre away. Furthermore a large number of them have schools only at a distance of more than 1 km. The non-availability of middle / high school in the vicinity places further limitations on educational motivations and aspirations of ST children. Several micro studi... also reveal the continued state of abysmal provision in many tribal poc' ts.

What we can surmise from the overall scenario is that though there has generally been a marked improvement in provision over the last few decades, there are still areas and caste and tribe groups that are left out of the provision net. The micro studies referred to above provide better indication about who and where these groups are located. It is critical to address the need of these educationally neglected groups.

Impact of Structural Adjustment Policies on Educational Provision and Implications for Scheduled Castes and Scheduled Tribes: Structural adjustment policies have led to following developments in education:

1. Privatisation—i.e. the expansion of private funded educational institutions at all levels of education,
2. Narrow skill/knowledge based education geared to meeting the demands of the economy,
3. Budget cuts on education and slashing of teacher salaries in the interests of economy measures and positions, and
4. Aadopting narrow market oriented definitions and discourses of excellence,
5. Aadvocating foreign borrowing for funding of basic educational commitments and making education a component of the safety net,
6. Iinvolving NGOs as a support or replacement for the state delivery system, and
7. Advocation of a state withdrawal from all social sectors including the sector of education. Studies have noted that private schooling are playing a growing role in elementary education, a fact that government reports and statistics obscure.

There is proliferation of private schools for the poor in urban, mofuzzil and rural areas. Unrecognised schools, which are not accounted in official statistics, have mushroomed in cities, towns and in the larger villages. The NCERT survey estimated around 38,000 unrecognised primary schools in rural India.

The policy of privatisation in education has enabled access of SC/ST children to private schools. However, the overwhelming majority of SC children continue to avail mainly of government schooling. According to the Sixth All-India Educational Survey, 91.3 per cent of SC children in rural primary schools and 64.6 per cent in urban areas were in schools managed by government and local bodies. At the middle stage, a relatively larger proportion of Scheduled Caste children were enrolled in privately managed schools, though expectedly this is more in urban (49.6 per cent) as compared to rural areas (32.9 per cent).

There is a distinct trend towards SC enrolment in private elementary schools. As much as 32 per cent of the increase in primary school enrolment among Scheduled Caste boys was accounted for by private unaided (PUA) schools between 1986 and 1993. In rural areas PUA schools accounted for a relatively smaller proportion of the increase in enrolment during this period, around 7 per cent for Scheduled Caste boys and 4 per cent for Scheduled Caste girls. However, the commercialisation and commodification of education that privatisation entails, results in poor educational effects for SC/ST children. In a desperate bid to stay in the struggle for mobility, they avail private education in the faith that it is better quality education. In actuality however, private education for the poor is largely of an inferior quality. The cost is exorbitant and the sacrifices made to meet them are not eventually worth them.

State response to growing public demand for 'quality' education has been to launch innovative efforts on behalf of hitherto neglected segments, such as Lok Jumbish of Rajasthan and EGS of Madhya Pradesh etc. They have had some visible positive impact. In Madhya Pradesh for instance, the number of formal primary schools increased from 16,548 in 1990-1 to 18,716 in 1998-9. During the same period Alternative Schools, 10,626 EGS schools, and 1133 TWD schools have been established. As a result number of schools nearly doubled from 19,295 in 1992-93 to 34, 131 in 1998-99. There is also the case of West Bengal however, where the state government sponsored alternative system of Shishu Shiksha Kendras is having encouraging results. However, impacts of alternative schools and educational innovations need to be continuously and carefully assessed. Leclerq's critical evaluation of functioning of the Education Gurantee Scheme in SC and ST dominated districts of Madhya Pradesh sounds a worthy caution.

7.2.2. Poor Implementation of Positive Discrimination

A crucial dimension of unequal provisioning is the woeful implementation of the enabling programmes meant to facilitate and support the schooling of SC and ST children. For several years after independence, many of these programmes had a very limited implementation, and their operation suffered from stark bureaucratic apathy. Yearly reports of the Commissioner for SC/ST and of other groups set up from time to time to look into welfare of these groups and academic studies have brought the situation to light. It is undeniable that despite several shortcomings, special schemes had a key role to play in facilitating social mobility and status change for SC and ST and the creation of political leadership. However, the coverage of programmes continues to be inadequate and there is no monitoring arrangement for the actual operation of these programmes, quantifying achievement targets and determining financial outlays. Thus, the actual benefits are limited and accrue largely to the relatively more powerful and better off SC and ST groups. Poor implementation reduces them much more. Quantitative expansion usually occurs as a result of political pressures and enhanced awareness. Gross inadequacies continue to exist aggravated by the changing socioeconomic context and nature of the state.

7.2.2.1. Pre-Metric Scholarships

While the programme of scholarships and stipends has significantly grown, there are some weaknesses which have to be noted carefully. The coverage under the assistance programme increases as one moves up the educational ladder. Every SC and ST student subject to certain conditions is eligible for a pre-metric scholarship. But at the higher secondary level the coverage is much smaller and there is hardly any assistance at the elementary level. This has created a situation in which those people who have been able to cross the initial hurdle at the primary and secondary level are able to move up with comparative ease but those who are unable to cross even the first hurdle are doomed for life. There is also great delay in receipt of scholarship.

7.2.2.2. Ashram Schools

Despite the fact that the vast majority of tribal children study in government day schools, a fair-sized achievement both in terms of money and coverage is claimed for Ashram schools. The SC/ST Commissioner reports have provided some data on the functioning of the schools. The inefficiency, mismanagement, nepotism and corruption besetting the Ashram Schools are well documented by B.K. Roy Burman years ago and B.D. Sharma more recently. They have commented upon the shortcomings of the voluntary agencies who run Ashram schools, pointing out the sub-standard level of education given in these institutions, poor hostel facilities, the use of inmates as unpaid, forced labour, etc. Other observers have also noted evils rampant in the system.

A few recent studies have given detailed accounts of the appalling living and educational conditions prevalent in ashram schools in Gujarat, Karnataka, Maharashtra and Andhra Pradesh. Poorly constructed structures, overcrowding, lack of basic provisions such as toiletries, uniforms and fans for children, alienating environments, inadequacy of number and quality of teaching staff, lack of regular inspection are some of the problems that have been highlighted. Clear vested interests from politically- influential sections among tribal groups as well as others have developed in sanctioning and management of Ashram schools leading to many malpractices and much corruption. On the whole, the schools have reached out to very small proportions. Only the relatively better off tribal groups seem to access them and there are limits to how much they can increase general access for tribals. For girls insecurity has been mentioned as a major deterrent.

7.2.2.3. Hostels

Provision of hostels is crucial for increasing access to middle and higher levels of education. Coverage of hostel schemes has substantially risen, indicating that a genuine demand for separate lodging and boarding arrangements exists for facilitating the pursuit of education among SC/ST communities. Reports of Commissioner of SC/ST – attest to this. Systematic studies are few and far between. One study conducted among centrally sponsored hostels in Maharashtra and Gujarat showed over utilisation and over crowding and that living conditions are unhygienic, quality of food poor and medical facilities nil, for the residents. With the increased demand for hostels, caste based organisations are now important providers of such facilities. We have gathered from personal accounts as well as studies that there is a trend towards increasing politicisation in the provisioning and functioning of such hostels and the need to address the issue of how conducive the environment is for students.

7.2.2.4. Mid Day Meal Scheme

Though the scheme does not fall in the purview of positive discrimination policies, we consider it here due to its potential importance for enrolment of largely impoverished SC/ST children. The scheme which originated in Tamil Nadu in 1982 is currently implemented across the country. A recent study conducted in Chattisgarh, Rajasthan and Karnataka noted an immense positive impact in terms of higher enrolment and attendance levels. Apparently it signified the end of classroom hunger. The study however did not specifically report on SC/ST children. Interestingly however, a study evaluating the scheme's recent performance in Tamil Nadu itself, suggests that it may not be currently having a significant impact on educational attendance or enrolment. Moreover, it noted that implementation is poorer in schools whose social composition is predominantly Scheduled caste.

7.2.3. Poor Physical Infrastructure of Schools

A majority of studies suggest that physical/infrastructure facilities are totally inadequate and particularly deplorable in schools accessed by SC/ST, including the private schools. As mentioned earlier the majority of SC/ST children are in regular government schools. Buildings are dilapidated or badly in need of repair and basic furniture and teaching equipment is nonexistent or of pathetic quality. There are of course state and regional variations. The poorest of physical infrastructure and basic amenities afflict schools in remote tribal areas. There is also a high incidence of very poorly and irregularly functioning schools. We have reports from rural Punjab, Orissa, and Rajasthan's SC and Tribal dominated districts that reveal shortage of basics such as classrooms, drinking water facilities and teachers. Reports of neglect, indifference, greater teacher absenteeism from dalit and tribal dominated schools have accumulated, pointing to the grim reality that exists on the ground. Exceptions too have been noted, for example studies of Garhwal, Himachal Pradesh, Gujarat, Maharashtra and Kerala show that there are several regions in which the SC/ST have a fairly good provision for education. In certain areas in Maharashtra for e.g., Silla Parishad schools are fairly good.

Further, it is important to break the common misconception that rural schools are necessarily worse than urban. There are indications from Maharashtra that government rural schools may be in far better shape than urban municipal schools. This is so because most rural schools have a mix of higher and lower castes/classes whereas in urban areas where the choice of school is greater, the municipal schools cater almost exclusively to the poor, lower castes and tribes.

7.2.4. Inadequacy of Teachers

A highly inadequate teaching force has been a most critical element of unequal provisioning. Teacher-pupil ratios in schools frequented by SC/ST have been much higher than those in other schools meant for higher caste villagers. Multigrade teaching often amounts to very limited teaching or no teaching at all !

The problem of insufficient number of teachers has been compounded by the problem of unmotivated teachers, which is reflected in the phenomenon of teacher absenteeism. Teachers for SC and ST children primarily belong to non-SC or non tribal backgrounds. They are highly irregular in attending since they live outside the villages. This is a common feature in schools located in remote areas. There are reports of 'paper schools' which remain closed during the year and yet others for years on end especially in remote tribal areas. This is the situation particularly in remote tribal areas. A study of tribal education conducted in eighteen villages from seven states showed that teacher absenteeism was rampant in tribal areas of Orissa and Madhya Pradesh. It was common for teachers to mark fictitious attendance of children. Leclercq noted that in the EGS school in SC and ST dominated district of Madhya Pradesh multigrade teaching was generalised. The quantity of teaching was problematically low and quality was equally a key deficiency.

Dysfunctional and poorly organised school environments, inadequate number of teachers, inadequate teaching quantum ranging from absence of teaching to the adoption of most conventional and uninteresting teaching methods together makes for a situation where the teaching transaction is poor and inadequate. Poor teacher competence is also a critical negative factor. Even trained teachers are not necessarily 'good' teachers. Both their knowledge and skill levels are unsatisfactory. Kerala too is no exception to the situation of low teacher quality! At the same time however, poor working conditions which can demotivate and demoralise even the most motivated of the primary school teacher need to be highlighted. Teachers are expected to work in isolation under harsh conditions. Worse still their teaching function is dislodged by compulsion to perform all kinds of government work. Bureaucrat-teacher relationships undermine the dignity and status of the primary school teacher, which in turn interferes with their teaching role.

In comparison to the state and much private effort on behalf of the underprivileged, the missionary effort, although not free from inadequacies, appears far more efficiently organised – both in terms of the quality of education provided and the management of institutions. This is perhaps the principal reason for the major influence they wield in educational and other matters in Scheduled Tribe areas. Several studies have noted significant educational progress among Christian tribals or in areas where missionaries are active in school provision. Contemporarily, neo-right Hindu organisations have emerged as major contending forces and are aggressively pursuing tribal constituencies through a vast network of schools in several states.

7.2.5. Teaching Learning Conditions

Teaching- learning material- blackboards, chalk, texts and other reading material, laboratory equipment, instructional aids are always in short supply, of poor quality or simply nonexistent.

While everyone expects education to respond effectively to old and new challenges, we have seen that all essential ingredients of education are missing! The infrastructure for education and its quality is worsening by the day. Current policy changes such as budget cuts, ban on the new recruitment of teachers, and a growing reliance on contract teachers have compounded the crisis caused by historical neglect. Despite some quantitative gains considerable qualitative setbacks are being experienced by neglected regions and peoples.

Further the "minimum levels of learning" model compromises quality in no uncertain measure. The exclusive focus on the 3 R's creates an unhealthy dichotomy alluded to by Lawton, between the cognitive and affective domains. Issues of educational quality are integral to both "effective" equal opportunity and democratic value formation, but are grossly neglected.

7.3. Curriculum, Pedagogy and Sc & St Children

This section firstly examines curriculum as a mediator of dominance and hegemony, exploring ideological issues in the selection and structuring of knowledge and in pedagogic practice. Secondly we focus on the issue of representation of subaltern groups, culture and ideologies. The concept of curriculum is used here to designate the experiences pupils have under the guidance of the school. Most issues in this area are predicated upon the assumption that appropriate school experiences can indeed make a significant difference to learning and lives of SC/ST children. Content of curriculum and internal operations are thus key issues that need to be addressed. Also very important are related areas of pedagogic methods, assessment and evaluation.

In India, curriculum and the content of education have been central to the processes of reproduction of caste, class, cultural and patriarchal domination-subordination. In post independence educational policy, modification of content supposedly aimed at indigenisation resulted in Brahmanisation as a key defining feature of the curriculum. Brahmanisation has been evident in the emphasis on,

1. 'Pure' language,
2. Literature and other "knowledge" of society, history, polity, religion and culture that is produced by higher castes which reflects Brahmanical world view and experiences and Brahmanical perspectives on Indian society, history and culture, and
3. High caste, cultural and religious symbols, linguistic and social competencies, modes of life and behaviour.

Furthermore, the overarching stress has been on eulogising mental as against manual labour. The heavily gendered nature of school curricular content was evident in that women's specialised knowledge and skills systems found no place in it or in the general curricular discourse. Rather they were used for devaluation and stereotyping of the female sex in curriculum. Curriculum is thus urban elite male-centric and bereft of the country's rich cultural diversity. There has been a corresponding devaluation of "lesser" dialects, cultures, traditions, and folklore of dalits and adivasis as also of peasantry.

The second defining feature of the curriculum on the other hand, was its 'colonial' character which privileged western modernisation. The ideology however was adopted in truncated, superficial ways – the emphasis being on the incorporation of knowledge of Western science and technology, vis. That of the "hard Western sciences", the English language and Western styles of life. The pursuance of liberal, democratic socialist values even though enshrined in the Indian constitution was largely notional in the curriculum.

Curricular structure and culture of the colonial model has remained unchanged. The defining features of the structure are: full time attendance of age specific groups in teacher supervised classrooms for the study of graded curricula. Full day schools, compulsory attendance, unconducively long time–span of classes and vacations, served as deterrents, being ill suited to educating SC/ST children, especially in the initial years when access was just being opened up and availed. Poor and SC/ST households depended on children for domestic work or other productive work whether or not to supplement household earnings.

Today, things have changed substantially and large numbers of parents are prepared to forego children's labour and send them to school. However school organisation and curricula have not been sensitive as yet to fundamentally different economic situations, life aims and social circumstances of children belonging to poorer strata households or communities in the shaping of the school structure. Culturally, school norms of attendance, discipline, homework, tests and exams, and cognitive ethnocentric demands of concentration on and memorisation of the content of the text by 'rote', all prove problematic for SC/ST children (personal account, teacher M.P.). Furthermore, the curriculum itself as a tool of cultural dominance and hegemony has an alienating and intimidating impact.

7.3.1. Curriculum and the Scheduled Castes

For the Scheduled Castes who have sought education as a mechanism to transform as well as enter "mainstream" (read dominant) society, the central questions are of representation of their knowledge and culture and the critiquing of dominant knowledge and value systems of their lived reality and of social relationships based on dominance/ subordination and exclusion. Dominant forms of inequality and hierarchy are made invisible in the discourse on common nationhood and common and equal citizenship, which the school curriculum propagates. But for the Scheduled Castes the heart of the matter is structural oppression, not cultural difference. Thus understandings of oppressive aspects of our traditional and contemporary structures, the historical construction of groups and communities are made invisible by the curriculum and not subjects of key curricular importance.

Krishna Kumar's studies have focused attention on how the dominant groups' ideas about education and the educated get reflected in the curriculum. Following the curriculum, Indian texts uphold symbols of the traditional, male dominated feudal society and its obsolete cultural values and norms. However, that the value content of education is out of tune with the reality of the changing, dynamic India is a matter of choice – a choice consciously or unconsciously made by those selecting textbook material from the available body of literature and by those creating it. Worthwhile knowledge is that which is linked to the values and lifestyles of dominant groups!

Ilaiah has vividly described how knowledge and language are rooted in and structured around productive processes of lower castes and around sociocultural surroundings of their habitat. This knowledge and skill based vocabulary, which is very highly developed, finds no place in the school curriculum. Nor do stories, music and songs, values, skills, knowledge, traditions, cultural and religious practices. Contemporary dalit literature is similarly disregarded. Lives, values and norms of upper caste Hindus which are strange and alienating for the lower castes, continue to be dominantly present. To quote from Ilaiah, "right from early school upto college, our Telugu textbooks were packed with these Hindu stories. Kalidasa was as alien to us as the name of Shakespeare. The language of textbooks was not the one that our communities spoke. Even the basic words were different. Textbook Telugu was Brahmin Telugu, whereas we were used to a production-based communicative Telugu. It is not merely a difference of dialect; there is a difference in the very language itself".

The dominance of epistemology and content of the politically powerful intellectual classes makes curricular knowledge ideologically loaded. While Gandhi, Tagore and Krishnamurti – all from the high castes have received national attention as indigenous educational philosophers, education has not incorporated the anti-caste-patriarchy and anti-egomaniac discourses of Phule, Ambedkar, Periyar or Iyotheedas. Curriculum does not reflect upon the historical significance of caste, gender and tribe, nor of the challenges posed to it by dalit epistemology, knowledge and protest. This should have been done through literature and social science curricula.

Phule saw education as a potent weapon in the struggle for revolutionary social transformation. For him, the purpose and content of education were radically different from both Brahmanical and colonial models of education. His ideal was an education that would bring an awareness among lower castes of oppressive social relations and their egomaniac moral and belief systems that pervaded their consciousness..... An education that would instill western secular values, encourage critical thought and bring about mental emancipation. It would fulfil practical needs but would be broad based enough to inspire a social and cultural revolution from below. During the course of the long struggle of dalit liberation, Ambedkar developed an ideology that incorporated a critique and reinterpretation of India's cultural heritage, a rich philosophy drawn from a wide range of social thought and an action programme which lay an equal stress on social and cultural revolution as it did on the economic and political one. Like Phule, he defined the purpose of education in terms of mental awakening and creation of a social and moral conscience. Education was also a means of overcoming inferior status and state of mind, of wresting power from the powerful. Thus, the Ambedkarian agenda for education included:

1. Creation of capacities for rational and critical thinking,
2. Socialisation into a new humanistic culture and ideology,
3. Development of capacities and qualities necessary for entry and leadership in modern venues of work and politics, and

4. Inculcation of self-respect and aspirations to respectable lifestyles in which demeaning traditional practices would have no place.

Clearly Phule-Ambedkarian ideology went way beyond narrow modernisation and technocratic impulses. It gave pre-eminence to ideology and values, Western in origin but critically adapted towards emancipation of India's downtrodden. Ilaiah, in fact, argues that these values are equally indigenous, constitutive of lived-in realities of dalit bahujans. Dalit and non-Brahman leaders drew on western philosophical traditions to build an ideology and praxis of revolutionary transformation of the Hindu social order. It aimed at establishing a socialist social order underpinned by a new morality, based on values of liberty, equality, fraternity and rationality.

School curriculum in India failed to reflect these expressions of new moral order. It does not need any great study to show that the national or state school curricula or teacher education curricula were never guided by these radical visions. The Scheduled Castes and their issues and problems have remained peripheral to the curriculum and their representation if at all has been weak and distorted.

7.3.2. Curriculum and the Scheduled Tribes

Like the SC, curriculum does not acknowledge cultural rights of the Scheduled Tribes who are denied their own culture and history. School curriculum fails to take account of tribal cultures as autonomous knowledge systems with their own epistemology, transmission, innovation and power. Kundu gives the example of children being set to write essays on the circus, or being trained to write letters through mock missives to the police asking them to take action on disturbance by loudspeakers during exams. While adivasi children may know a great deal about animals, they are unlikely to have ever seen a circus; where the police are usually feared as oppressors and electricity is erratic, if at all available, enlisting police support in keeping noise decibels down is a most unlikely situation. Not only are the knowledge and linguistic and /or cognitive abilities that Scheduled Tribe children possess ignored e.g. the capacity to compose and sing spontaneously, to think in riddles and metaphors and their intimate knowledge of their environment but schooling also actively encourages a sense of inferiority about Scheduled Tribe cultures. Like the Scheduled Castes, Scheduled Tribes rarely feature in textbooks, and when they do, it is usually in positions servile to upper caste characters; or as 'strange' and 'backward' exotica.

The 'cultural discontinuity' between school and home draws attention to the rigidity of school organisation and the emphasis on discipline and punishment in contrast with socialisation practices and the lives of children, as reasons for non-attendance. Sujatha cites the case of community schools in Andhra where there was closer interaction with parents, weekly holiday was in tune with the local weekly bazaar, and school holidays coincided with tribal festivals. The school was observed to show positive results.

7.3.3. Language Question

Despite several policy documents and a constitutional provision (350A) recognising that linguistic minorities should be educated in their mother tongue at primary level, there is practically no education in Scheduled Tribe languages. This includes even those like Santhali, Bhili, Gondi or Oraon which are spoken by over a million people. Although states in India were organised on linguistic grounds, political powerlessness of Scheduled Tribes prevented the formation of states based on tribal languages. They are confined to minority status within large states and are compelled to learn the state language in school. Primary teachers are predominantly from non-ST communities. And despite the pedagogic significance of initial instruction in the mother tongue, teachers do not bother to learn the tribal language even after several years of posting. The general picture at primary level is often one of mutual in comprehension between ST students and their non-ST teachers. Several studies have pointed to the significance of the language question at the primary levels.

Quite apart from the pedagogic problems this creates such as destroying the child's self esteem, and reducing the possibilities of successful learning in later years, the denigration of Scheduled Tribe languages amounts to denigration of Scheduled Tribe world views and knowledge. The education system with its insistence on a common language as a means of achieving a common nationhood has been instrumental in the destruction of tribal language, culture and identity.

Even outside the school, educated youth often speak to each other in the language of the school, perhaps to mark themselves off from their 'uneducated peers'. Several languages, especially those spoken by small numbers, are dying out. Loss of a language means the loss of a certain way of knowing the world. Experiences of schooling of tribal children in Madhya Pradesh, Andhra Pradesh and Maharashtra have revealed the displacement of Bundelkhandi, Gondi and Warli by Sanskritised Hindi, Telugu and Marathi respectively.

Depending on levels of cultural absorption and adaptation however, several Scheduled Tribes may not look to schools to teach in their home language. Indeed, for many Scheduled Tribe parents, the main advantage of schooling is that it gives access to the new languages, new occupations and a new life and enables interaction with the non-tribal world. But wherever Scheduled Tribes have been politically mobilised to celebrate Scheduled Tribe identity, they have been more clear and open in their demand for education in indigenous languages.

7.3.4. Alienating Impact of School Regimen

The school regimen of timing, discipline, hierarchy is especially alien to tribal children socialised in a world where individuality is respected from early on, and where parent-child interactions are relatively egalitarian. Kundu points out that testing procedures too are based on urban middle class values – the competitiveness and system of rewards that examinations represent is often culturally anomalous to Scheduled Tribe children who are brought up in an atmosphere of sharing. Furthermore, learning among ST children is usually intimately connected to the work process – children learn the names and medicinal uses of many plants and trees while accompanying their parents on foraging trips in the forest. When children are away at school, especially when they are sent to residential schools, they lose connection with this world of labour and their capacity to learn from it. Several studies have attested the alienating effects of language, school structure and ethos.

7.3.5. Hindu Nationalist Influences on Curriculum

In the recent past a serious concern has been the 'Hinduisation' of the curriculum, its adverse implications for all children but most particularly to religious minorities and SC/ST. A deliberate policy move towards Hinduisation of the school which occurred at the behest of neoright national government's policy meant its specific framing within Vedic values and thought. However, even prior to that when there was no overt intent of curriculum or text to be grounded in dominant religious culture, the fact that most educational action teachers are Hindu made curriculum Hinduised. It influenced the manner in which annual days or other school events are celebrated. Breaking a coconut and lighting incense at the base of the flag pole on Republic or Independence Day is common practice. Additionally, distinctive Scheduled Tribe names are changed to standard Hindu names.

7.4. Hidden Curriculum and Sc/St Children

The term "hidden curriculum" is used to mean the tacit teaching of dominant cultural norms, values and disposition towards maintenance of ideological hegemony. Within the Indian school scenario, the concept might actually be a misnomer because processes of cultural domination and caste class, tribe and gender relations that shape school organisation, culture and classroom interaction are all too visible.

In the school and in classrooms, teacher-pupil interaction is central to teaching and learning processes. Teacher's social background (caste, religion, language), affect their interactions with students. Middle class higher caste teachers are very unhappy with the environments of schools for the poor and are poorly motivated to teach children of the poor, particularly of SC/ST background, who are 'derogatorily' categorised as uneducable.

We have now an appalling body of evidence that suggests that teacher's preconceptions, bias and behaviour, subtle or overt, conscious or unconscious, operate to discriminate against children of SC/ST background. Teachers are observed to have low expectations of SC/ST children and girls and a condescending and downright abusive attitude to poor children from slums. Teachers also have stated or unstated assumptions of "deprived" and "deficient" cultural backgrounds, languages and inherent intellectual deficiencies of SC/ST children. They follow discriminatory pedagogic practices of labelling, classifying and teaching styles and operate on the basis of "realistic" perceptions of low caste children's limited cognitive capacities and life chances. For e.g. teachers beliefs about Mushar children in Bihar are that they are just not interested in education and that they do not have any 'tension' in life. Such presumptions set effective and in the teachers' view legitimate limits to their teaching effort. Levels of hostility and indifference to dalit/tribal cultural traits and value systems are high. Discriminatory behaviour manifests itself in numerous ways. Teachers perceive dalit and adivasi children in a negative light, see them as unclean, dishonest, lazy, ill-mannered etc. The children could be criticised for their clothes, the dialect they speak, the abhorment of uncouth habits of meat eating and alcohol consumption, the ignorance of their parents and even the colour of their skin! They are punished and shouted at in efforts to discipline and "civilise" them!

Several studies have noted that SC children do not encounter practices related to untouchability in school. However others point to varied forms of direct and subtle discrimination. For instance, Artis, et al. find that in village schools of Gujarat, SC children are forced to sit at the back, actively discouraged to participate in class, are subject to food and water taboos. Similar experiences exist for village schools in Karnataka. Tribal children too are victims of 'caste like' discrimination as a study conducted in the tribal village of Harda (M.P) has pointed out. Teaching Korku children is considered as good as 'teaching cows' by teachers. Non-adivasi children do not mix with them or drink water from the same tap! In relation to dalits, teachers refuse to correct their notebooks. Complaints to headmaster results in beating of children. Indeed teacher violence against dalit children is widely reported.

Like the children, dalit and tribal teachers also suffer humiliation and discrimination. They are largely isolated or compelled to form their own separate social circles. They also find themselves succumbing to dominant religio-cultural practices in a bid to avoid conflict and gain acceptance. A disturbing tendency noted by several studies and further substantiated by poignant personal narratives is the use of children as servants by high caste teachers. Children are assigned a range of menial tasks – from cleaning and sweeping the school to fetching "paan" and cigarettes for the teacher. They assign

SC/ST children menial jobs and shift the onus of low learning on children and their families. Tribal children have been punished for talking in their own languages. There is an undue obsession with language purity and correctness. Placing disadvantaged students in 'better quality' schools doesn't seem to solve the problem. Studies have suggested that feelings of isolation, alienation and experiences of discrimination do neutralise the impact of better facilities.

References

Human Rights Watch, *Broken People: Caste Violence Against India's "Untouchables"*. New York: Human Rights Watch. 1999.

Jaffrelot, Christophe. *India's Silent Revolution: The Rise of the Lower Castes.* C. Hurst & Co. 2003.

Kothari, Rajni. *Caste in Indian Politics.* Orient Longman.2004.

Kundu, Amitabh. "Reservation, Anti-reservation and Democracy." *Economic and Political Weekly.* Vol. 25, No. 45. November 10, 1990.

Mahar, J. Michael, (ed.) *The Untouchables in Contemporary India.* Tucson. The University of Arisona Press. 1972.

Parvathamma. *Scheduled Castes and Tribes: A Socioeconomic Survey,* Ashish, Delhi. 1984.

Pauline Kolenda. *Caste in Contemporary India: Beyond Organic Solidarity* Menlo Park. Benjamin/Cumming Publishing Co. 1978.

8

Planning for the Development Scheduled Communities

Relegation of a defined section of a society to inequality is found perhaps only in India. Nowhere in the world has any particular section been devoid of basic human rights, dignity of labour and social equality on the basis of classification that finds its root in religious writings. In India, the Hindu society is divided into various castes on the basis of their occupation. In the lowest rank of this classification are the Scheduled Castes (SCs) who were condemned to perform the menial and unclean tasks on behalf of the society. As they were exclusively assigned the role of performing unclean tasks on behalf of the society, they came to be treated as outcasts or "untouchable". It is this social stigma that pushed them down to the bottom of the social ladder alienating them from the mainstream of the society and assigning them to a position lower than several depressed classes who also suffered from social, economic and educational deprivation.

Since the caste system attains its sanctity in religious writings, emancipation from the rigid classification has been difficult to achieve for the lower groups. The belief in religion has singularly contributed to this difficulty. The Scheduled Castes (SCs), as they came to be described in the Government of India Act 1935, have suffered social, economic, cultural and political inequalities for centuries.

Under the customary rules of the Hindu social order, the untouchable were denied rights to property, pursue business (except the polluting occupations), education and employment (excluding the manual labour). The consequences of these traditional restrictions in the past are to be seen, even today in terms of lack of ownership of agricultural land, business or non-land capital assets, in education and ultimately in high incidence of poverty among them.

A look at the recent available data brings out these facts quite clearly. About three-fourths of the SCs live in rural areas, where the main source of livelihood is either farming, wage labour or some kind of non-farm business. In 2000, only 16 percent of all SC households cultivated land as owner-cultivator as against 41 percent among non-SC/ST households. Only 12 percent carry out some kind of business, which indicates access to capital. Taking both farm and non-farm activities, only about 28 percent of rural households had got some access to capital assets as compared to 56 percent for non-SC/ST households.

Inadequate access to agricultural land and capital leaves no option to SC workers except to resort to manual wage labour; consequently, it leads to enormously high level of (manual) wage labour among the SCs, i.e., 61 percent as compared to only one-third for others in rural areas. Among them, in urban areas, one-third are casual labours as against only 7 percent among the non-SC/STs. The unemployment rate (based on current daily status) in 2000 were two times higher among the SCs (5.5%) as compared with non-SC/STs.

With higher incidence of wage labour, associated with high rate of underemployment, the SCs tend to suffer from low income and greater level of poverty. In 2000, about 38 percent of SC households were below the poverty line in rural areas as compared to only less than 20 percent among non-SC/STs households. The incidence of poverty was as high as 50 percent among agricultural labour as against 40 percent among non-agricultural labour. In urban areas also, the poverty among SCs was about 38 percent, which was much higher as compared with 19 percent for non-SC/STs. The incidence of poverty was quite high among casual labour about 60 percent. The former untouchable also leg far too behind in education 37 percent as against 57 percent for others in 1991.

The arguments in support of remedies against discrimination that are mainly based on historical denial of equal opportunity, due to practices of caste and untouchability based exclusion and discrimination toward untouchable and seeking provision for equal rights, safeguards against violation of equal rights and strategies for equal access or opportunity through reservations or affirmative action.

Not only the untouchability arrested the growth of personality of untouchable but also comes in the way of their 'material well-being'. It deprived them of certain civil rights. The untouchable is not even a citizen. Citizenship is bundle of rights such as personal liberty, personal security, right to hold private property, equality before law, liberty of conscience, freedom of opinion, and speech, right of assembly, right of representation in country's government and right to hold office under the state. The untouchability of untouchable puts these rights far beyond their reach.

Depressed classes cannot be employed in the army, navy, and police because such employment is opposed to the religious notion of majority. They cannot be admitted in schools, because their entry is opposed to the religious notion of majority. They cannot avail themselves of government dispensaries, because doctors will not let them cause pollution to their persons or to their dispensaries. They cannot live cleaner and higher life, because to live above their prescribed station is opposed to the religious notion of majority.

So rigorous was the enforcement of the social code against the depressed classes that any attempt on the part of depressed classes to exercise their elementary rights of citizenship only ends in provoking the majority to practice the worst forms of social tyranny known to history. What is worse that this servility and bar to human intercourse, due to their untouchability, involves not merely the possibility of discrimination in public life, but actually works out as a positive denial of all equality of opportunity and the denial of those most elementary of civic rights on which all human existence depends. Unequal treatment has been the inescapable fate of the untouchable in India and that in a country like India where it is possible for discrimination to be practised on a vast scale and in a relentless manner, fundamental rights have no real meaning for untouchable.

Ambedkar had dealt in detail the logic and reasons behind these measures against discrimination and in particular on (a) equal rights, (b) legal safeguards against violation of rights, (c) strategies for fair share and participation, and (d) developmental and empowering measures to compensate for historical exclusion.

Ambedkar suggested dual remedies:

(i) a set of policies/ remedies relating to safeguards against discrimination, and

(ii) strategies to overcome deep rooted deprivation caused by historical exclusion and isolation of untouchable.

Ambedkar, also suggested fundamental measures for addressing the problem of structural inequalities and special developmental measures of equalisation, particularly in the spheres of education, and economic empowerment of the historical denial of right to education, employment and right to property in the past. These include distribution of agricultural land through State ownership, State ownership of key basic industries, banks and insurance. Ambedkar also suggested constitutional obligations on the State to undertake developmental measures and the participation of depressed classes to influence the Government policies through representation in legislature, executive and public services in the form of reservation policy.

8.1. Constitutional Safeguards

On attaining Independence, the Constitution of India provided Six Fundamental Rights to its Citizens.

8.1.1. Planning Commission

The untouchable benefited immensely out of these provisions. The overall development of the Scheduled Castes has been a declared concern of the successive governments in independent India. Efforts in this direction have aimed at the social, economic and political upliftment of this group to bring them at par with other sections of society through various safeguards and provisions. Since independence, new strategies for accelerated development have been evolved and programmes implemented with a view to bring the Scheduled Castes in the mainstream of the Indian society.

Recognising the relative backwardness of SCs in the society, the Constitution of India guarantees equality before the law and enjoins the State to make special provisions for advancement of socially and educationally backward classes. It also empowers the State to make provisions for reservation in appointment or posts in favour of SCs/

STs. The Constitution of India also states categorically that untouchability is abolished and its practice in any form is forbidden. Further, the State is required to promote with special care the educational and economic interests of weaker sections in particular the exploitation of SCs. Reservation of seats in democratic institutions and in services is another measure of positive discrimination. It also empowers the State to appoint a commission to investigate into the conditions of socially and educationally backward classes and to specify the castes to be deemed as SCs.

The forces of urbanisation, social and protective legislation, positive discrimination and other measures taken by the Government, have led to gradual improvement in occupational mobility and living standards over the years, but the living conditions of the majority of Scheduled Castes continue to show socioeconomic backwardness.

8.2. Socioeconomic Status of SCs

The Scheduled Caste (SC) population, according to 2001 Census, is 166.6 million constituting 16.23 per cent of the total population of India. They are mainly concentrated in Uttar Pradesh (35.1 million), West Bengal (18.4 million), Tamil Nadu (11.8 million), Andhra Pradesh (12.3 million) and Bihar (11.3 million). These States account for 53.36 per cent of the total SC population of the country. While Uttar Pradesh has the highest concentration of SC population (28.9%) in terms of absolute number, Punjab with 28.9 per cent SC population occupies the first position in terms of percentage of SC to the State population.

The major occupational groups of SCs can be categorised into:

- Agricultural labourers.
- Landless.
- Those with petty extent of agricultural land.
- Marginal and small cultivators including share croppers and other tenants.
- Fishermen.
- Traditional Artisans.
- Leather workers.

— Weavers.

— Other artisans.

— Civic Sanitation workers (scavengers and sweepers), and Traditional Dais.

— Urban marginal labour.

— The educated.

These occupational groups may be put into two broad categories:

— Those engaged in land based activities.

— Those engaged in non-land based activities.

Population and Decadal Growth Rate of SCs and STs 1971-2001 The SC population in the country in 1971 was 80 millions which has increased to 166.6 million in 2001. SC population had a decadal growth rate of 20.5% during 1991 and 2001 as in the case of general population though it had experienced higher growth rates during 1981 and 1991.

Sex Ratio: The Sex Ratio (females per 1000 males) for SCs has declined over the last 30 years. The declining sex ratio of SCs could be attributed to higher female mortality and their limited access to health services. Such developments are surely a matter of concern for gender equality within the disadvantaged group.

The SC population in the country in 1971 was 80 mil Literacy: According to 2001 Census, the literacy rate among Scheduled Caste population is 54.7% as compared to 64.80% among total population. However, literacy among Scheduled Caste female is quite low i.e., 41.90% against 53.70% of general female, which is a cause of great concern. Growth rate of literacy among SC females between the two decennial Census 1991 and 2001 is 18% points. However, 456 districts out of total of 582 districts inhabited by SCs, the literacy among SCs is less than average literacy rate of non-SC/ST population. The literacy rate among the SCs continues to be much lower than the all India level for the States : Bihar (28.5%), Rajasthan (52.2%), Madhya Pradesh (58.6%), Uttar Pradesh (46.3%) and Andhra Pradesh (53.5%).

8.3. Gross Enrolment Ratios

The enrolment ratio in classes I-VIII indicates 84.8% for general population and 69.63% for SCs. The dropout amongst the SCs is much higher in classes IVIII & I-X (59.42% & 73.13%) as against the general population (31.47% &62.69%). The drop out rate is much higher amongst the SC girl students.

8.4. Economic Status

Majority of the Schedule Caste population lives in rural areas, which is characterised as an agrarian economy. The poverty ratio, the size of the land holding, occupational classification and number of main workers and its pattern are important parameters to judge the rural economy. Most of the SC families are still below poverty line. Majority of them are engaged in low wage and even obnoxious and degraded occupations like sweeping and scavenging. Their skill base is rather weak.

Along with the general population, the percentage of both SCs living below the poverty line has indicated a declining trend from 1993-94 to 1999-2000. The need for special attention for SCs welfare and development was realised that the Scheduled Castes suffer from the dual disabilities of severe economic exploitation and social discrimination. While they constitute 16.2 per cent of the total population of the country, their proportion is much larger more than twice in the poverty groups of the country, most of the Scheduled Castes are below the poverty-line. Accordingly, thrust has to be on the economic development of the Scheduled Castes.

In respect of the Scheduled Castes the strategy is to take up programmes for the Scheduled Castes in different occupational categories, especially poverty groups. The Scheduled Castes are mostly landless labourers, marginal and small farmers, leather workers, fishermen, artisans like weavers and those who follow strenuous occupations like rickshaw pullers, cart pullers, etc. The approach is to reach the flow of benefits to the Scheduled Castes through individual family and group-oriented programmes. For this, new need-based programmes require to be taken up and existing programmes reoriented to suit the specific developmental requirements and handicaps of the Scheduled Castes in different occupational groups.

Most of the key health indicators indicate a gap of 5 to 10 points difference between SCs and general population. Infant mortality rate

(IMR) is 83 for SCs and 67.6 for general population. Child mortality is also quite high amongst the SCs which are 39.5 in comparison to 29.3 for general population. The data reveals that 20% of SCs are only cultivators and 45.61% SCs are agricultural labourers.

8.5. Socio-Economic Development of SCs During Five Year Plans

8.5.1. Progress during First Five Year Plan

The population of the 779 scheduled castes in India was 498.37 lakhs. This figure does not include backward groups which are not mentionec in the schedule "other backward classes" population was 546 lakhs ir 1951. Article 340 of the Constitution has empowered the President tc appoint a Commission to determine the conditions of backward group: not included in the schedule of castes who could be considered to be socially, economically and educationally backward.

Untouchability, being an age-old institution, has taken roots in the psychology and social structure of certain communities. Its eradication is incomplete so long as it receives a mental recognition and persists indirectly in some form in the social structure. A four fold programme is, therefore, necessary, vis., removal of untouchability by law; removal by persuasive and educative processes through social education ; the practice of democratic behaviour in social and recreational life ; and opportunities afforded by the State and private agencies for self-development and expression and for the betterment of health, education, economic life, and living conditions. Improved living conditions, education, and participation in a society with extensive economic interdependence and facilities for communication, movement, and contact, will in due course of time lead to a total integration of these groups with the rest of the country.

The State Governments have been provided a sum of Rs.10 crores for the benefit of scheduled castes during the period of the Plan. The Central Government has also provided a further sum of Rs. 4 crores for expenditure during the remaining period of the Plan. The general aim is to follow intensive programmes rather than to dissipate the limited resources on loosely conducted activities over a wide area. Provision is made for the more liberal disbursement of money under different heads to institutions working in this field, and an effort was made to improve efficiency by channelling expenditure through effective and well-supervised organisations. Since most of the Harijans live in isolated colonies, they offer good scope for the organisation of community centres. Measures for achieving the welfare of the scheduled castes are circumscribed by the amount of available resources.

8.5.2. Progress during Second Five Year Plan

In this plan period "backward classes" were described as the four sections of the population:

— Scheduled tribes who number about 19 million.

— Scheduled castes who number about 51 million.

— Communities formerly described as 'criminal tribes' who number a little over 4 million.

— Other socially and educationally backward classes who may be declared as such by the Central Government in the light of recommendations made by the Backward Classes Commission.

The welfare of Harijans (scheduled castes) was mainly the responsibility of State Governments. The Constitution provides several safeguards for the protection of the interests of scheduled castes. Development programmes for scheduled castes have been formulated with the object of improving their social status and providing them fuller educational and economic opportunities.

The Constitution has abolished untouchability and has forbidden its practice in any form. State Governments and all-India voluntary organisations with help from the Centre have undertaken extensive propaganda and publicity with a view to mobilising public opinion against untouchability. Nevertheless, the practice still persists indirectly in some form or other although on a greatly reduced and diminishing scale. With the enactment of the Untouchability (Offences) Act and its enforcement from June, 1955 the practice of untouchability has been made a cognisable offence.

In the Second Five Year Plan, Rs. 21.28 crores have been earmarked for the welfare of scheduled castes. Besides this a sum of

Rs. 6.25 crores has been allocated for Centrally sponsored schemes which include housing, drinking water supply, economic uplift and aid to voluntary organisations and publicity for removal of untouchability. The special programmes proposed for Harijans are intended to supplement the general development. Programmes in each State.

The special provisions made in favour of backward classes should be so utilised as to enable them to derive the maximum advantage from general development programmes and to make up as speedily as possible for retarded progress in the past Departments concerned with the welfare of backward classes in States should make special efforts to get all the other development Departments to consider ways by which their programmes can produce marked impact on the welfare of backward classes. They should utilise the resources available to them so that the general and special programmes -operated in a manner complementary to one another.

8.5.3. Progress during Third Five Year Plan

The problems of scheduled castes and other backward classes are essentially those of economically weaker sections of the community, who suffer also in larger or smaller measure from social disabilities. Of the outlay of Rs. 114 crores in the Third Plan, provided for the welfare of backward classes, about Rs. 42 crores are intended for schemes of educational development, Rs. 47 crores for economic uplift schemes and Rs. 25 crores for health, housing and other schemes.

Development programmes for the welfare of backward classes, for which provision is made in the Five Year Plans, are intended to supplement benefits accruing from programmes of development in different fields such as agriculture, cooperation, irrigation, small industries, communications, education, health, housing, rural water supply and others. One of the principal lessons of the past decade is that for a variety of reasons, in the ordinary course, the weaker sections of the population are not able to secure their fair share of the benefits of provisions made under different heads. To enable them to do so, it is desirable that the normal patterns of assistance should provide, wherever necessary, for an element of special consideration for the weaker sections and, in particular, for the backward classes. The Third Plan provided about Rs. 114 crores for the backward classes sector in total and for SCs development Rs.40 crore had been allocated.

8.5.4. Progress during Fourth Five Year Plan

In the Fourth Five Year Plan, the emphasis was on consolidation, improvement and expansion of the services so that the process initiated in the earlier plans is accelerated. The objective of integration with the rest of the society is proposed to be related mainly to the equalisation of opportunities for development.

Programmes for the welfare of backward classes should be fully integrated with the development plans of the district which would take into account the physical features and resources, the institutional structure and local conditions and circumstances. The large number of individual schemes in States in the backward classes sector need to be woven together and integrated with general development schemes so that the effort will be of a magnitude which produces an impact.

Each State should review its legislative and executive measures for providing house-sites to members of the Scheduled Castes and other weaker sections and conferring proprietary rights on homestead land already occupied by them. Those members of the Scheduled Castes who are landless should at least be provided with house sites, if resources do not permit the grant of housing aid to them for construction of houses. Mixed settlement of various communities should be encouraged. Adequate funds for this purpose should be provided in the general sector and the programme of housing in the backward classes sector should be fully integrated with the general village planning and layout.

8.5.5. Progress during Fifth Five Year Plan

Before the Sixth Five Year Plan no clear strategy for the economic development of Scheduled Caste emerged notwithstanding the fact that formal decisions were taken for earmarking of outlays in their favour in proportion to their population. The only funds available upto the end of 1979-80 for development of SCs were provided under the Backward Classes sector. It has been reported that only Rs.433.24 crores were set for the purpose. Of this amount, 48% was spent on educational schemes, another 26% on health, housing, drinking water supply and grants in aid to voluntary organisations working amongst SCs and STs. The remaining 26% was spent on economic development schemes for the SCs.

In other words, only about Rs.112.6 crores were spent on economic development of SCs upto the end of 1979-80. Since the members of SCs have been too weak to take initiative, it is the State which has to take remedial measures to correct the society's inbuilt discrimination against them. They are trapped in the circle of deprivation due to caste structure. The SCs are usually engaged in unpleasant and menial jobs. Their basic disabilities stem from their low social status and are interrelated. It is in this segment of society that one finds greater illiteracy, poorer health, poorer nutrition, poorer housing, as well as exploitation by large land-holders generally the upper and middle level castes, money lenders, village traders and businessmen. In spite of constitutional directives and a number of legislative and executive measures taken by the Government, the situation of the Scheduled Caste did not improve appreciably during the period prior to Sixth Plan mainly due to lack of economic support.

8.5.6. Progress during Sixth Five Year Plan

Sixth Five Year Plan is the first plan which gave due emphasis for the development of SCs in terms of Special Component Plan. Special Component Plan is a Sub Plan of the Annual Plan and Five Year Plan targeting the SC population especially the proportion among the people below the poverty line in the country, and about 84% of them live in the rural areas. In effect any programme for economic development of SCs is a very important part of the poverty-alleviation programme.

In the Sixth Five Year Plan, the stress has been given through the new strategy of Special Component Plan on providing adequate economic development. The Special Component Plan has been formulated as a mechanism for channelising a due share of benefits in physical and financial terms from the various programmes of every sector in favour of SCs. Realising the meagerness of the flow of fund to the development of SCs compared to the enormity of the problem, the strategy of Special Component Plan has been evolved for earmarking of outlay for the development of SCs by all the sectors in all States and UTs except those which have no or negligible SC population and by all Central Ministries.

— The Special Component Plans of the States and Central Ministries (SCP)

— The Special Central Assistance (SCA) to Special Component Plan (SCP).

— Scheduled Castes Development Corporations in the States (SCDC).

The approach in the matter of development of SC families in the Sixth Plan period has been two-fold : cluster approach and saturation approach. Although SC population lives dispersed all over, it is still possible to identify and list out villages in a Block, district and State in the order of one size of the SC population in absolute numbers. In other words, the list should include villages in decreasing order of size of the SC population. Those villages having the largest population of SCs should be at the top in the list.

The development programmes should be taken up in that priority. For instance, in the State of Gujarat out of a total of about 18,000 villages nearly 1110 villages have about 50% of the total state population of SCs. Hence, executing the development programme, clusters of villages from these 1100 villages should be selected. Secondly, under saturation approach in every village taken up for development among these, all deserving SC families should be covered under one or another suitable programme or a combination of programmes with all necessary linkages and backup services.

8.5.7. Progress during Seventh Five Year Plan

The strategy of the Special Component Plan (SCP) for the development of scheduled castes, which is aimed at their socioeconomic and educational development and also at improvement in their working and living condition geared up and intensified. The thrust of the programme was on economic development through comprehensive and integrated beneficiary-oriented programmes for individual families and groups of families of scheduled castes for raising their income and enabling them to cross the poverty line. Basti-oriented schemes so as to bring about a significant and tangible improvement in the working and living conditions, in the inhabitation and Bastes of scheduled castes; liberation of scavenging without reduction of income and employment of the existing municipalised as well as private sanitation workers.

Educational development so as to remove the flag in education of scheduled castes at every stage; promotion of occupational mobility of the scheduled castes so that the disproportionate burden on them in occupations like agricultural labour and other unpleasant and strenuous work is removed so that human resources are optimal developed and utilised; elimination of exploitative middlemen layers; special attention to scheduled castes women and children.

Administrative and personnel reforms so as to orient personnel and the delivery mechanism and other public institutions towards the scheduled castes, sensitise them to the problems and needs of the scheduled castes and make them efficient and setting up of a beneficiary participant system with all management skills. 75 per cent of the SC families to be enabled to cross the poverty-line by the end of the Seventh Plan including those who have been so enabled successfully in the Sixth Plan. Adequate per-family investment and strong backup services and linkages are necessary during the Seventh Five Year Plan. The package of assistance was to be so designed that it is capable of generating the additional income necessary to enable each family so assisted to cross the poverty-line.

The objective of the family-oriented programmes may not only be to raise the scheduled caste families above the poverty-line but also to help the beneficiaries, as far as possible, to diversify their traditional occupations and eliminate the disproportionate burden on them in unpleasant and low paid occupations like agricultural labour and optimal develop and utilise human resources. The main focus was on development of different occupational categories especially agricultural labourers, marginal and small farmers, leather workers, fishermen and vulnerable groups.

With this end in view, implementation of the cluster-cum-saturation approach which was evolved during the Sixth Plan was intensified to ensure the total coverage of all eligible families, in village clusters, identified on the basis of the size of the scheduled caste population. Emphasis was made to use all agencies, government and voluntary, to carry out this enormous task. In order to give a boost to the arrangements for economic support to the Special Component Plan, banks and other financial institutions were involved in a big way and adequate quantum of funds under Special Central Assistance has to be earmarked.

The institutions must be strengthened and used as one of the main planks for the economic development of scheduled castes. In the scheduled caste Bastis, essential facilities like drinking water, drainage, street-lighting, link roads, health institutions, primary and adult educational institutions, where lacking will have to be provided on a priority basis. For scheduled caste families in urban areas, self-employment schedules and schemes for endowing them with assets where they are settles, should be given importance and institutional finance arranged for them.

The degrading practice of scavenging should be eliminated as per a time-bound programme during the Seventh Five Year Plan period by adequately intensifying the programme of conversion of dry-latrines into water-borne ones and, at the same time, ensuring that civic sanitation workers ("scavengers") who are in the employment of Municipal Bodies are retained in employment and given alternative work, while private scavengers are provided alternative employment or self-employment by imparting skills wherever necessary.

The States should evolve appropriate administrative structure and personnel policies for development of scheduled castes. At the district level, the Collectors should be made responsible for formulation and implementation of the Special Component Plan. The implementation machinery to be adequately strengthened to make the delivery system effective. Both in formulation and implementations phases, involvement of representatives of beneficiary-participants should be ensured; in this matter, voluntary agencies working for them were encouraged to associate themselves with developmental programmes.

Of the total outlay of each State Plan, a total outlay amounting as a percentage of State Plan, to not less than the population-percentage of the scheduled castes in that State should be set apart as the State SCP; schemes and programmes should be formulated to the extent of this amount in accordance with the objectives and priorities of SC development; and corresponding outlays should then be distributed sector-wise as SCPs of the respective sectors. Of the outlay in the Central Plan, not less than 15 per cent should be similarly set part for development of scheduled castes as SCP; schemes and programmes should be formulated to the extent of this amount in accordance with the objectives and priorities of scheduled caste development and corresponding outlays should then be distributed sector-wise for implementation by Central Agencies or through State agencies as appropriate, as the SCPs of respective Central Sectorial Plans. The Central Ministries should also indicate the actual expenditure incurred on the SCP during a particular year. Separate accounts should be maintained in respect of all schemes under the SCP by opening a separate budge head. The funds thus becoming available in each State for the development of scheduled castes, should be used purposefully and realistically co-related to the development needs of the scheduled castes.

8.5.8. Progress during Eighth Five Year Plan

There has to be an intensification of efforts to bridge the gap in the levels of development of the Scheduled Castes, Scheduled Tribes, Backward Classes and other sections of the population so that by the turn of the century these disadvantaged sections of the population are brought on par with the rest of the society in all spheres of national endeavour. Problems of access for Scheduled Castes to programmes and services have to be identified and removed.

Elimination of exploitation of Scheduled Castes and removal of all forms of oppression of Scheduled Castes must receive high 14 priority. Untouchability, suppression of rights, usurious money lending, land alienation, non-payment of minimum wages, and restrictions on right to collect minor forest produce have to be removed to enable these people to avail of the benefits of development efforts. Problems of Scheduled Castes have to be tackled by suitable streamlining of the mechanism of planning and implementation of programmes of Special Component Plan and the schemes specifically targeted for the welfare and development of Scheduled Castes. The strategy of Special Component Plan for Scheduled Castes will be reviewed inter-alia to make them effective instruments of planning to ensure real and tangible flow of benefits to the target group, both individuals and families.

Re-orientation of administrative structure at all levels for functional coordination, integration and effective delivery of services will be necessary. There is considerable inter-caste in the levels of socioeconomic development of Scheduled Castes in the social and economic organisation of their life. It is essential that planning gives full cognisance to these variations and responds to their specific problems and needs and the sociocultural values of the community through decentralised participatory planning.

Alleviation of poverty through sustained employment and generation of incomes is vital so that at least the basic needs are met. National poverty alleviation programmes will have to ensure that the Scheduled Castes are able to derive adequate benefit. Skill development programmes will be necessary to improve their earnings and help them to diversify into trades and occupations.

It will also be necessary to provide assistance to Scheduled Castes in the matter of choice of projects, marketing, procurement of raw materials, and introduction of new technologies. Elimination of scavenging and rehabilitation of scavengers will be an important programme in the Eighth Plan. Education, training and other incentives will be provided to children of parents engaged in unclean occupations so that they can prepare themselves for occupations, which provide better incomes and a higher social status. Occupations like tanning and leather work would be modernised with improved technology to remove the stigma attached to these professions and to produce goods which have a better market.

Women belonging to the Scheduled Castes are in a far worse situation by all development indicators. Poverty and deprivation affect them more adversely. Although they work along with men, they are not recognised as producers in their own right. The strategy for the development of Scheduled Castes will have to include a major thrust for the benefit of womenfolk.

Voluntary organisations will need to be promoted and assisted to play a partnership role in the designing and implementation of programmes. Their role in advocacy and acceleration of the process of change and development and in playing a constructive role of intermediaries in general and in innovating new programme structures, in organising and preparing the people and in giving them a stake in the success of their endeavours, in particular, has to be recognised. Voluntary organisations can also help in the training of grassroots level workers and in mobilising community resources.

8.5.9. Progress during Ninth Five year Plan

While the major objective of SCP and TSP is to ensure the much needed flow of funds and benefits for the welfare and development of these two categories in proportion to their population, which is now 16.5% in respect of SCs and 8.1% in respect of STs, as per the 1991 Census, SCA to SCP and TSP extends financial assistance to States and UTs as an additive to their SCP and TSP for filling up of the critical gaps in the family based employment-cum-income generation programmes. The flow of funds during the Eighth Plan for SCP under Central and State sectors was to the tune of 27.8 % and 10.8% respectively against the target of 16.8%.

The Special Central Assistance (SCA) to States/ UTs, as an additive to SCP and TSP, was enhanced during the Eighth Plan so as to strengthen the efforts of States in filling up the gaps under the family-based income generation projects. The SCA to SCP was enhanced from Rs.930 crore in the Seventh Plan to Rs.1125 crore in the Eighth Plan, indicating 21 per cent increase. The details of the flow of funds from he Central and the State Sectors to SCP for SCs, TSP for STs and the SCA to SCP and TSP, during the Seventh and the Eighth Five Year Plans.

Despite the fact that the strategy of SCP has been in operation for more than fifteen years, they could not influence all those concerned towards the right perspective. Further, lack of effective monitoring to ensure that all these concerned earmark funds under SCP and that the funds received under SCP and SCA to SCP are utilised both effectively and purposefully is another area of concern in this regard.

8.5.10. Progress during Tenth Five Year Plan

Funds to the extent of Rs. 1,646.00 crore (10.63 per cent) from 14 Ministries/Departments at the Central level and funds to the extent of Rs. 42,308.97 crore (12.20 per cent) from 22 States/UTs are flowing to SCP. This indicates that efforts need to be made to improve the implementation of SCP at both the central and state levels to reach the expected level.

A quick review of the earmarking of funds under SCP brings forth certain issues like while some Ministries/Departments being regulatory in nature are not able to earmark funds for SCP, some others having activities which are non-divisible in nature, are finding it difficult to earmark funds under SCP. In respect of SCA to SCP, it was observed that non-release of SCA funds on time by the State Finance Departments to the State/nodal departments of Welfare has been adversely affecting the smooth running of various income generation programmes that are undertaken for SC families living below the poverty line. Such delays are not only affecting the beneficiary families but also causing predicament to the nodal department, as they are not able to make full use of the allocated funds, and finally resulting in unspent funds. Often, such unspent SCA funds, as reported, are getting diverted to other purposes leaving the earmarked/ intended purposes unattended to.

To look into all the related issues, a Central Standing Tripartite Committee was set up by the Planning Commission in May 1999 with the representatives of the Planning Commission, National Commission for SCs, the nodal Ministry of Social Justice & Empowerment and the concerned Central Ministries/Departments.

The Committee has reviewed formulations of SCP of the 14 Central Ministries/Departments (Agriculture and Cooperation, Environment and Forest, Urban Development and Poverty Alleviation, Rural Development, Indian Systems of Medicine and Homeopathy, Non- Conventional Energy Sources, Water Resources, Public Enterprises, Animal Husbandry & Dairying, Sugar and Edible Oils, Drinking Water Supply, Statistics and Programme Implementation, Food Processing and Power) and advised that all the Ministries/Departments should put in their special efforts to revive the otherwise routinised SCP.

It also suggested that the formulation of SCP should be right at the plan formulation stage through identification of schemes and earmarking of funds so that a systematic monitoring of the utilisation of earmarked funds can be planned for. Similar Committees are also coming up at the state level. So far, 6 states vis., Andhra Pradesh, Bihar, Madhya Pradesh, West Bengal, Punjab and Gujarat have set up such Committees. Other States/UTs are also expected to come up soon with such Committees to review the progress of the implementation of SCP and SCA to SCP on a continuing basis.

8.6. Scheduled Caste Sub Plan (SCSP)

Inspite of the Constitutional safeguards and developmental planning launched since 1951, through the First Five Year Plan the SCs lagged behind the general population in various socioeconomic indicators. The Sixth Plan has identified the lack of economic support as the main cause of extremely slow pace of development of the Scheduled Castes during the earlier plans.

Thought it was inherent in the earlier five year plans that the benefits of economic development resulting from the investments in agriculture and industry in particular would, incourse of time trickle down to the poorest of the poor, the search of a new strategy during the Sixth Five Year Plan. The new strategy so evolved is a combination of the following three instruments: The Special Component Plan of the States and Central Ministries (SCP), The Special Central Assistance, (iii) The Scheduled Castes Development Corporations in the States (SCDCs). The Sixth Plan marked a shift in the approach to the development of SCs.

Special emphasis was laid on the implementation of the newly launched SCSP for SCs facilitating easy convergence and pooling of resources from all the other developmental sectors in proportion to the population of SCs and monitoring of various developmental programmes for the benefit of SCs. The Scheduled Caste Sub Plan is designed to channelise the flow of benefits and outlays from the general sectors in the plan of the States and Central Ministries for the development of Scheduled Castes in physical and financial terms.

These plans are envisaged to help poor Scheduled Castes families through composite income generating programmes during the Sixth Plan period. Such family oriented programmes are to cover all the major occupational groups amongst Scheduled Castes such as agricultural labourers, small and marginal farmers, share croppers, fishermen, sweepers and scavengers, urban unorganised labours below the poverty line.

In addition, the Special Component Plans also seek to improve the living conditions of Scheduled Castes through provision of drinking water supply, link roads, house sites and housing improvements, establishment of such services as primary schools, health centres, veterinary centres, panchayat gras, community halls, nutrition centres, rural electrification, common work places, common facility centres etc. In the scheduled Caste bastis under the Minimum Needs programme to improve their access to social, educational and other community services and earmarking outlays for this purpose in appropriate sectors.

The Scheduled Caste Sub Plan (SCSP) launched for the Scheduled Castes expected to facilitate easy convergence and pooling of resources from all the other development sectors in proportion to the population of SCs and monitoring of various developmental programmes for the benefit of SCs. While the essential features of SCSP are the same as in the TSP except for the fact that its dynamics had to be regulated in tune with the fact that SCs are spread all over the country and have no territorial specificity.

8.6.1. Scheduled Caste Sub Plan (SCSP) Aims and Strategy

The strategy of Scheduled Caste Sub Plan (SCSP) since evolved in 1979 is aimed at:

- — Economic development through beneficiary oriented programmes for raising their income and creating assets;
- — Basti-oriented schemes for infrastructure development through provision of drinking water supply, link roads, house sites, housing etc.
- — Educational and Social development activities like establishment of primary schools, health centres, vocational centres, community halls, women work place etc.

The strategy of Scheduled Caste Sub Plan envisages to channelise the flow of outlays and benefits from all the sectors of development in the Annual Plans of States/UTs and Central Ministries at least in proportion to their population both in physical and financial terms.

Implementation of SCSP and TSP is not being done uniformly in all States/UTs. Different States have adopted different mechanisms without exploring effective mechanism which can ensure quantification of funds for SCSP and TSP, monitoring of expenditure, avert diversion of funds to unintended ventures etc. The State Governments exercise their quantification as 'Divisible' and 'Non-Divisible' components. Effective quantification is made only from the

'Divisible' component scheme wise. As a result of this, the actual flow of funds to SCSP and TSP from the total State Plan becomes much lesser than what should have been as per the percentage of the population of SCs and STs to the total population of the State.

8.6.2. Implementation of SCSP

The special strategy of Scheduled Caste Sub Plan (SCSP) for SCs has been receiving special attention, right from their initiation in the Seventies, as these are the most effective mechanisms to ensure flow of funds/ benefits for SCs from the other general development sectors.

During the period of appraisal, certain issues regarding non-earmarking of funds and the consequences thereof, have also come to surface. Firstly, some Ministries/Departments are allegedly regulatory in nature and as such, it is not possible to earmark SCSP; secondly, activities of some Ministries/Departments are being non-divisible in nature, SCSP was not earmarked. To look into these and other related issues of SCSP, SCA to SCSP, a Central Standing Tripartite Committee consisting of the representatives of the Planning Commission, National Commission for SCs & STs, and the concerned Ministry/Department, was set up in May 1999.

The committee, thus set up, has already completed the task of reviewing the SCSP formulations of the Central Ministries/ Departments of Agriculture and Cooperation, Environment and Forest, Urban Employment and Poverty Alleviation, Rural Development, Indian System of Medicine and Homeopathy, Non Conventional Energy Sources, Water Resources, Public Enterprises, Animal Husbandry & Dairying, Sugar and Edible Oils, Drinking Water Supply, Statistics and Programme Implementation, Food Processing and Power. Similar Committees are also coming up at the State level. 6 States/UTs vis., Andhra Pradesh, Bihar, Madhya Pradesh, West Bengal, Punjab and Gujarat have already set up such committees.

Despite the fact that the strategy of SCSP has been in operation for more than seventeen years, they could not influence all the concerned in its right perspective. Further, lack of effective monitoring to ensure that all the Ministries/Departments both at Central and State levels earmark funds under SCP and the funds received under SCP and

SCA are utilised effectively and purposefully, is another area of concern in this regard.

Just as the States, the Central Ministries/ Departments are also expected to formulate SCSP component and ensure that the flow of SCSP in their plans are at least in proportion to the SC population of the country. As on date, only 17 Central Ministries/ departments are able to formulate SCSP. Many of the Ministries/Departments are unable to provide funds to SCSP on the basis of population proportions. Some Ministries/Departments have expressed their inability due to the non divisibility of their programmes/ projects and budgets. During Fifth Plan and Sixth Plan no allocation was made under SCSP for the Central Sector. However, allocation of Rs. 751.33 (4.25%) and Rs 3614.66 crore (7.67%) had been allocated under State Sector.

Allocation under Central Sector had been made only during Seventh Plan onwards. A sum of Rs. 1070.17 crore (1.08 %) which include allocation for TSP also made for the Seventh Five Year Plan whereas State Plan allocation was much higher constituting 8.28% of the total allocation of the State Plan. Similarly, during the 8th Five Year Plan, Central Sector allocation was only 3.36% whereas State allocation for SCSP was 11.26%.

It was observed that during the Ninth Five Year Plan under the Central sector allocation for SCSP had been picked up (10.63%) which was almost on line with the allocation under State Sector (11.24%). The SC and ST population was 16.5% and 8.1% respectively as per 1991 census. It is observed that in all the Five Year Plans allocation under SCSP has not been made as per the proportionate percentage of Scheduled Castes in the State and at the Central level.

8.6.3. Special Central Assistance (SCA)

The Ministry of Social Justice & Empowerment (M/SJ&E) is providing 100% grant under the Central Sector Scheme of SCA to SCSP as an additive to SCSP to the States/UTs to fill the critical gaps and vital missing inputs in family oriented income generating schemes with supporting infrastructure development so as to make the schemes more effective. The objective of the SCA is to provide additional support to Below Poverty Line (BPL) SC families to enhance their productivity and income. SCA could also be utilised for infrastructure development in the blocks having 50 percent or more of SC population. SCA is released to these States/UTs on the basis of the following criteria:

- — SC Population of the States/UTs : 40%.
- — Relative backwardness of the States/ UTs :10%.
- — Percentage of SC families in the States/ UTs covered by Composite economic development programmes in the State Plan to enable them to cross the poverty line : 25%.
- — Percentage of SCSP to the Annual Plan as compared to SC population percentage of the States/UTs : 25%.

8.6.4. Problems Associated with Old Methodology

The problems associated with old methodology are :

- — States/UTs were quantifying funds only from the divisible sectors/programmes.
- — Plan outlays from schemes/programmes were not reaching the SC habitations which are outside the villages/towns.
- — Priority sectors and need based schemes/programmes for the benefit of SCs like education, health, technical/ vocational training were not devised based on the needs.
- — Development schemes/programmes of infrastructure relating to roads, major irrigation projects, power and electricity sector mega projects are not accruing any direct immediate benefits to SCs.
- — Schemes related to minor irrigation, asset creation, housing and land distribution were not given importance.

The allocations made were only notional in nature showing supposedly benefits accruing to the SCs welfare and development from the general sectors. The funds allocated were not budgeted and released in time. The expenditure in many of the States/UTs was not even 50% of the allocated funds. No proper budget heads/sub-heads were created so the funds were diverted to the other general sectors from SCSP funds. As the Secretary, Social Welfare was not made a nodal Officer, there was no controlling mechanism and the planning, supervision and allocation of funds to the priority sectors.

The State Governments of Maharashtra and Uttar Pradesh have pioneered a special mechanism as regards SCSP to ensure its effective operationalisation for the benefit of SCs since a long time. The following measures have proved effective in a few States in the formulation and implementation of Scheduled Caste Sub Plan (SCSP):

— Earmark funds for SCSP from the total State Annual and Five Year Plan outlays at least in proportion to their respective population in the State.

— Designate the Social Welfare Department in the State as nodal department for the formulation and implementation of SCSP with full autonomy in the selection of Schemes, allocation of funds and diversion of funds from one scheme to another within the overall allocations.

— These nodal departments to be entrusted with responsibility to take all policy decisions regarding administration of development programmes, including budgeting of funds, making and release of allocations for development schemes and powers to review, monitor and supervise the implementation of all the programmes for the SCs.

— Establish State level, District level and Block level Standing Committees to monitor the implementation of various schemes under SCSP of all departments.

8.6.5. Present Status

As on today, 27 States/ UTs and only 17 Central Ministries/ Departments have been practising in formulation of SCSP. A Standing Tripartite Committee was constituted in the Planning Commission in 1999 to review the implementation of the Special Strategy of SCSP for SCs, TSP to STs and to resolve various policy related issues in respect of Central Ministries/ Departments as well as State Governments. The Central Standing Tripartite Committee (CSTC) reviews the implementation of SCSP and TSP and guides the nodal Ministries of Social Justice and Empowerment and Tribal Affairs in ensuring of earmarking of funds by the service oriented Central Ministries/ Departments and States/UTs.

References

Ainapur, L. S. *Dynamics of Caste Relations in Rural India.* Rawat Publications. Jaipur. 1986.

Bandyopadhyay, Sekhar. *Caste, Culture, and Hegemony: Social domination in Colonial Bengal.* Sage Publications. New Delhi. 2004.

Banerjee, Biswajit and J.B. Knight, "Caste Discrimination in Indian Urban Labour Market" *Journal of Developing Economics.* 1985.

Bashiruddin Ahmed. *Caste and Electoral Politics.* Asian Survey. Vol. 10, No. 11, Elections and Party Politics in India: A Symposium. Nov., 1970. pp. 979–992.

Blunt. E.A.H. *The Caste System of North India.* S.Chand Publishers. 1969.

Chalam, K.S. "Caste Reservation and Equality of Opportunity in Education" *Economic and Political Weekly.* Vol. 25, No. 41. October 13. 1990.

National Commission for Scheduled Castes and Scheduled Tribes. Fourth Report 1996-97 & 1997-98, vols. I &II, Delhi. 1998.

National Commission for Scheduled Castes and Scheduled Tribes. *Highlights of the Report for the Years 1996-97 and 1997-98.* New Delhi. Government of India, 1999.

Report of the Commissioner for Scheduled Castes and Scheduled Tribes, 1974. New Delhi: Government of India Press. 1977.

Susan Bayly. *Caste, Society and Politics in India.* Cambridge. Cambridge University Press. 1999.

Bibliography

Ainapur, L. S. *Dynamics of Caste Relations in Rural India*. Rawat Publications. Jaipur. 1986.

Bandyopadhyay, Sekhar. *Caste, Culture, and Hegemony: Social domination in Colonial Bengal*. Sage Publications. New Delhi. 2004.

Banerjee, Biswajit and J.B. Knight, *"Caste Discrimination in Indian Urban Labour Market" Journal of Developing Economics*. 1985.

Bashiruddin Ahmed. *Caste and Electoral Politics*. Asian Survey. Vol. 10, No. 11, Elections and Party Politics in India: A Symposium. Nov., 1970. pp. 979–992.

Beteille, Andre. *Caste, Class and Power: Changing Patterns of Stratification in a Tanjore Village*. New Delhi. Oxford University Press. 1996.

Bloch, Francis, and Vijayendra Rao, *"Statistical Discrimination and Social Assimilation," Economics Bulletin*, 10(2), 2001, Pp: 1-5

Blunt. E.A.H. *The Caste System of North India*. S.Chand Publishers. 1969.

Chalam, K.S. *"Caste Reservation and Equality of Opportunity in Education" Economic and Political Weekly*. Vol. 25, No. 41. October 13. 1990.

Conlon, Frank F., *"Caste by Association: The Gauda Sarasvata Brahmana Unification Movement," The Journal of Asian Studies*, Vol. 33, No. 3, Pp: 351-365, May 1974.

Das, Veena, *Structure and Cognition: Aspects of Hindu Caste and Ritual*, Second Edition, Oxford University Press, Delhi, 1982.

Francine R. and M.S.A. Rao (eds.). *Dominance and State Power in Modern India*, Vol. II, Delhi, OUP. 1990.

Frankel Francine R. and M.S.A. Rao (eds.) *Dominance and State Power in Modern India*, Vol. I, Delhi, OUP. 1989.

Ghurye, G. S. *Caste, Class and Occupation*. Popular Book Depot, Bombay. 1961.

Gupta, S.K. *The Scheduled Castes in Modern Indian Politics: Their Emergence as a Political Power.* New Delhi. Munshiram Manoharlal Publishers Pvt. Ltd. 1985.

Human Rights Watch, *Broken People: Caste Violence Against India's "Untouchables".* New York: Human Rights Watch. 1999.

Jaffrelot, Christophe. *India's Silent Revolution: The Rise of the Lower Castes.* C. Hurst & Co. 2003.

Jenkins Rob. Where the BJP Survived : Rajasthan Assembly Election, 1993, *Economic and Political Weekly,* March 12. 1994.

Karve Iravati and V.M. Dandekar. *Anthropometric Measures of Maharashtra,* Poona, Deccan College. 1951.

Kothari Rajni (ed.) *Caste in Indian Politics,* New Delhi, Orient Longman. 1970.

Kothari, Rajni. *Caste in Indian Politics.* Orient Longman.2004.

Kumar, Dharma, *Land and Caste in South India,* Manohar Publishers, New Delhi, 1992.

Kundu, Amitabh. *"Reservation, Anti-reservation and Democracy." Economic and Political Weekly.* Vol. 25, No. 45. November 10, 1990.

Lele Jayant K. and Rajendra Vora (eds.). *State and Society in India,* Delhi, Chanakya. 1990.

Mahar, J. Michael, (ed.) *The Untouchables in Contemporary India.* Tucson. The University of Arisona Press. 1972.

Michael, S.M., (ed.) *Untouchable: Dalits in Modern India.* Boulder. Lynne Rienner Publishers. 1999.

Miguel, Edward, *"Tribe or Nation? Nation Building and Public Goods in Kenya versus Tansania," World Politics,* 2004, 56 (3), 327-362.

National Commission for Scheduled Castes and Scheduled Tribes. Fourth Report 1996-97 & 1997-98, vols. I &II, Delhi. 1998.

Omvedt, Gail, *Dalits and the Democratic Revolution: Dr. Ambedkar and the Dalit Movement in Colonial India,* Sage Publications, Delhi, 1994.

Palshikar Suhas. *Politics of Marginalised Groups,* (Report submitted to UGC), Dept. of Politics and Public Admn., University of Pune. 2000.

Pandian, J., *"Political Emblems of Caste Identity: An Interpretation of Tamil Caste Titles," Anthropological Quarterly,* Vol. 56. No. 4, Pp: 190-197, October 1983.

Parvathamma. *Scheduled Castes and Tribes: A Socio-economic Survey,* Ashish, Delhi. 1984.

Paul R Brass, *The Politics of India since Independence*, Cambridge, Cambridge University Press, 1990, pp 210-11.

Pauline Kolenda. *Caste in Contemporary India: Beyond Organic Solidarity* Menlo Park. Benjamin/Cumming Publishing Co. 1978.

Pradhan M.C. *Political Systems of the Jats of Northern India,* London, OUP. 1966.

Professor Parmaji, *Caste Reservations and Performance : Research Findings*, Warangal, Mamata, 1985, pp 174 -75.

Ramaiah, A (6 June 1992). *"Identifying Other Backward Classes"* (PDF). Economic and Political Weekly. pp. 1203–1207.Munshi, Kaivan and Mark R. Rosensweig, "Traditional Institutions Meet the Modern World: Caste, Gender, and Schooling Choice in a Globalising Economy." *American Economic Review* 96(4):1225-1252, September 2006.

Rao, Vijayendra and Michael Walton, *"Culture and Public Action: Relationality, Equality of Agency and Development,"* Chapter 1 in (V. Rao and M. Walton – eds.) *Culture and Public Action*, Stanford University Press, Stanford, 2004.

Report of the Commissioner for Scheduled Castes and Scheduled Tribes, 1974. New Delhi: Government of India Press. 1977.

Roy Ramashray and Richard Sisson (eds.) *Diversity and Dominance in Indian Politics,* Vol. 2, New Delhi, Sage. 1966.

Srinivas M.N. *The Dominant Caste and Other Essays,* Delhi, U.P. 1989.

Susan Bayly. *Caste, Society and Politics in India.* Cambridge. Cambridge University Press. 1999.

Index

Gupta, S.K. *The Scheduled Castes in Modern Indian Politics: Their Emergence as a Political Power.* New Delhi. Munshiram Manoharlal Publishers Pvt. Ltd. 1985.

Human Rights Watch, *Broken People: Caste Violence Against India's "Untouchables"*. New York: Human Rights Watch. 1999.

Jaffrelot, Christophe. *India's Silent Revolution: The Rise of the Lower Castes.* C. Hurst & Co. 2003.

Jenkins Rob. Where the BJP Survived : Rajasthan Assembly Election, 1993, *Economic and Political Weekly,* March 12. 1994.

Karve Iravati and V.M. Dandekar. *Anthropometric Measures of Maharashtra,* Poona, Deccan College. 1951. .

Kothari Rajni (ed.) *Caste in Indian Politics,* New Delhi, Orient Longman. 1970.

Kothari, Rajni. *Caste in Indian Politics.* Orient Longman.2004.

Kumar, Dharma, *Land and Caste in South India*, Manohar Publishers, New Delhi, 1992.

Kundu, Amitabh. *"Reservation, Anti-reservation and Democracy." Economic and Political Weekly.* Vol. 25, No. 45. November 10, 1990.

Lele Jayant K. and Rajendra Vora (eds.). *State and Society in India,* Delhi, Chanakya. 1990.

Mahar, J. Michael, (ed.) *The Untouchables in Contemporary India.* Tucson. The University of Arisona Press. 1972.

Michael, S.M., (ed.) *Untouchable: Dalits in Modern India.* Boulder. Lynne Rienner Publishers. 1999.

Miguel, Edward, *"Tribe or Nation? Nation Building and Public Goods in Kenya versus Tansania," World Politics,* 2004, 56 (3), 327-362.

National Commission for Scheduled Castes and Scheduled Tribes. Fourth Report 1996-97 & 1997-98, vols. I &II, Delhi. 1998.

Omvedt, Gail, *Dalits and the Democratic Revolution: Dr. Ambedkar and the Dalit Movement in Colonial India,* Sage Publications, Delhi, 1994.

Palshikar Suhas. *Politics of Marginalised Groups,* (Report submitted to UGC), Dept. of Politics and Public Admn., University of Pune. 2000.

Pandian, J., *"Political Emblems of Caste Identity: An Interpretation of Tamil Caste Titles," Anthropological Quarterly,* Vol. 56. No. 4, Pp: 190-197, October 1983.

Parvathamma. *Scheduled Castes and Tribes: A Socio-economic Survey,* Ashish, Delhi. 1984.

Paul R Brass, *The Politics of India since Independence*, Cambridge, Cambridge University Press, 1990, pp 210-11.

Pauline Kolenda. *Caste in Contemporary India: Beyond Organic Solidarity* Menlo Park. Benjamin/Cumming Publishing Co. 1978.

Pradhan M.C. *Political Systems of the Jats of Northern India,* London, OUP. 1966.

Professor Parmaji, *Caste Reservations and Performance : Research Findings,* Warangal, Mamata, 1985, pp 174 -75.

Ramaiah, A (6 June 1992). *"Identifying Other Backward Classes"* (PDF). Economic and Political Weekly. pp. 1203–1207.Munshi, Kaivan and Mark R. Rosensweig, "Traditional Institutions Meet the Modern World: Caste, Gender, and Schooling Choice in a Globalising Economy." *American Economic Review* 96(4):1225-1252, September 2006.

Rao, Vijayendra and Michael Walton, *"Culture and Public Action: Relationality, Equality of Agency and Development,"* Chapter 1 in (V. Rao and M. Walton – eds.) *Culture and Public Action*, Stanford University Press, Stanford, 2004.

Report of the Commissioner for Scheduled Castes and Scheduled Tribes, 1974. New Delhi: Government of India Press. 1977.

Roy Ramashray and Richard Sisson (eds.) *Diversity and Dominance in Indian Politics,* Vol. 2, New Delhi, Sage. 1966.

Srinivas M.N. *The Dominant Caste and Other Essays,* Delhi, U.P. 1989.

Susan Bayly. *Caste, Society and Politics in India.* Cambridge. Cambridge University Press. 1999.

Index